GUIDE TO TEACHING PERCUSSION

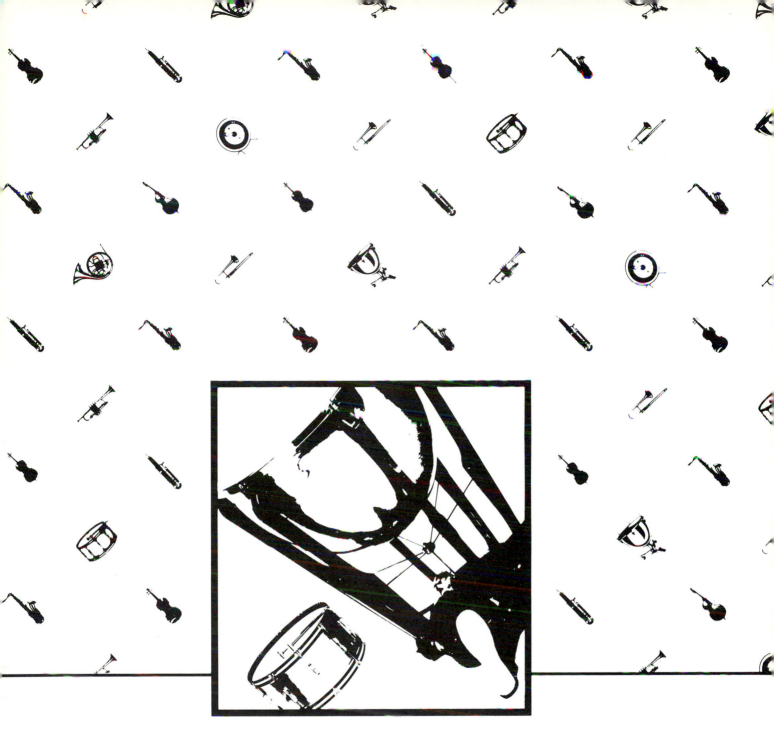

GUIDE TO TEACHING PERCUSSION

RONALD A. HOLLOWAY
HARRY R. BARTLETT
CALIFORNIA STATE UNIVERSITY, SACRAMENTO

REVISING AUTHOR
JOHN J. PAPASTEFAN
UNIVERSITY OF SOUTH ALABAMA

FOURTH EDITION

wcb

WM. C. BROWN COMPANY PUBLISHERS
DUBUQUE, IOWA

MUSIC SERIES

Consulting Editor
Frederick W. Westphal
California State University, Sacramento

Contents

v

Preface to the Fourth Edition

The intent of the *Guide to Teaching Percussion* is to present as much practical and theoretical material as possible concerning percussion instruments, their playing techniques and teaching procedures. To this end, more than fifty instruments are treated in the book. The information has been drawn from the authors' experiences as both players and teachers of percussion instruments, and from the published and unpublished writings of a multitude of other teacher-musicians. Throughout this revision a concerted effort has been made to avoid controversy arising from differences in pedagogical philosophy. When newer or different techniques have been introduced, it has been with the knowledge that they are accepted by the majority of today's percussionists, but do not necessarily represent the only point of view.

The *Guide* has been developed as a textbook for use in the pre-service and in-service training of instrumental music teachers, and as such will serve as the basic textbook for the percussion methods/techniques classes at the college level. Teachers already in the field should find the *Guide* a source of new ideas and a ready reference for solution of the many and varied problems which arise in conjunction with the interpretation and performance of percussion parts, and in a similar manner for the studio teacher. The needs of advanced percussion students, professional percussionists, and conductors, composers and arrangers of music have been kept in mind too. For these readers the descriptive information on the standard and more esoteric percussion instruments, their typical idiomatic usages and playing techniques, and the glossary of terms in four languages should prove worthwhile.

The philosophy underlying the *Guide* may be summarized as follows:

1. Percussion technique should be developed to produce musical results.

2. Recommended techniques and styles should be those most generally used by artist-percussionists currently active in music performance.

3. Though the snare drum may rightly be considered the basic percussion instrument, the ability to execute the "original 26 rudiments" does not necessarily make a percussionist.

4. Demonstration-emulation is the best method for teaching skills such as those neuromuscular coordinations used in manipulating sticks, mallets and beaters.

5. Percussion teaching should impart the feeling of pride on the part of the student in performing every assignment, no matter how small, with care and musical feeling.

The procedure in each of the chapters has been to begin with pertinent historical data, introduce the basic playing techniques and conclude with teaching procedures and suggestions. To help the reader develop clear and accurate concepts of the various physical actions used to produce the tones of the percussion instruments, liberal use has been made throughout of photographs and diagrams.

For this fourth edition, the entire text has been carefully reviewed. Special thanks go to William H. Vits with the Grand Rapids Symphony Orchestra and Ronald J. Crocker, Kearney State College. In some instances the fourth edition has been reworded, in others expanded, and in still others it has been revised completely. Some new figures have been added. Newer techniques of performance have been introduced throughout. Since many recent innovations have occurred in nearly all percussion instruments, solo and ensemble music, method books, sticks, mallets and other striking implements, and of course in the entire realm of marching percussion, these areas have been given additional attention.

The assistance of the following organizations and individuals in the preparation of this book is gratefully acknowledged: The Ludwig Drum Company, the A. Zildjian Company, Slingerland/Deagan, LP (Latin Percussion, Inc.), Rogers Drums and the Wenger Corp. for furnishing photographs of their products for inclusion; Boosey & Hawkes, Inc. for permission to reproduce the percussion parts of *Variations on a Korean Folk Song* by John Barnes Chance, photographer Weldon Pollard for the photographs in the first edition, and to Len Cramer for the additional photographs for the second and third editions; to Richard F. Bartlett for the drawings and diagrams; and to Jere O'Boyle of Musicopy, San Francisco for the music autographing.

CHAPTER 1

Introduction

BASIC CONCEPTS OF PERCUSSION PLAYING

Tone Production

The sound-producing vibration of any percussion instrument is made by a quick, resilient blow. The drumstick, beater, or mallet must "get-on-and-get-off" the vibrating drumhead, bar, or plate. However, this concept should not be carried to extremes. The vibrating body *must* be adequately set into motion to produce a proper and characteristic tone on the instrument. Any lingering of the beater on the surface tends to stop the vibration. See Figure 1.1. Percussion instruments must be struck (played) in such a way that the tone is drawn out of the instrument rather than pounded into it.

Three factors influence the tone quality of percussion instruments: (1) the physical properties of the instruments themselves: resonance of the materials, adjustments of the heads and snares, choice of sticks, beaters, or mallets; (2) the place at which the surface is struck; and, (3) the manner in which the surface is struck.

To achieve good quality of tone from percussion instruments, it is imperative that the vibration be free and not interfered with by stiff, lingering strokes.

Attack and Release of Tones

The character of the percussion instruments demands that the start of a tone be accented slightly. The attack, even at *pp* volume, should be crisp, definite and fall precisely on the beat, or fraction thereof, as dictated by the music. Snare drum rolls, for example, require a slight accenting of the initial blow to set the drumhead into vibration, thus starting the tone at precisely the right instant. The larger the instrument, the slower it "speaks." The bass drum, large tam-tams (gongs), large cymbals, and timpani thus require great care in timing by the player.

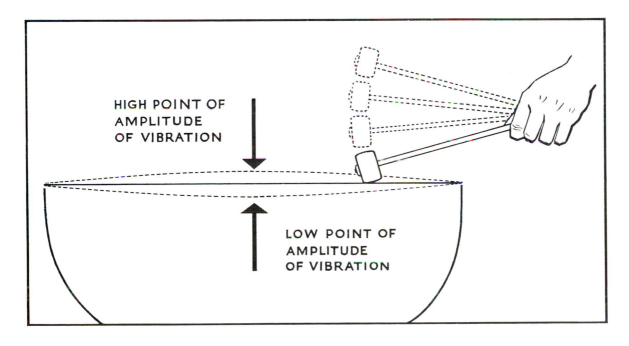

HIGH POINT OF
AMPLITUDE
OF VIBRATION

LOW POINT OF
AMPLITUDE
OF VIBRATION

Figure 1.1. Vibration of drumhead.

The stopping (release) of the tone is done by pressing or grasping the vibrating surface with the finger tips or hands. Damping is the term used in percussion playing to refer to the stopping or release of tone.

The following are important applications of the concept of damping:

1. Allow the tone to ring for the written duration of the note, then damp it. (Exceptions are noted in succeeding chapters.)
2. Damping should be instantaneous and complete.
3. Drumheads not being played upon will ring sympathetically, so there must also be damping of these heads at such places in the music as general pauses, cut-offs at ends of fermatas, and final notes.
4. The snare drum requires damping in many passages. Even though the snare drum has only a short after-ring, no sound should spill over into a general silence.
5. The tone must be allowed to project before being damped, even on notes marked *staccato, sfz,* or *secco* (dry, short).
6. A tie or slur mark after a triangle, cymbal, bass drum, chime, bell, or timpani note means to let the tone ring considerably longer than the written value of the note. For example:

Dynamic Contrasts

Musical percussion playing demands careful attention to the dynamic level at all times. Second in importance only to rhythm is the percussion section's function of underlining the dynamics. The imaginative contrasting of louds and softs, crescendi and diminuendi, etc. is the most effective way that the percussionist can communicate his feeling for the music. By the same token, there is nothing less musical than percussion which remains on the same volume level throughout a whole piece (or even a whole concert!). Don't be afraid of *ff* or *sfz.* The composer wanted the percussion to be powerful at such points. By the same token, some of the most beautiful and effective utilization of percussion occurs at the opposite end of the dynamic spectrum. All too often, *piano* and *pianissimo* parts are overlooked by both performer and composer.

Accents

The rhythmic security of the entire ensemble is strengthened when the percussion emphasizes the natural accents and exaggerates the artificial (written in) accents.

The accent marks within parentheses in the following rhythmic figures indicate where the natural emphasis would occur in each given bar.

Solo bass drum booms and cymbal crashes are usually marked with an accent, and these notes should be played *sfz* with *full* power.

Stickwork

The instruments of percussion which are played with sticks, hammers, or mallets in both hands utilize the natural and efficient basic technique of alternating the sticks. In rudimental snare drum parlance this is called "hand-to-hand" playing. There are many exceptions to this principle, however. The term "rudimental drumming" applies to snare drumming only. The principles of rudimental stickwork do not apply to other instruments of percussion to any great extent, but for the snare drum the alternation of single strokes is *the* very fundamental rudiment. Because this hand-to-hand principle of stickwork dominates, we may draw up the following rules for snare drum stickwork:

The right stick leads. There are two widely used systems of snare drum stickwork: 1) the strict alternation of R (Right Hand) and L (Left Hand), starting with either hand; 2) the *"right-lead"* system of sticking for snare drum. The latter is a policy of sticking which puts the right stick on the first beat in a measure and on all strong and principally accented beats. Weak beats, pick-up beats, and such fractional parts of beats as the eighth note off the beat are played by the left. The right-lead stickwork system can be likened to the normal bowing patterns of string instruments: the R stick corresponds to the down-bow, the L stick to the up-bow. The right-lead system is recommended. Its advantages are: it is *a system,* and hence preferable to the haphazard stick indications given in many method books; it has few exceptions in duple meters, some in triple (3/4, 3/8, 9/8); this system is based on practical performance practices and not on a "strengthen-the-left-hand" theory. Unfortunately, the right-lead system does not take into account the very special problems which are sometimes encountered by left-handed players.

Idiomatic figures of snare drum rhythm are always played with the same sticking. By adhering to this principle, stickwork is soon eliminated as a problem, and thus sight-reading becomes easier. Improved rhythmic precision usually results when little or none of the player's conscious focus is directed to stickwork. In the case of young beginning players, it is strongly recommended that the habit of playing the typical snare drum rhythms consistently with the same sticking be developed from the start. See pages 45 to 48 for a more complete discussion of snare drum stickwork.

Rhythm, Beat, Tempo and Time

One of the most basic functions of the percussion is to provide a rhythmic foundation for the ensemble. This is especially evident in music with a regularly recurring beat such as marches, dance-like pieces, and jazz. The percussion in such cases performs the function of establishing and holding the beat.

The percussion player, therefore, should have or develop a metronomic "beat-sense" in order to time his sounds with precision. Secondly, he must possess a fine sensitivity to rhythmic patterns. He must be able to maintain a steady tempo over a long time span. In short, rhythmic precision is expected of the percussion section. Three important factors in this matter of rhythmic precision are:

1. The beginning student must concentrate from the very start on the perfecting of his "beat-sense." In all his playing he should feel the pulse of the beat to the point of exaggeration. Physical manifestations in addition to counting aloud such as toe tapping, and other bodily movements usually help to make the student "beat-conscious" and should be encouraged. Needless to say, these devices should not be carried over into public performances.

2. Precision in timing requires fine neuromuscular coordination. Mechanical mastery over problems of stick control must be developed before truly fine timing is possible.

3. The recognition, comprehension, and execution of rhythm, i.e., *groupings* of beats and *divisions* within a beat, is not the exclusive province of the percussion player, yet he is properly looked upon as a specialist in matters of rhythm.

FUNCTIONS OF THE PERCUSSION INSTRUMENTS

The Percussion Section (Fr. batterie, It. batteria, Ger. Schlagewerk)

The percussion section in the modern orchestra usually consists of a timpanist, a snare drummer, a bass drummer, a cymbal specialist, and a mallet-instrument specialist. Very often one or more all-around performers are included. The concert band percussion section usually includes a timpanist, two snare drummers, a bass drummer, a cymbal player, and a mallet-instrument player, and sometimes one or more additional players. The marching band section varies in make-up with the size of the band. The large marching units employ one or more bass drummers, one or two cymbal players, four to six snare drummers, two tenor drummers, and one or two bell-lyra players as a basic section. Contemporary new tonal sounds are being added to this conventional marching band percussion instrumentation through the use of portable timpani, timp-tom duos and trios, differently pitched bass drums, Latin American instruments, and keyboard mallet percussion.

In each of these ensembles there is considerable variation. For example, a symphonic orchestra sometimes needs to augment its basic section in order to meet the requirements of particular compositions. The make-up of the band percussion section will vary depending upon the size of the band.

One of the most important functions of the orchestra or band percussion section is that of providing a *rhythmic basis* for the ensemble. This function is most obvious in march and dance-like music, but is nearly always present to some extent. Perfect rhythm (precision in time) is to be expected of the percussionists.

The second function of the percussion is that of *underlining dynamic nuance.* The possibilities for shading the volume of sound in the percussion instruments are probably greater than in brass, woodwinds, or strings.

The third task for the percussion section is the *providing of a variety of tone color* to the total ensemble timbre. Beginning with the introduction of the kettledrums into the orchestra, c. 1670, composers have become increasingly aware of the coloristic possibilities of percussion instruments. Rimsky-Korsakov, Mahler, Ravel, Debussy, Stravinsky, and Bartók are among the nineteenth and early twentieth-century composers who have exploited percussion timbre. Much contemporary music places the timbre function above rhythmic and dynamic usage, as witness certain works by Boulez, Nono, and Berio, to name but a few.

The Percussion Ensemble

Special mention should be made of the spectacular increase in percussion ensemble activity at all educational levels. Gordon Peters, principal percussionist with the Chicago Symphony Orchestra, has written a brilliant work which captures the essence of this important movement and includes objectives and suggestions for the implementation of a viable percussion ensemble program.[1]

Historically

The latest major historical development in the realm of percussion instruments has been the evolution of the percussion ensemble as a separate entity in the United States. This period can be said to have commenced formally with the premiere performance of *Ionization* by Edgar Varèse, which was performed in New York City under the baton of Nicolas Slonimsky on March 6, 1933. This work demands 13 players and 42 different instruments. It could be classed in the experimental and "effect" school of composition. Immediately it set up a trend in percussion ensemble composition that led to such unconventional sounds as "glissando on the xylophone resonators," "strike timpani bowls," "break ginger ale bottle," "rub resined-glove over snare stick held on center of bass drum," etc.

Some of the other proponents of this "school" of writing have included William Russell, Henry Cowell, John Cage, Lou Harrison, and Gerald Strang. The surge of interest in this type of percussion ensemble, however, diminished temporarily, only to be revived again after World War II.

The type of percussion ensemble that flourished during the interim period in the 1930's was the rudimental, military-type, consisting of at least one and usually two field drums, a bass drum, and a pair of cymbals. With the advent of the first individual, school-band drumming contest in 1929, the way was paved for the rudimental percussion ensemble.

In 1937 the first evidence of ensemble activity was found in the National Regional Contests when six drum ensembles were entered. By 1941, 102 such ensembles were entered. Today, these types of ensembles make up only a minor portion of percussion ensemble entries at most contests across the nation. With the restrictions of this type of instrumentation, the function of the rudimental drum ensemble has been limited almost exclusively to contests and the parade band.

Another type of percussion ensemble came into existence in the United States around 1930—the marimba ensemble. John C. Deagan, manufacturer of keyboard percussion instruments, organized a fifteen-instrument/fifteen-player ensemble to play the larger theaters around Chicago. In 1933 Clair Musser played at the Century of Progress Exposition in Chicago with a 100-instrument-player group.

It was not until around 1950 that dynamic and constructive directions were evolved for the percussion ensemble. The University of Illinois School of Music in that year was the first institution to give formal credit to percussion ensemble classes. In charge of this pioneering work was Paul Price, who has since contributed greatly to percussion ensemble work in the United States, including the establishment of a publishing firm devoted exclusively to the publication of percussion music.

The Percussion "Chiros"

There has been considerable speculation about the reasons for the awakening of the percussion "leviathan." It is perhaps simply "chiros," a term coined by theologian Paul Tillich to describe the occurrence of an event or the evolution of something brought about by many events or influences happening collectively and simultaneously and resulting in a new phenomenon. Some of the circumstances involved in the percussion ensemble chiros could be:

(1) a new awareness, by the public, of recordings made according to the latest Hi-Fi and Stereo fads (2) the feeling that percussion is the only unexplored field of instrumental music, (3) the increasing attention focused on percussive music because of the pace and noise of the times,—although some observers of contemporary music contend that this renewed interest in rhythm and percussion instruments is merely a natural cyclical reversion.

I feel, however, that the simple factor of natural historical development is involved, in addition to these stated reasons. The attitudes of many of our theologians of the day toward music, and percussion instruments particularly, have in most cases become greatly liberalized. Also, the influences of multiple cultures are cross-fertilizing all the national societies of the world now because of trends begun during World War II and accelerated through the past two decades by TV, jet travel, satellite communications, and the unholy combination of affluence and small wars around the world. Seen specifically in terms of the United States, it is safe to say that U.S. citizens are vitally interested in other cultures in an unconscious effort to evolve their own: Americans love to emulate!

Educationally

Percussion ensembles today are found principally in educational institutions, including colleges, universities, conservatories, high schools, and grammar schools. Programs of this nature are increasing in number at more and more schools each year. The many and varied benefits derived from such activity perhaps can be illustrated best by reviewing the multiple objectives of these various programs.

Objectives of Percussion Ensemble Programs

1. To provide a more personal musical expression for the percussionist through a regulated and constant chamber ensemble experience with his own instruments.
2. To supplement the most important aspect of the percussionist's training—private lessons and studies with competent and experienced instructors.
3. To focus particularly on the melodic and harmonic aspects of percussion instruments (the marimba, xylophone, vibraphone, bells, chimes, and timpani) to compensate for many students receiving only rhythmic training on the snare drum.
4. To serve as a step toward marimba ensemble work, through which medium the percussion student can experience the finest literature of other instrumental ensembles, including the orchestra (through transcriptions). In this objective lies the key to achieving the highest degree of musical development, appreciation, and reward for the percussion student.
5. To provide an ensemble experience for jazz arrangements. Many percussionists never get an opportunity to participate in this significant area of musical experience, but the "jazz feeling" is acquired only through actual experience and participation. Abilities of jazz techniques and feeling are now expected of the concert (sometimes called "legit") percussionist and vice-versa.
6. To promote a greater degree of musicianship, instrumental and stylistic versatility, and flexibility.
7. To further imbue the percussion student with the concepts of color, imagination, sensitivity, phrasing, artistry, and ensemble as pertains to the playing of the instruments and hence inspire the percussionist to greater confidence, pride, and enthusiasm.
8. To improve sight-reading.
9. To provide an organized and functional laboratory where percussion parts to orchestra, band, and wind ensemble repertory can be studied and rehearsed.
10. To acquaint the percussion performer with a wider variety of playing techniques and to make use of developed skills on percussion instruments infrequently used in band and orchestra scores.
11. To improve percussion playing in the larger organizations through the transfer of training acquired in the percussion ensemble.
12. To develop a greater sense of group responsibility through group participation.
13. To initiate an activity that can be extended throughout life.
14. To stimulate the formation of percussion ensemble programs in other school-instrumental programs.
15. To focus students' attention on the pedagogic value of percussion ensemble training in their own learning experience and in their future work as teachers.
16. To promote greater interest among young talented percussionists to inspire them to serious study of all the percussion instruments.
17. To help expose the student percussionists to as many different styles of music as possible, including the rudimental-military types of ensembles, but only to the degree that a balanced percussion ensemble program will permit.
18. To raise the standards of percussion ensemble repertory by educating percussionists to the existing repertory which will raise their threshold of musical discrimination and ultimately result in a demand for more profound compositions for percussion ensemble.
19. To encourage percussion students to compose percussion ensemble works in order to gain a deeper insight into their instruments. Too frequently overlooked is the development of the percussionist's imagination as pertains to the functional aesthetic-coloristic roles of this family of instruments.
20. To promote the composition (and performance) of high-caliber percussion ensemble works through the sponsorship of percussion ensemble composition contests and the commissioning of composers to compose such works.
21. To promote the composition and use of both absolute percussion music, where no instruments foreign to the percussion section are utilized, *and* works including instruments other than percussion.
22. To encourage the composition of works featuring percussion instruments for soloist or ensemble with orchestra or band accompaniments or both.
23. To give the instructor more opportunity to observe students' performance in relation to each other and thereby improve the effectiveness of their performance in the larger instrumental ensembles.
24. To promote the employment of bona-fide percussionists to teach percussion rather than persons whose major instrument is other than percussion.
25. To promote a change in the erroneous traditional attitude that percussion is not as important as the other sections of the orchestra. This would be done by explaining the history, functions, and untapped potentials of percussion instruments.
26. To provide students and teachers of composition and orchestration with opportunities to gain a clearer understanding of the use of percussion instruments and the notation for such insruments.

27. To encourage percussion instrument manufacturers to improve the quality of their instruments and sticks.
28. To bring to audiences a "new" musical experience and entertainment that is both aurally and visually fascinating.
29. To improve the general organization and efficiency of the percussion section in the band and orchestra.

INITIATING A PERCUSSION ENSEMBLE PROGRAM

Music directors find that giving their students small ensemble experience provides them with a more subtle vehicle through which to develop an awareness of phrasing, balance, and expression which in turn will be reflected in the larger musical organization. Ensemble programs, however, often have been "grounded" on the argument that "the curriculum allows no further scheduling of new activities." This is often merely a defensive excuse for some other reason; it is a common axiom of the logistics of human activities that allowance always can be made in any schedule or program for something that those in authority deem good and beneficial.

Percussion students should be given the privilege of a chamber music program just as other instrumentalists are. Besides giving the percussionists a more subtle musical experience, it gives them an opportunity to develop techniques on a greater variety of instruments than is possible in the larger musical organization. For instance, the director can break in a prospective timpanist by having him play timpani in the ensemble. Also, the exposure of comparative playing abilities of the players on different instruments develops a healthy competitive environment.

Convincing the Administrators

The primary obstacle to a formal percussion ensemble program coming into existence on the college level is sometimes the school administration. Administrators must be indoctrinated in the background and educational importance of this program.

First, the administrators must be impressed with the value of such a program in the overall instrumental ensemble program. To accomplish this, the administrators could hear a performance of a percussion ensemble. This could be a group from the school involved, a visiting percussion ensemble from another school, or a professional group. Many college percussion ensembles have annual tours and are delighted to find new audiences. A school assembly program of such a group, particularly one where the players demonstrate the instruments, is a superb educational opportunity for *all* students.

The impact of personal observation of such a fascinating group plus some background in the objectives and result of such a program often are sufficiently convincing

to administrators. Also, use of recordings, pictures, percussion ensemble programs, and printed reviews of works performed elsewhere will help in selling the idea. Student expressions in favor of such a program are difficult to ignore.

The administrators must then be made to realize that to pursue such a program means an expansion in the budget allowed for the percussion department, for additional instruments may have to be purchased, old instruments may have to be brought into use again and repaired, and percussion ensemble music will have to be purchased. This music is no more expensive (in many cases, less expensive) than music for other instruments.

Finding the Teacher

At the outset a program outside of regular school hours is better than none at all. In high schools the music director's time seems to have more and more demands made upon it. If the director is unable to spend sufficient time with such a program, a student conductor or an advanced student might be used at first. Perhaps the director already has a faculty assistant who could carry on this work. Another alternative is to have a percussion specialist visit the school regularly to coach percussion ensembles and perhaps also give private percussion lessons.

If at all possible, college percussion ensemble programs should be made formally a part of the curriculum, that is, taught with academic credit attached.

Finding someone who has the time to coach a percussion ensemble program is another consideration, for these reasons: 1) many music directors are not qualified to perform such a task because their percussion education has been inadequate, many times through no fault of their own, 2) some percussion instructors themselves are inadequate when it comes to this new task because they lack prior experience with percussion ensembles, and 3) some instructors simply lack the background in interpretive, conducting, and administrative skills needed to head such a program.

Finding the Hall

The physical facilities for a percussion ensemble program must also be considered. A rehearsal room that is close to the storage area for percussion instruments will save many rehearsal minutes.

The problem of possibly disturbing others with rehearsals must certainly be considered: acoustics and percussion are not always compatible!

Ensemble rehearsals can be scheduled during the band and orchestra rehearsals whenever the director is rehearsing works or sections where all or part of the percussion section is not needed. Percussion ensemble rehearsals, however, should never take the percussionist out of the band or orchestra rehearsal when needed there nor should regular *sectional* rehearsals be supplanted by them.

At the grammar school level a beginning percussion class can eventually include simple ensemble playing, first with the practice pads and drums and later with the addition of any other instruments called for.

Better Overall Motivation

There may be some initial reticence on the part of the percussion students who have never participated in ensembles. This would stem mainly from the student's fear that the ensemble would take too much time from other studies. Once the student has participated in such a program, however, and realizes the benefits to be derived, overall motivation is so enhanced that it carries over into other studies and even results in some students asking for more ensemble practice!

Matters related to the staging of percussion ensembles require planning ahead, because a different arrangement of instruments is necessary for each piece. Drawing charts that indicate the placement of instruments for each piece will soon facilitate moving instruments between pieces. To save time it is best to request that players be set up for the piece(s) to be rehearsed *before* the appointed hour of rehearsal. One way to call rehearsals is to announce "downbeat at such-and-such a time".

Finding the Music

Finding repertory to accommodate a specific number of players from semester to semester is another problem to be resolved. Today there is an abundance of music to choose from, and in some cases parts can be doubled or divided between players. If there are not enough percussion players to cover all the parts, other instrumentalists can be recruited.

In the choice of repertory the conductor-coach of an ensemble must be very discerning. Much ensemble music is of inferior musical worth, principally because of the comparative newness of the medium of percussion chamber music. At the outset of the evolution of this repertory, many percussionists without composition training or talent or both were attracted by publication offers as were many young composition students who wished to become famous overnight and have works published. But more serious composition talents have now been attracted to this medium of expression, and, as each year passes, finer works are being evolved at all levels of difficulty. Some works, even if of questionable musical worth, do serve certain laboratory needs by challenging the players technically. Most publishers are now including percussion ensemble music in their catalogues.

. . . And Starting Young

There is one other type of percussion ensemble in existence today whose objectives are not primarily to teach people how to play percussion instruments, but rather to teach young people of early school age (and sometimes adults) the basic elements of music and to appreciate musical art works through the use of percussion instruments.

Carl Orff[2], more known today as a prominent German composer, has evolved a set of seven books, called *Music for Children,* in which he basically gets the children to translate speech patterns from nursery tunes and such into rhythmical patterns which are "experienced" on specially built percussion instruments.

Charles Bavin[3] of England has evolved a system in which both young and older students get acquainted with the best musical literature by playing along with great music—either live or recorded—on a percussion instrument of some kind.

Satis Coleman[4] of the United States has also evolved some practical educational schemes for young children in learning about music through activity with percussion instruments.

The Jacques-Dalcroze School of Eurhythmics[5] has for years integrated percussion, rhythm, music, and movement in its course of study for both young children and adults.

Whatever obstacles or problems may exist in connection with a percussion ensemble program, regardless of age or academic level, this ensemble activity pays rich dividends in developing motivation and musical development. It is essential to the development of the serious percussion student.

Percussion in Dance Music and Jazz

One of the earliest functions of the drums was to furnish a repetitive beat to accompany dancers. With the development in America of the dance orchestra came a series of inventions which enabled the bass drum, cymbals, snare drum, and other percussion instruments to be manipulated by a single player. Early jazz bands used the drums mainly as a time-beating adjunct which worked in close cooperation with the bass, piano, guitar, and other chord instruments to form the *rhythm section.* Since about 1940 there has been a trend toward setting the drums free from their monotonous duty of time-beating. The progressive jazz drummer today functions more as an equal partner with the other instruments in melodic and solo rhythmic "fill-ins" rather than merely as a keeper of the beat.

Since dance band and jazz combo experience form a part of most high school music programs, it behooves the instrumental music director to keep abreast of the tremendous strides which are being made in the field of dance band, stage band, and jazz drumming. The author believes that all percussion students should be given training and on-the-job experience in this idiom. The rhythmic drive and precision acquired through jazz playing is a requisite and valuable skill in all areas of percussion playing.

In addition, the interest of young percussion students can often be stimulated and maintained by dance band experience.

Soloistic Possibilities. Nearly all of the major percussion instruments can be used in solo roles. The most satisfactory solo instrument of the percussion family is the marimba, which has a more mellow and resonant tone than its close relative, the xylophone, and lends itself to four-mallet chordal style. Several composers have written important works for the solo marimba, such as Paul Creston's *Concertino for Marimba and Orchestra,* Robert Kurka's *Concerto for Marimba and Orchestra,* and Darius Milhaud's *Concerto for Marimba, Vibes, and Orchestra,* Gen Parchman's *Concerto for Marimba and Orchestra,* Basta's *Concerto for Marimba and Orchestra* and Aldana's *Concerto for Marimba and Wind Orchestra.* Several major works have evolved for solo xylophone including *Fantasy on Japanese Wood Prints* by Alan Hovhaness, *Sonata for Xylophone* by Thomas Pitfield and *Concerto for Xylophone and Orchestra* by Toshiro Mayuzumi.

Among the drum group, the snare drum is the traditional solo instrument. A great wealth of solo material is available, chiefly of a rudimental nature designed to display the drummer's technique and command of the rudiments.

However, there are also a number of substantial non-rudimental solos for snare drum including Jay Collins' *Tabula Rasa* for solo snare drum with piano, Ellis Kohs' *Sonata for Snare Drum and Piano* and Warren Benson's *Three Dances for Solo Snare Drum.*

The timpani solo repertory is rapidly expanding. Some excellent accompanied and unaccompanied pieces have been written in recent years ranging in difficulty from very easy to virtuoso level. Tcherepnin's *Sonatina for Three Timpani and Piano* (Orchestra), Elliot Carter's *Eight Pieces for Unaccompanied Timpani,* Gutche's *Timpani Concertante, Concertino for Timpani and Tape* by Jan Hanus and Donald White's *Concertino for Timpani, Winds and Percussion* are examples of large scale solo works.

Other major works for the timpani include *Sonata for Timpani* by John Beck, *Improvisation Del Quiché* by Jay Collins, *Paukenzeit* by Jay Collins, *Concerto for Timpani and Orchestra* by Harold Farberman, *March for Two Pairs of Kettledrums* by André and Jacques Philidor, *Timpani Concerto* by Sam Raphling, *Konzert für Pauken und Orchester* by Werner Thärichen, *Three Etudes for Five Timpani* by Raymond Helble, and *Concerto for 5 Kettledrums and Orchestra* by Robert Parris. There is even a work for six (!) timpani: *March and Polonaise* by Julius Tausch. Robert Muczynski's *Three Designs for Three Timpani* was written expressly for the high school timpani soloist.

Multi-percussion solos for all grade levels are available. These works are exciting to perform and to hear. They provide a fine challenge to those individuals striving to become the "complete or total percussionist." The better solos demand great attention to overall musicianship—a quality sadly lacking in far too many percussionists.

MUSICIANSHIP IN PERCUSSION PLAYING

Goal of Instruction Is Musicianship

In teaching percussion students the techniques of the various insruments, one must emphasize continually that beyond mere technical competence lies a higher goal—namely, *musicianship.* Highly paid professional players in symphony, jazz, recording, and theater work are masters of their craft in a technical sense, true. But they are more than technicians. In nearly every case their outstanding qualification is their basic musical feeling, which can truly be called artistry.

Can the elements which constitute musicianship be taught? The answer is *yes,* provided, of course, that the student is responsible, alert, and willing to persevere and that the instructor himself possesses and communicates thorough musicianship.

There are certain specific aspects of musicianship which the teacher and the student should check on in their day-to-day, month-to-month work. Musical playing is not mystery, nor a divine gift, nor simply long experience. Rather it can be conceived as a complex of factors which can be isolated and pursued as specific goals of instruction. Constant careful attention to the following factors of musicianship, plus the factor of practical, on-the-job experience, is the foundation upon which good percussion playing (and teaching) rests. A good musician develops and possesses:

1. Sensitivity to the expressive quality of music.
2. Sensitivity to sounds (the natural sounds as well as strictly musical).
3. The urge to experiment with sounds (at a high level: improvise, compose).
4. The urge to analyze patterns of organized sound (*hearing* music).
5. A keen sense of pitch.
6. A keen sense of time (tempo, rhythm).
7. A keen sense of timbre (color).
8. A keen sense of volume (dynamics).
9. A knowledge of tonal expectancies (progressions of tones, resolutions, logic of tones in motion).
10. A sense of tonality (key feeling, tonal center).
11. An acquaintance with the literature (*all* styles and historical periods).
12. The ability to discriminate (evaluate music).

13. A knowledge of performance practices and traditions.
14. Solo and ensemble performance skill.
15. Skill in reading music.
16. The ability to memorize music.
17. Skill in following a conductor (flexibility).
18. The ability to recognize and be cognizant of musical lines (phrases).

Of these facets of general musicianship, the most important for the percussionist are:

1. Sensitivity to time, rhythm, "beat-sense," tempo feeling.
2. Sensitivity to dynamics.
3. Sensitivity to timbre differences.
4. Urge to experiment with sounds.
5. Skill in reading music.
6. Skill in following a conductor.
7. The ability to recognize and be cognizant of musical lines (phrases).

Unfortunately, many percussionists are guilty of ignoring item 7 of the above listing. In their formative years of training, string, wind, and brass players are continually made aware of the necessity for accurate phrase interpretation. All too often, percussionists are permitted to concentrate on individual notes and idiomatic rhythmic figures failing to realize their obligation, along with the other instrumentalists, to contribute to the forming of complete musical statements (phrases). Playing the "musical line" is an absolute necessity for the percussionist performing contemporary literature.

Technical Facility as Means to Musical Ends

In recent years much progress has been made toward the teaching of musical percussion in our school music programs. However, in far too many of these programs most percussion instruction still is limited to technique. In many cases this nonmusical orientation is due to the overemphasis of the "original 26 Rudiments." Some music educators seem to feel that technical mastery of these somewhat archaic snare drum beats constitutes an adequate background for the band or orchestra percussionist. This is not to deny the "rudiments" their rightful place in a percussionist's training, but they should not become an end in themselves (nor for that matter should technique).

Sight-reading is an important aspect of the student's development that is usually given far too little attention. And yet sooner or later the student will be faced with the need to perform with little or possibly even no rehearsal time at all. Thus the essence of sight-reading skills. Sight-reading is a skill that must be developed by careful prac-

tice, by reading duets with another person, for instance. Sight-reading is usually the weakest area in a percussionist's background.

What, then, should be the relationship of technique to well-rounded percussion playing? The answer may be discovered by looking into the actual on-the-job demands made of the performing percussionist. At every level, from the elementary school band to the professional symphony orchestra, the percussion section cannot stand on technique alone. Musical percussion playing involves all of the aspects of general musicianship. The percussion problems which beset band and orchestra directors are usually more musical than technical. Matters of accenting, dynamic contrast, steadiness of tempo, proper choice of instruments, and accurate reading are common problems. Actual manipulative problems are much less frequent. There have been many cases in our symphony orchestras where wind or string players have been rather quickly and satisfactorily converted to percussion players. School music directors, in emergency situations, have often been pleasantly surprised to find that with only a minimum of practice a string or wind player can substitute for an ailing timpanist, bass drummer, or triangle player. These situations illustrate the relationship between musicianship and technique.

On the other hand, technical facility cannot be overlooked. The foregoing paragraphs are not meant to imply that technique is unimportant, or that we should de-emphasize completely the teaching and practice of snare drum rudiments, scales and arpeggios on the mallet instruments, legato rolls on the timpani. It is certainly true that fine players are masters of their instruments in a technical sense. Endless hours of practice, practice of the most monotonous and self-disciplined kind, have gone into the building of these facile techniques. The technical mastery which is so painstakingly acquired is a most valuable possession. It is valuable not for itself but because it is a *means to express musical ends* in the performance of music. It enables the player to *express his musical feeling.* Technical competence liberates the player so that all of his *attention and thought can be directed toward interpretation.*

Technique, considered as a means to musical ends, does make up a large part of the young player's instrumental study. Instruction in correct basic techniques is the responsibility of the teacher, and required home practice is pretty much confined to basic techniques with beginning students. This is practical and sound. In the band or orchestra rehearsal, however, it is the director's job to see that the techniques are applied in musically sound ways. By his attitude the skillful instructor imparts the idea that technical virtuosity is not an end in itself, but rather serves the ends of musicianly performance.

THE CLASS APPROACH TO PERCUSSION TEACHING

Values of the Class Approach

It seems hardly necessary to justify class instrumental teaching today when one considers the fine work that instrumental teachers are accomplishing by class instructional means. In addition to the important factors of ensemble experience from the start and competitive motivation, the percussion class may function very nicely as a true percussion ensemble. Once the basic snare drum techniques have been worked out on the practice pads and snare drums, simple snare drum duets, trios, and literature for snare drum, bass drum, and cymbals can be played by the class. Other instruments are added as they are studied. Additional advantages of the class approach for percussion are:

1. Rotation of the students on the various percussion instruments is workable in the class prior to actual band or orchestra experience.
2. The class approach is a good way to inculcate desirable habits of section routine and stage deportment.
3. The habit is formed of keeping one's eye on the conductor (instructor). Percussion sections often fail to maintain that all-important sight-line to the conductor's stick.
4. Students gain familiarity with the conductor's beat patterns in advance of band or orchestra membership.

Selection of Percussion Students

The selection of students for the percussion class is a problem which is largely a matter for the instructor to solve, as school situations vary greatly. If there is opportunity for a screening of applicants, some of the following suggestions may prove helpful:

1. A class of from four to eight students is easiest to work with. Twelve should be considered the maximum number.
2. The general intelligence of each student should be checked. Most schools have cumulative record cards which the teacher may consult. In the absence of I.Q. scores, a rough but quick method would be for the teacher himself to administer a short reading comprehension quiz. A word of warning, however. There is, as yet, no positive means of predicting musical success on the basis of verbal intelligence. Studies have shown that there does exist a low, but positive, correlation between musicality and intelligence.
3. Work habits, seriousness of purpose, enthusiasm, and other personality traits should be considered. Moti-

vation and drive to attain a certain goal are probably the most important factors in the student's musical growth.
4. Marching in time to music is a quick way to spot students who have a very deficient beat-sense. Prospective drummers who are unable to march in time are best eliminated at the outset.
5. To identify students with a good beat-sense, the instructor should set a tempo in single taps with a stick or hand clap and have the student maintain that steady beat. A more refined but similar test is the duplication of various rhythm patterns dictated by the instructor.
6. Prior or current study of another instrument, particularly the piano, should be considered. This is recommended especially in recruiting timpani prospects.
7. Despite the well-meaning intentions of school administrators and counselors, the acceptance of students in the percussion class for physical therapy or psychotherapy is to be discouraged as a practice.

Drum Pads and Other Physical Equipment

Certain basic equipment is needed for properly carrying through a successful percussion class. Each student should provide himself with a quality metronome (preferably a model which is equipped with a loud audio *and* a flashbeat option), *Stick Control* and *Mallet Control* by George Stone, a junior percussion kit consisting of 2½ octave chromatic bells with a stand, appropriate mallets, Firth SD-1 general purpose sticks, a lightweight music stand and a tuneable practice pad. It is *absolutely essential* that beginning percussion students also become involved with pitches from the outset, as this activity will greatly enhance their musical development and transition to the study of timpani at some later date.

Whatever physical set-up is decided upon, the instructor should allow enough space so that he can circulate easily among the students and offer extra assistance as needed. It is very important that each player's instrument be almost belt high as he stands in playing position. As a general rule of thumb, the drum or practice pad should be set approximately a hand's width below the belt. This will, of course, depend on individual physiological characteristics such as arm length, etc.

Figure 1.2 shows three set-ups which have been used effectively.

Suggested lists of basic instrumentations are given here as a guide for instructors of elementary beginning classes, junior high, and high school groups. College and university music departments should be equipped with a full inventory of standard percussion instruments.

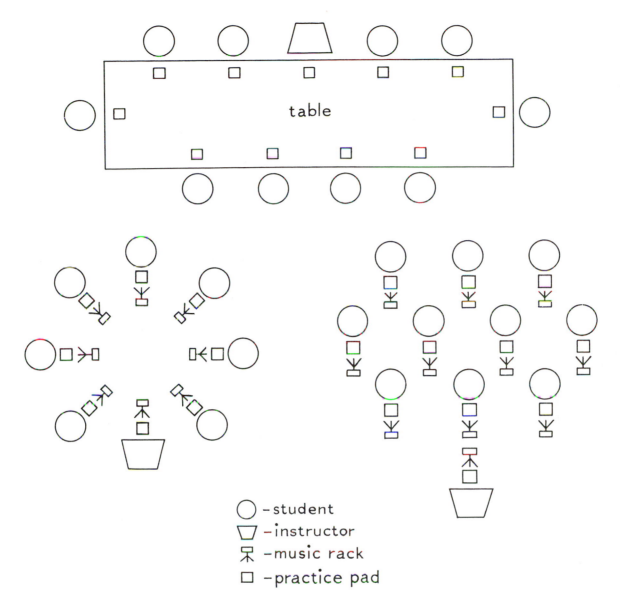

Figure 1.2. Three set-ups for beginning percussion class.

TABLE I ELEMENTARY (BEGINNING CLASS)

Several orchestra type snare drums with stands

Bass drum

Pair of cymbals

Miscellaneous small instruments including triangle, tambourine, woodblock, castanets, etc. with a trap table.

TABLE II JUNIOR HIGH SCHOOL

Several orchestra type snare drums with stands

Bass drum

Pair of cymbals

Suspended cymbal with stand

Set of bells and/or xylophone or marimba

Pair of timpani (pedal tuning)

Miscellaneous small instruments including triangle, tambourine, woodblock, castanets, etc. with trap table

TABLE III HIGH SCHOOL

Several snare drums, both orchestra and field types

Two or more tenor drums

Concert bass drum

Marching bass drums (2–3)

One large pair of cymbals

Figure 1.3. The University of South Alabama, Mobile Percussion Ensemble—Dr. John J. Papastefan, founder and director.

One smaller pair of cymbals
One or two suspended cymbals with stands
Tam-tam (gong)
Set of bells
Xylophone, marimba, vibraphone
Set of tubular chimes
Four timpani (pedal tuning)
Dance band drum set
Miscellaneous small instruments including triangle,
    tambourine, woodblock, castanets, etc. with trap
    table

The set-up for a percussion class using a full complement of percussion instruments should be the same as that used in the band or orchestra percussion section.

Sequence of Studies

Since snare drum technique is basic to all percussion playing, it is the logical starting point for all players. Mastery of the snare drum handholds and arm, wrist, and hand motions makes easier the mallet played instruments and timpani technique. Practice pads should be used for the first several lessons. Snare drums should be used in the class, if available, after the first few rudiments can be played fairly well. Following the first group of lessons on

essential snare drum techniques, the selected textbook should be introduced. Do not attempt the learning of reading skills until stick control is well developed.

Accurate reading of the most common snare drum figures is the second stage of percussion class study. The exercises introduced should include single strokes, taps, and flams. Reading material containing rolls should be delayed until the students can execute the long and short stroke rolls satisfactorily. Rote learning of remaining rudiments should then proceed concurrently with graded reading material. The class period at this stage should be divided between rudiment drill and reading practice.

The introduction of the bass drum and the cymbals should be made after some degree of reading skill has been achieved, and the snare drum roll can be executed fairly well. For creating interesting ensemble effects, various combinations of snare drums, bass drums, and cymbals can be used. For reading practice, this combination of instruments can make use of the drum parts to actual band and orchestra scores. Most instruction books contain many study pages scored for snare drum, bass drum, and cymbals. Later, easy percussion ensembles scored for this combination can be learned. In many elementary school situations this basic snare drum-bass drum-cymbals group will constitute a year's class work, and will enable most students in the class to proceed the next year to band or orchestra.

If the class can be continued a second year, much can be done in the areas of mallet-played instruments, timpani, and the so-called "traps" or miscellaneous small percussion instruments. Musically satisfying percussion ensemble work utilizes many instruments and so it follows that the ideal course of study would include instruction on all of the standard instruments prior to the student's enrollment in performing groups.

Since this sequence of class work is not always possible to schedule, the band and orchestra sectional rehearsals provide an alternative solution to the problem of *when* to carry out the necessary instruction for the mallet instruments, the timpani, and the small instruments.

Finally, it is realized that technical instruction is a day-to-day process carried on within the framework of full band and orchestra rehearsals. Conscientious instructors and students can make application of much of the material of the *Guide* while working out specific problems encountered in the music being studied. Individual practice of techniques is, of course, required for real mastery.

The foregoing paragraphs have dealt with the class instructional approach as it may be applied to the learning of percussion instruments. The realities of school music life being what they are, most work must necessarily be carried on in large groups. Good results can be achieved by this means, especially with the snare drum. However, the rather specialized techniques of the xylophone, marimba, vibraharp, and especially the timpani, indicate private instruction whenever and wherever a *competent* teacher can be found. Because a school normally has access to only one set of bells, one xylophone, one pair of timpani, etc., it is somewhat of a problem to carry on advanced work on these instruments in a class setting.

Note

1. Gordon B. Peters, *The Drummer: Man,* rev. ed. (Wilmette, IL: Kemper-Peters Publications, 1975), pp. 210–220.
2. Orff, Carl and Gunild Keetman. *Music For Children* (Orff-Schulwerke), in seven volumes. English adaptation by Doreen Hall and Arnold Walter., New York, 1950. Assoc. Music Publ. (G. Schirmer).
3. Bavin, Charles. *The Percussion Band from A to Z.* London, 1953.
4. Coleman, Satis N. *Creative Music for Children,* New York, n.d.
5. Rosenstrauch, Henny. *Percussion, Rhythm, Music, Movement.* Availability: Miss Henny Rosenstrauch, 5628 Forbes St., Pittsburgh, Pa. or Volkwein Music House, Pittsburgh.

CHAPTER 2

Functional Classification of Percussion Instruments

System of Classification

Historical and pedagogical literature contains varied and confusing classifications of the numerous percussion instruments. Starting from the basic definition of percussion instruments as *those musical instruments whose sound is produced by striking,* writers have offered differing systems for subgrouping this large and extremely heterogeneous family.

Curt Sachs[1] classifies percussion instruments under two headings, membranophones and idiophones. The membranophones basically are drums, whose construction includes one or two stretched membranes (skins, heads). The shells may be of wood, metal, bamboo, gourd, etc. and their general shapes are tubular, kettle (hemispheric), and frame. Plates and bars are used in the construction of the idiophones, which are instruments made of naturally sonorous substances not requiring additional tension as do membranes. Idiophones can be made of metal, wood, plastic or composition, and assume a variety of shapes like plates, tubes, rods, strips, blocks, and bars. Some idiophones, like the pair of cymbals, are played by striking together while others are struck with sticks, mallets, or rods. Further differentiation is made between an idiophonic instrument like the xylophone which is a set of bars, or plates, and others, like the triangle, which are single rods, or bars. Still other idiophones are sounded by means of shaking (maracas), scraping (guiro), and friction (sandpaper blocks).

A somewhat more useful system for classifying the instruments of percussion has been adopted by writers on musical acoustics[2,3,4] who find it convenient to subgroup the instruments according to *whether or not they emit a definite pitch.* Thus the timpani, xylophone, marimba, vibraphone, bells, and chimes would fall into one category while the bass drum, snare drum, cymbals, tam-tam, triangle, and the dozens of more primitive and exotic instruments would fall into the non-pitch category. Percussionists take exception, however, to the acousticians' relegation of the non-pitched instruments to the status of mere noisemakers.

Because each of the sonorous materials commonly used in constructing the instruments of percussion produces a unique and identifiable timbre, composers and orchestrators often think of the percussion family as made up of three subgroups: the membranes (including all the drum-type instruments), the metals (including the cymbals, tam-tam or gong, triangle, bells, vibraphone, chimes), and woods (xylophone, marimba, woodblock, temple blocks, and various gourd instruments).

The most practical classification of the percussion instruments is derived from their functions in the orchestra and band and their general manner of playing. Thus, a table may be drawn up as follows:

I. Drums with definite pitch:
    timpani (kettledrums)
    concert or tuneable tom-toms, roto-toms
    timp-toms (marching bands)
II. Drums with indefinite pitch:
    snare drum
    field drum
    tenor drum
    tambour de Provence
    tom-tom
    bass drum
III. Cymbals:
    pair of crash or hand cymbals
    suspended cymbals
    sizzle
    Chinese
    swish
    sock cymbals (hi-hat, afterbeat, etc.)
    antique cymbals (crotales)
    finger cymbals
IV. Mallet-played instruments:
    xylophone
    marimba
    vibraphone (vibraharp)
    bells (glockenspiel, orchestra bells, campanelli)
    chimes
    bell-lyra

V. Miscellaneous percussion instruments, including the so-called "traps" and sound-effects:
triangle
tambourine (tambour de Basque)
tam-tam (gong)
woodblock
castanets
metal castanets
Chinese temple blocks
anvil
auto horn (claxon)
ratchet (raganella, crécelle)
sandpaper blocks
siren
slapstick (whip)
sleighbells
thunder sheet
wind machine
steel plate
brake drum
horse hooves (coconut shells)
bird whistles (cuckoo, canary, etc.)
lion roar (string drum)
dog bark (puita)
police whistle
jingles
marching machine

VI. Latin-American rhythm instruments:
claves
maracas (shakers)
guiro (notched gourd, reco-reco)
cowbell (cencerro)
bongos
timbales
quijada (jawbone)—vibra-slap
conga drum (tumba, tumbadora)
chacalho (metal shaker)
cabasa (gourd shaker with rattles)

VII. Dance band drum set:
small bass drum (14″×22″) with foot pedal beater
small snare drum (5″ × 14″)
sock cymbals (hi-hat, afterbeat) with pedal mechanism
crash cymbal (17″ or 18″ diameter)
ride cymbal (20″ or 22″ diameter)
small tom-tom (9″ × 13″)
large tom-tom (16″ × 16″)
cowbell, woodblock

A comprehensive reference table follows which lists the instruments of percussion with their French, Italian, and German equivalent designations, basic techniques, acoustical features, and characteristic usages.

I. DRUMS

	ACOUSTICAL FEATURES	BASIC TECHNIQUE	CHARACTERISTIC USAGES
Timpani (kettledrums) Fr. timbales It. timpani Ger. pauken 	Head may be tuned to definite pitches by hand screws, pedals, chain or other mechanism. The greater the tension on the head the higher the pitch. Head vibrates as a whole and in segments. The vibration is resonated by the hollow hemispherical metal shells, called bowls.	Striking the heads with various types of timpani sticks which have felt-covered, felt disc, or wooden ends. Tones sustained by means of single stroke roll.	In classical music the pair of timpani were tuned to the tonic and dominant of the tonality and reinforced the bass line and brass passages. Beginning with Beethoven, tunings other than tonic and dominant were used, and solo passages given to the timpani. Nineteenth century composers scored for three, four and more timpani, and called for rapid changes of pitch. The modern timpanist requires at least four machine-tuned timpani and at times as many as six. Lightweight marching machine timpani have been developed for use in marching bands. The kettles are completely portable and give added tonal color and depth of sound to the marching band percussion section.
Snare Drum (side drum) Fr. caisse claire It. piccolo cassa Ger. kleinetrommel	Top (batter) head tuned slightly *lower* than bottom (snare) head by a major 2nd or minor 3rd. Vibration from batter head is transferred to snare head. The gut or wire snares rattle crisply against the snare head. As in all two-headed drums, the diameter governs the pitch (highness or lowness) and the depth of the shell governs the volume (loudness).	Striking the top (batter) head with snare drumsticks. Tone sustained by means of rapidly alternating double strokes, called the *roll*.	Marking rhythm figures, especially repetitive march and dance patterns. Underlining dynamics, often by means of the roll.
Field Drum (parade drum, street drum) Fr. tambour militaire It. tamburo militare Ger. militartrommel	Same as for snare drum, except that shell is proportionately deeper.	Same as for snare drum.	Playing marching beats. In concert music used when deep and military snare drum tone is indicated.
Tenor Drum Fr. caisse roulante It. cassa rullante Ger. ruhrtrommel 	Top and bottom head, but no snares. Both the diameter and depth of shell are greater than those of the snare drums.	Same as for snare drum and field drum, except that in marching band and drum corps, hard felt-ended sticks are used.	Very much like a tom-tom in sound. Used in marching bands and drum corps to furnish a sound midway in depth between the snare drum and the bass drum.

Tambour de Provence (Fr. only)

Top and bottom heads, but with only one thick cord (snare) under bottom head.

Striking with large snare drumsticks.

Called for only in French scores. Bizet's *L'Arlésienne Suite* is an instance. Also used in Milhaud's *Suite Francaise*.

Tom-tom

Top and bottom heads which are tuneable. Sizes range from 7'' × 13'' to 18'' × 18''.

In more recent years, a demand for definite pitches as opposed to simply highs and lows has arisen. Concert or tuneable tom-toms have been developed to satisfy this demand. Usually in a group of four, these single headed drums are tuned like a "hand screw" timpani and are high pitched (in the timbale and bongo range).

Striking the top head with snare drumsticks or hard felt sticks.

The concert tom-toms are played in the same manner as regular tom-tom.

Used chiefly in the dance band drum set-up. Also used to imitate primitive or exotic drums in concert music.

The concert tom-toms are utilized primarily in percussion ensembles and chamber music; however, parts occasionally are being written for these instruments in orchestral and band scores.

Timp-toms (see Figure 10.5)

A grouping of two or three one headed, portable, tuneable drums ranging in size from 10'' depth by 14'' diameter to 16'' depth by 28'' diameter.

Striking the head with wooden timp-tom or hard felt mallets utilizing the matched grip.

The timp-tom duos or trios are utilized by marching units to extend the lower color range of the percussion section.

Bass Drum

Fr. grosse caisse
It. gran cassa, cassa grande
Ger. grosse trommel

Size varies with type of ensemble in which it is used. Both heads tuned fairly loosely, so that very lowest frequencies predominate. No definite pitch is desirable.

Playing surface is struck with one or two bass drum mallets. Marching bass drum may use wood mallets. Bass drum roll is produced with smaller, matched mallets, but *not* with timpani mallets. Drum set bass drum played by means of a foot pedal.

Marks the strong beats in march and dance music. Underlines the dynamics in other types of music. Provides the lowest frequencies to reinforce the bass instruments. Dramatic use of solo "booms" and rolls is common.

II. CYMBALS

Cymbals (pair of clashed cymbals)

Fr. cymbales
It. piatti
     cinelli
Ger. becken

A good pair of cymbals are matched to complement one another in order to bring out the greatest number of frequencies. This simultaneous sounding of a wide range of frequencies accounts for the brilliant, crashy tone characteristic of fine cymbals.

The cymbals are held by means of loose rawhide straps and are sounded by clashing one against the other.

Cymbals are ancient instruments which were brought into the orchestra during the classic period. (Beethoven-*Scherzo* from *Ninth Symphony*) being at that time chiefly associated with Turkish military music. Subsequent composers have employed the cymbals mainly to add brilliance to the band and orchestra timbre, and to help in marking the rhythm in marches and dance music.

Suspended cymbal
Fr. cymbale suspendé
    cymbale libre
It. piatto sospeso
Ger. becken frei

ACOUSTICAL FEATURES

The sound of cymbals varies with their diameter and thickness. In the case of the suspended cymbal a third very important variable is the choice of beater. Each type of beater brings out a different set of frequencies. A further variable is the playing spot, i.e., edge, top, or dome.

Variations in construction and additions to the regular suspended cymbal create further variable sounds such as attaching rivets at its circumference (sizzle cymbal), having the edges turned up with a squarer crown (Chinese cymbal), or combining both of the above (swish cymbal).

BASIC TECHNIQUE

The single cymbal is mounted on a floor stand which allows it to vibrate freely. It can be struck with mallets, drumsticks, timpani sticks, wire brushes, triangle beater, or even a coin.

CHARACTERISTIC USAGES

Used chiefly for very dry, choked crashes and, by means of a single stroke roll, for assisting in creating tremendous crescendi. A characteristic rhythm figure

is played by dance and jazz drummers on the top of a large suspended cymbal, using the right stick or brush.

Sock cymbals (high-hat, afterbeat cymbals)
Fr. crotales
It. crotalo
Ger. antiken Zimbeln

The characteristic sound is a "ching" or "chup" as the cymbals contact each other.

The sock cymbal set-up consists of a pair of 14" or 15" cymbals clashed by means of a foot pedal mechanism. Sticks or brushes can be used on the top or edges while the cymbals are being operated by the left foot.

Used in dance music and jazz exclusively. In 4/4 measure it is played on the afterbeats, using the left foot. The rhythm figure

is sometimes played on the sock cymbals.

Antique cymbals
Fr. crotales
It. crotalo
Ger. antiken Zimbeln

Antique cymbals are very thick in comparison with their diameters, being essentially circular bars. They have a definite pitch, and are usually used in pairs pitched a fifth apart. They emit a clear bell-like tone.

These tiny cymbals are not struck as are regular cymbals. If both are to sound, they are struck one edge against another edge at a single point. If only one is to sound, the other cymbal is muffled by holding with the fingers. An alternative is to strike the single cymbal with a triangle beater.

Used sparingly by a few composers for coloristic purposes, (Debussy-Afternoon of a Faun). Pitches are specified in scores requiring use of antique cymbals. Some contemporary band scores such as Husa's Music for Prague 1968 call for their use. Often used in percussion ensemble scores.

Finger cymbals
Fr. cymbales doigts
It. cinelli dito
Ger. fingernbecken

Finger cymbals are thinner than antique cymbals. They do not emit a definite single pitch, but produce a cluster of very high frequencies with very little volume or carrying power.

Same as for antique cymbals.

Rarely called for in symphonic scores. Limited use by modern composers of small ensemble and percussion music. Berio's Circles is an example.

III. MALLET-PLAYED INSTRUMENTS

Xylophone
Fr. xylophone, clagnebois
It. silophono, sticcato
Ger. holz und strohinstrument xylophon strohfiedel

The xylophone consists of a series of chromatically tuned wooden or synthetic bars mounted on a frame. A 2½ to 4 octave range is usual, the majority of xylophones having a range of 3½ octaves, F4-C8. The bars are arranged in two banks, corresponding to the piano keyboard's white and black keys. Most xylophones do not have resonators, although the so-called concert model is an exception. Typical xylophone tone quality is hard, brittle and rather piercing. The xylophone sounds one octave higher than written.

The xylophone was at one time chiefly a solo instrument. Vaudeville era performers developed a facile and brilliant technique. In band and orchestra scores the xylophone is used sparingly, typically to play short melodic lines of a dry, angular and brittle nature.

Striking the bars with mallets, one in either hand. To sustain a note the rapidly alternating single stroke roll is used.

Marimba

Prototype marimbas developed both in Africa and South America. There is a certain similarity of appearance to the xylophone, but the marimba's tone quality is more mellow due to the wider and flatter wooden bars, and also to the softer mallets used. An additional feature is the resonating tube mounted beneath each bar to aid in amplifying and sustaining the sound. Range is usually from A2 to C7, 4⅓ octaves.

The marimba is widely used as a solo instrument. In the low register it can sound almost organ-like when played with the four-mallet tremolo. The marimba does not have the penetrating tone quality of the xylophone, and for this reason is seldom used in band and orchestra. However, concerti for marimba and orchestra have been written by Creston, Kurka, Basta, Milhaud, and Parchman.

Striking the bars with mallets (normally softer than xylophone mallets), one in either hand. Chordal style used in solo playing employs two mallets in each hand. The roll is the same as that of the xylophone.

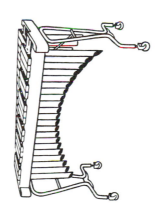

Vibraphone (vibraharp)
It. vibrafono

The "vibe" has the same keyboard layout as the wood-barred instruments, but the bars are made of a metal alloy. The most distinctive features of the vibraphone are a sustaining pedal which is operated by the foot, and the electrically driven "vibrato" mechanism which consists of discs on a shaft which alternately open and close the resonating tubes. Range is usually 3 octaves, F3 to F6.

In concert music the vibraphone is employed mainly to play bell tones, chords and arpeggios. In jazz the instrument has become a popular solo and ensemble instrument, often used without the "vibra" to produce a sound which is cooler and less lush than its normal quality.

Techniques are basically like those of the xylophone and marimba, except that the tremolo (roll) is not needed to sustain tones. Instead, the damper pedal is used as it is in piano playing. The roll is occasionally used for effect and to avoid tone decay.

Bells (orchestra bells)

Fr. jeu de timbres
     jeu de clochettes
It. campanelli
Ger. glockenspiel

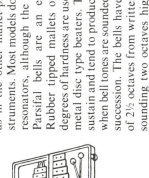

The small metal bars are mounted as in the other mallet-played instruments. Most models do not have resonators, although the so-called Parsifal bells are an exception. Rubber tipped mallets of various degrees of hardness are used, as are metal disc type beaters. The tones sustain and tend to produce a clang when bell tones are sounded in quick succession. The bells have a range of 2½ octaves from written C5–C8 sounding two octaves higher than usually written.

Technique basically same as for xylophone and marimba.

Bell tones, singly or in octaves, arpeggios, and diatonic melodic lines are common.

Chimes

Fr. carrillon
It. campani
Ger. glocken

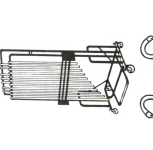

The metal tubes sound somewhat like carillon bells, but have fewer overtones. The tones sustain themselves so long that rapid passages sound blurred. Chimes equipped with a damper pedal make hand damping unnecessary, but for the other type, damping is the main problem. Control of the volume is another problem. C5 to G6, 1½ octaves.

The top ends of the tubes are struck at an angle with a laminated wood or chamois covered chime mallet. Some passages require two mallets. The more recent models are equipped with a damper pedal to help overcome the problem of discordant clang.

Single bell tones, church bell effects, and repetitive arpeggiated figures are common.

Bell-lyra (glockenspiel)

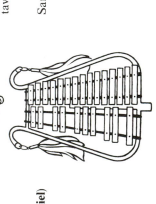

Same as for bells.

This marching band version of the orchestra bells is held in a sling in front of the player with the keyboard extending from low to high in the direction of march. Two pyralin or hard rubber mallets are used.

The bell-lyra doubles the melodic line in marching band music.

IV. MISCELLANEOUS PERCUSSION INSTRUMENTS

Triangle

Fr.   triangle
It.   triangolo
Ger.   triangel

A steel rod bent into the form of a triangle producing a small bell-like tone when struck by a metal beater. Several sizes and diameters of triangles are needed for various effects and dynamic levels. Various weights of beaters produce varying tone qualities.

The triangle is suspended by a narrow gut string attached to a clamp which is detached from the music rack and held about head high for playing position. The metal beater rod may strike the outside of the right leg of the triangle or the inner side of the lower leg. A roll can be executed by rapid alternating strokes between closed ends of the triangle.

This very ancient instrument came into the orchestra along with the cymbals during the eighteenth century. It is a coloristic instrument, contributing a delicate and ethereal timbre to the ensemble. Sometimes it is used simply to add a dash of metallic sound to the percussion timbre.

Tambourine

Fr.   tambour de Basque
It.   tamburo basco
      tamburino
Ger.   becken tambourin

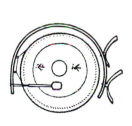

The tone quality of a tambourine is dependent upon the diameter, the tension of the head, and the number of jingles attached. The tambourine is a hybrid, being partly drum and partly tiny pairs of cymbals.

For ordinary playing, the tambourine is held in the left hand and its head is rapped sharply by the fingers and thumb of the right hand formed into a small tight ball of flesh. The roll is produced either by shaking with a rotating wrist motion, or by moistening the right thumb tip and rubbing it around the outer perimeter of the tambourine head.

In modern scores the tambourine is used chiefly for the sake of its individual sound in marking the rhythm. In light concert music it is often used when a Spanish or Gypsy flavor is desired. The tambourine is also used in the Brazilian samba.

Tam-tam (gong)

Fr.   tam-tam
It.   tam-tam
Ger.   tam-tam

A circular, slightly convex metallic disk with the edges turned inward, the tam-tam or gong (in modern day symphonic organizations, these terms are used interchangeably) may range in size from ten to forty inches in diameter. Naturally, the larger instruments will produce a darker, more resonant sound. The larger instruments do not "speak" quickly, the tone seeming to reach its maximum volume a second or two after impact. The after-ring is lengthy and careful damping is necessary.

The tam-tam is struck with a large heavy chamois or felt covered beater which is usually weighted with lead. Most tam-tams sound best when struck a few inches off center.

Although the tam-tam still suggests the Orient, it is now called for in scores of all types. The sound is serious and awesome. Loud gong crashes are often used to mark a climax.

	ACOUSTICAL FEATURES	BASIC TECHNIQUE	CHARACTERISTIC USAGES

Woodblock
Fr.   bois
It.   legno
Ger. holz

A woodblock is a rectangular block, hollowed out for resonance. Various sizes give a range of high-low sounds. For best resonance, blocks should be mounted to another percussion instrument or stand.

The woodblock may be struck with soft xylophone mallets or drumsticks on its top surface, or it may be played with two sticks. The tips or the shoulders of the snare drumstick may be used, depending upon the volume and tone quality desired.

The woodblock is mainly a color effect and is suggestive of Oriental music. It is also used to suggest "ricky-tick" vaudeville and early Dixieland orchestras.

Castanets
Fr.   castagnettes
It.   castagnetta
Ger. kastagnetten

Castanets are a pair of small shells of hard wood or plastic which create a "clacking" sound when struck together.

Percussionists do not attempt to play the castanets in the manner of the Spanish dancers. Instead, the shells of the castanets are mounted opposite one another separated by a broad wooden handle. When the handle is shaken in mid-air against the opposite hand or against the knee, the castanets sound.

A better arrangement is to have the castanet shells attached by a spring to a piece of resonant wood so that they can be played by striking with the fingertips or with drumsticks.

Castanets are used almost without exception for the purpose of imparting a Spanish flavor to a composition or arrangement. Repetitive rhythm figures are typical.

Metal Castanets
Fr.   castagnettes de fer
It.   castagnetta ferra
Ger. metallkastgnetten

Metal castanets are finger cymbals mounted opposite each other so that they can be clashed together by squeezing the hand spring.

The pair of metal castanets is played by striking the flat surfaces against each other, preferably by means of a spring-type holder.

Repetitive rhythm figures are typical. The metal castanets do not produce as dry a sound as the wooden type, nor do they suggest a Spanish flavor.

Temple blocks (Chinese temple blocks)

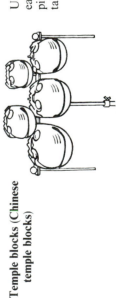

Usually a set consists of five blocks, each with a different pitch. The pitches are indefinite, but unmistakably "higher" or "lower."

The set of blocks is mounted with the lower pitched blocks to the left. They may be struck with soft xylophone mallets, felt timpani sticks or snare drumsticks. May be mounted either staggered or in straight line.

The temple blocks are another import from the Orient, and have been used to suggest Oriental atmosphere and as horsehoof imitations.

Anvil

Fr. enclume
It. incudine
Ger. amboss

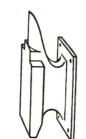

When struck, the anvil emits a heavy ringing metallic sound. A section of railroad track or other heavy metal objects can be substituted for an actual anvil. Percussion equipment companies have available for sale "concert anvils" consisting of a metal bar and beater. These are compact, easy to transport, and produce a very fine metallic sound.

The anvil is usually struck on its top surface with a small ball peen or regular hammer. Most real anvils sound best when struck on the tongue or tapered end.

Very limited call in the repertoire for the anvil. Its sound is suggestive of great force, fury, armor and battle. Verdi—*Il Trovatore* is a classic example. A modern work calling for anvil is Gene Gutche's *Holofernes Overture.*

Auto horn (claxon)

Pressing down the lever sounds the horn. In the bulb type of horn, a sudden squeezing of the rubber bulb sounds the horn.

Limited to descriptive music portraying traffic sounds. Gershwin—*An American in Paris* is an example.

Ratchet

Fr. crécelle
It. raganella
Ger. handratche

Pieces of flexible flat wood are sprung against a rotating geared wheel. It produces a very fast, grinding, clattering sound.

The ratchet clamp is usually attached to the bass drum hoop. To sound the ratchet, turn the handle clockwise.

This curious sound effect has been used by many composers in a variety of idioms. It has no clear associative or imitative qualities. Example is Honnegger—*Jeanne d'Arc.*

Sandpaper blocks

Two blocks of wood with medium or fine sandpaper attached which produce a "brushing" or "swishing" sound.

To maintain a steady volume of sound it is necessary to turn the handle at a constant rate.

One block is held stationary, the other brushed against it in rhythm.

Limited to train and steamboat imitations and soft shoe rhythms.

Siren

Fr. sirène
It. sirèno
Ger. sirene

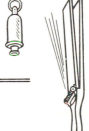

The small type used by theater drummers is held in the mouth and blown with the breath. The large fire sirens used in certain symphonic works are cranked.

Usually confined to funny music and descriptive background music. Most serious use of the large siren in Varèse—*Ionisation.*

Slapstick

Fr. fouet
It. frusta
Ger. peitsche

The action is similar to an actual whip crack in the case of the commonly used type of slapstick. Another model has two handles by means of which the two boards can be slapped shut.

Used in certain descriptive pieces.

	ACOUSTICAL FEATURES	BASIC TECHNIQUE	CHARACTERISTIC USAGES
Sleighbells Fr.　grelots It.　sonagli Ger.　schellen 	—	The most convenient way to play rhythm figures cleanly on sleighbells is to have them mounted on a flat board, which can then be shaken up and down. To play softly, contact several of the bells with the hands. This allows only two or three to vibrate.	Highly suggestive of sleigh rides, Christmas, Santa Claus, etc. Most serious use in Mahler—*Fourth Symphony*.
Thunder sheet 	—	A large sheet of metal is shaken to produce the thunder imitation.	Used to imitate thunder.
Wind machine 	—	This barrel-like machine is cranked to provide a friction sound which rises and falls in pitch with changes in the rate of cranking.	Wind imitation. Most serious use is in Strauss—*Don Quixote*.
Steel plate 	—	The plate is suspended with a heavy gut or cord, and struck with a metal beater such as a bell mallet or a small hammer.	Steeple bell imitations, fire alarm effects, and occasionally in modern scores they are employed simply for their own timbre. An example of the latter is Dorati—*Missa Brevis*.
Brake drum 	Certain brake drums have a very beautiful, clear and resonant sound.	Can be struck with metal bell mallets or a small hammer.	An ethereal and other-worldly sound.
Horse hooves (coconut shells) 	The best horsehoof imitation consists of two coconut shells fitted with leather handles at their tops.	These are clapped against a marble base in the characteristic rhythm.	Horsehoof imitations.
Bird whistles 	—	The canary imitation must be filled with water prior to use. In the type known as the cuckoo whistle, a plunger controls the pitch.	Literal bird call imitations.

Lion roar (string drum)

A single headed drum rather bucket-like in appearance, mounted on a base with a rosined string fastened through the head at its center.

A piece of leather is drawn along the string causing the head to vibrate and sound like a lion's roar.

Imitation of lion's roar. Example is Ganz—*Percussion Melange*.

Dog bark (Portuguese—*puita*)

Instrument consists of a hollow box, the top side of which is rosined and can swing back and forth.

The top side is moved back and forth sharply creating a frictional vibration.

Imitation of dog's bark. Most serious use is Villa-Lobos—*Choros #10*.

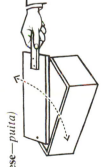

Police whistle

Whistle is blown forcibly with the breath.

Traffic noise sound effect. Ibert's *Divertissment* contains notes for the police whistle.

Jingles
It. sonaglieri

Consists of a pair of tambourine jingles mounted at the end of a rattan handle.

Played by tapping against the knee.

A pair of jingles is called for in Vaughn-Williams—*London Symphony*.

Marching machine

This box-like machine is cranked to allow blocks inside to fall against a sounding board.

Imitation of troops on the march.

V. LATIN-AMERICAN INSTRUMENTS

Claves (Spanish)

The cupped hand acts as a sound box. Both claves must be held very lightly in order to obtain maximum resonance.

One clave rests on the finger tips of the cupped left hand. The other is held lightly in the right hand. The right clave strikes the left on top, over the center of the left palm.

The claves beat is the basis of most of the Latin-American dance rhythms. It is usually one of the following repetitive two-measure phrases:

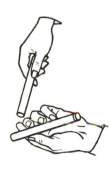

	ACOUSTICAL FEATURES	BASIC TECHNIQUE	CHARACTERISTIC USAGES

Maracas (Spanish)

Dried seeds, shot or tiny pebbles are used as the filler material which rattles against the sides of the gourd.

Shaking alternately, usually with an up and down motion, the rhythm of straight eighth notes.

Basic instrument (along with the claves) of the Latin-American dance rhythms. Used in the rhumba, bolero, cha-cha-cha, mambo, meringue, samba (both maracas held in one hand in samba rhythm).

Guiro (Spanish)
Gourd (English), also called rasper, scratcher, guaracha, reco-reco

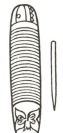

A guiro is a long gourd that is dried and hollowed out with grooves or ridges cut into its playing side and a thumb hole cut in the opposite side. When played it produces a raspy, scraping sound.

Sounded by scraping across the notched surface with a stiff wire set in a handle, with a stick, or even a comb. The volume of sound is controlled by the speed and pressure of the scraping action plus the type of scraper used.

Used mainly in sambas, but can also be used in the Cuban dance forms. Villa-Lobos, Varèse, and Stravinsky have scored for guiro.

Cowbell (English)
Cencerro (Spanish)

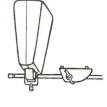

The cowbell produces a loud "bonk" when struck with the shoulder of the snare drumstick near its open end. A softer "tick" is made by striking the bell near its closed end using the tip of the drumstick. The cowbell should be muffled by wrapping with tape.

Can be held in one hand and struck with a snare drumstick, or attached by means of a clamp to a stand or to the bass drum hoop.

In Latin music, each dance has its distinctive cowbell rhythm. The cowbell usually maintains a one or two measure pattern, changing only at the end of definite sections. At times it may be utilized to create its own free-style rhythmic line for added color.

Bongos (Spanish)

Bongos are high pitched single headed drums always mounted in pairs. The sound produced is akin to a small tom-tom. The lower bongo should be at least a fourth lower than the smaller drum.

The pair of bongos are held between the knees, large bongo to the right. The heads are struck by the extended first and second fingers of each hand, usually at a point near the edge. The characteristic ringing "pop" on the high bongo is produced when the fingers contact the edge and the playing surface of the head simultaneously.

The bongos do not have a strict rhythm pattern to which they must adhere. The player is free to improvise in authentic Latin style.

Timbales (Spanish)

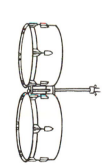

Timbales are a pair of metal-shelled, single headed drums mounted on a stand (sizes 6" × 13" and 6" × 14"). The sides, as well as the heads are used for producing sound. Striking the sides is called "paila" style. Although considered drums of indefinite pitch, the heads of the timbales may be tensioned to vary in pitch from a perfect fourth to a perfect fifth, as desired.

The timbales are played with cylindrical sticks, 3/8" wide by 12" long. Both sticks are held in a manner similar to the grip for the right snare stick. The player usually stands. The larger timbale is at the player's left (as opposed to the bongos).

Timbales maintain a steady beat pattern in Latin dances. Rim shot combinations are commonly used for fill-ins.

Note: The French word for timpani is 'timbales.'

Jawbone (English)
Quijada (Spanish)

The sound is caused by the loose teeth rattling in their sockets in this instrument which is simply the jawbone of an ass.

A commercially produced device called a vibra-slap is available on the market. It insures more consistency and strength of sound than the jawbone.

The jawbone is held in one hand and struck with the heel of palm of the other.

Used mainly in sambas. It plays the most simple of parts and is usually used only on single notes.

Conga drum (English)
Tumbadora, tumba (Spanish)

A single headed drum with a diameter of approximately 12 inches, the conga is a barrel-shaped, long tom-tom with a deep, low, somewhat hollow sound.

Can be suspended by means of a shoulder sling in front of the player, or set on a stand. The extended fingers and heels of the palms are used. A high pitched sound is made with the extended fingers striking at the edge of the head. A lower tone is made by striking with the heel of the palm near the center.

Used in nearly all Latin dance rhythms to provide a low pitched drum sound. The conga drum typically sounds the second quarter and final two eighths of each measure in Latin rhythms.

Shaker (English) also called metal
shaker
Chocalho (Spanish)
Chucala (Portuguese)

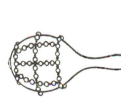

The sound is caused by the enclosed shot rattling against the sides of the tin shaker.

The shaker is played with an up and down motion of the forearm and wrist. It may be held in the center with one hand, or held at each end with both hands.

Not one of the essential rhythm instruments, but often used in sambas. Called for in several Villa-Lobos scores.

Cabasa (Spanish)

Large beads strung over the outer surface rattle against the hollow gourd.

Played by turning the gourd and slapping the beads with the opposite hand.

Used mainly in sambas and meringues.

Notes

1. Curt Sachs, *History of Musical Instruments* (New York: W. W. Norton & Co., Inc., 1940).
2. Wilmer T. Bartholomew, *Acoustics of Music* (Englewood Cliffs, NJ: Prentice-Hall, 1942).
3. Charles A. Culver, *Musical Acoustics* (New York: McGraw-Hill, 1956).
4. John Backus, *The Acoustical Foundations of Music* (New York: W. W. Norton & Co., Inc., 1969).

CHAPTER 3

Snare Drum

GENERAL DESCRIPTION

The genetic term *snare drum* includes drums of varying depths, diameters, and tonal qualities. Common to all are a cylindrical wood or metal shell, a calfskin or plastic head stretched over each end, and wire or gut cords called snares, which are stretched tightly across the bottom head. The drumheads are tucked over hoops, called flesh hoops and are held in place by counterhoops, called rims. Threaded rods may be turned to apply tension to the heads, and thus tune the drums. The top head is called the *batter head,* the bottom the *snare head*. When the batter head is struck with the drumsticks the air inside the drum is set into vibrations which are transferred to the snare head. The vibration of the snare head causes the snares to rattle crisply against it, thus producing the characteristic tone of the snare drum. The depth of the drum shell governs its volume and the diameter governs its pitch. The various types of musical organizations demand differing ratios of depth to diameter. A marching band therefore requires deep toned snare drums capable of producing a loud volume, while the jazz combo needs a snare drum of high pitch, crisp rather than deep toned, and relatively small volume. In recent years, however, the trend has been for drum corps and marching bands switching to 12-lug snare drums in order to withstand the increased head tension necessary to obtain the now preferred higher-pitched marching snare drum sound.

TYPES OF SNARE DRUMS

The *concert snare drum* ranges in depth from 6½″ to 8″ and is 14″ or 15″ in diameter. It is used in the symphony orchestra, the concert band, and is a good general purpose drum for school orchestras and bands. The shell may be made of wood or metal. It is commonly believed that the metal shell produces a more brilliant and penetrating sound. At least one major manufacturer of percussion instruments has re-introduced a concert snare drum model with a shell constructed from a single, solid sheet of brass, drawn and spun in a seamless configuration. It is believed that the solid brass shell has its own full resonance and a sound of pure brilliance. The same manufacturer has also developed two new concert snare drum shells from hammered bronze and from hammered chrome resulting in a dry, articulated sound. Wire snares are widely used, and are the most practical for school use. Most concert snare drums come from the manufacturer equipped with wire snares. A majority of symphonic band and orchestra players prefer the thin gut snares because they produce a drier tone than do the wire snares. Gut snares are less responsive, however, and also require more frequent adjustment. One manufacturer now markets a combination gut-wire set of snares, which has the advantage of gut tone with wire response. The most expensive concert snare drum models have provision for individual adjustment of each snare strand. A so-called tone control device, which is mounted inside the shell and presses against the batter head when a knob is turned on the outside of the shell, is a feature of some snare drums. The concert snare drum is mounted on a sturdy metal stand which is adjustable in height and degree of slant.

Courtesy Ludwig Drum Co.

Figure 3.1. Concert snare drum.

Courtesy Ludwig Drum Co.

Figure 3.2. Field drum.

The *field, or parade, snare drum* ranges in depth from 9″ to 14″ and 13″ to 16″ in diameter with the most frequently used sizes being 12″ × 15″ and 10″ × 14″. It is used primarily in drum corps and marching bands, but can be used in the concert band. Some orchestra scores call specifically for a field drum when the composer wishes to suggest the sounds of martial music. When used in marching units the drum is carried by a sling which passes over the player's right shoulder and allows the drum to ride at a slant over the left leg. Also available from various percussion companies is a device designed to hold field and tenor drums out and away from the body torso. This device, known as a "hi-stepper," allows the drummer freedom of leg and arm movement plus maximum carrying ease and control of the drum. Gut snares were formerly used on all field drums, but in recent years wire snares have become the rule rather than the exception. The field drum should be equipped with gut snares to achieve its true sound. Only for elementary age students would wire snares be advantageous, because they require less careful adjustment. Wire wound silk cord snares are still to be found occasionally, but are unsatisfactory. The combination wire-gut snares would be good for a field drum which is to be used in the concert band. It is possible to circumvent the adverse effects of humidity on gut snares by removing the snares and uniformly spraying them with Scotch Guard or a similar type product. A characteristic field drum sound can also be obtained from drums equipped with nylon snares. For concert playing the field drum should be mounted on a heavy duty snare drum stand.

The *dance band snare drum* is simply a small version of the concert drum. Changing conceptions of ideal tone for dance band, show, recording, and combo work have

Courtesy Ludwig Drum Co.

Figure 3.3. Dance band snare drum.

been responsible for the great variation to be found in dance drums. The trend generally has been toward a shallow, crisp, brilliant and responsive drum. Depth of tone and great volume are not needed for most pop, jazz, and recording work. The size of the most widely used dance drum is 5″ × 14″, although a few players seem to prefer the 6½″ × 14″ model. Dance band type drums are sometimes used in elementary school groups as concert drums, and are satisfactory for this purpose. They are not, however, at all adequate for secondary, college, or professional concert work. The shell of dance drums are constructed of either wood or metal. Most percussionists are now using the metal shell. Wire snares are best. For added responsiveness, 18 or 20 strand snare sets are often used on dance drums in contrast to the usual 12 strand sets found on most concert drums. The dance band snare drum is mounted on a stand which is adjusted to accommodate the sitting position of the player.

There is also a piccolo snare drum, 3″ × 13″, that allows for a unique "soprano" snare drum voice. It produces a crisp sound and is well-suited for very delicate playing of intricate rhythmic patterns. Occasionally a piccolo snare drum is specified in scores.

Figure 3.3a. Piccolo snare drum.

DRUMHEADS

Drumheads for the snare drum, historically, have been made of calfskin. In recent years, plastic heads have been replacing the calfskin heads. There was a period in their early development when the plastic heads were not too satisfactory; however, this is no longer true. Although there are still a few who claim better response and a truer snare drum sound is produced by playing on the calfskin heads, most educators and professional musicians now utilize the plastic heads. The following is a table listing comparative advantages of plastic heads over the calfskin heads:

Calfskin	*Plastic*
1. Subject to great variation in tension (and sound) by changes in the relative humidity.	1. Not affected by changes in relative humidity.
2. Subject to breakage through rapid changes in weather, puncture with drumsticks.	2. Less breakage, but care must be taken when mounting head. A rough edge on the drum shell may start a tear when tension is applied.
3. Longevity limited, as heads lose resiliency. Texture changes cause loss of responsiveness eventually.	3. Greater longevity, little change in resiliency with continued use.
4. Surface smooth and fairly hard textured when fresh, but becomes rough. Brushes rough up and eventually pierce head.	4. Surface texture very hard, and continued playing does not roughen head.
5. Considerable variation in uniformity from head to head.	5. Controlled uniformity in heads made by each manufacturer.
6. Stick response good when head is tuned properly and weather conditions optimum. Response poor in damp weather.	6. Stick response satisfactory. A harder "feel" to head is noted when first switching from calfskin head. Response same under all conditions.

In summary, the author recommends plastic heads for school use on the basis of their practicality and cost, which outweigh any slight disadvantage in tone quality.

The batter (top) heads for snare drums are thicker than the snare (bottom heads). Batter heads must be strong enough to withstand the impact of the sticks, while the snare head's thin gauge makes it extremely sensitive to vibration.

When purchasing drumheads, either calfskin or plastic, measure the diameter *inside* the rim. It is impractical for the player or instructor to mount drumheads on the flesh hoops. The time and skill required to mount drumheads is considerable, so it is well worth the extra dollar to buy the heads already mounted.

TENSION AND TUNING

Single and double tension are terms referring to the arrangement of tension rods on drums. In single tension drums both heads are affected when a single rod is turned due to its having claw hooks over both snare and batter counterhoops (rims). Such an arrangement is used only on the lower priced drums and is not recommended because it is not then possible to make the necessary adjustment of each head independently. Double tension drums have a separate tension casing attached to the shell for each tension rod. This arrangement provides for independent tuning at each tuning point on both the snare and batter heads.

The snare drumheads can be tuned in the following sequence of steps, beginning with the mounting of the head of the drum:

1. Loosen the tension rods until they can be pulled out.
2. Remove counterhoop and the head to be replaced.
3. Wipe off dust and dirt accumulated around edge of shell; make sure shell is smooth and completely free from rough spots.
4. Fit new head over shell, pressing flesh hoop down as far as it will go.
5. Remount and align counterhoop.
6. Replace tension rods and screw them down by hand until they are snug and height of counterhoop is even all the way around.
7. Using the drum key, give each rod one or two half-turns. Tune opposite, not adjacent, rods. Repeat process until head is fairly tight.
8. Test for sound with drumstick. Check evenness of counterhoop. Apply more tension if needed.
9. Final tuning of batter head should result in a head which can be depressed *only slightly* by pressing the thumb down in the center of the head.
10. In replacing and tuning the snare head it will be necessary to remove the snares. The procedure is then the same as for the batter head. The thumb should depress the head *slightly* less than for the batter head.

The most common tuning fault among school players is failure to tighten snare drumheads enough. Loose heads will not produce the typical snare drum sound. Remember the "rule of thumb"—the batter head should be depressable only very slightly; the snare head tighter.

It is best to change calfskin heads and set the tuning when the air is dry. If too much tension is applied when the air is moist a sudden change to dry weather may break the head. Once tuned carefully in dry weather, the snare drumheads should not be changed. It is *not* a good idea to tighten and loosen the snare drums each time they are used. Of course, if the drum must be played on a very humid day, it will be necessary to increase the tension by turning *each rod* an *equal* amount. Immediately after use on such a day, loosen the head by the same number of half turns used to tighten it before storing. Otherwise, a broken drumhead is likely to result when the humidity dips. Plastic heads once set will need only a very occasional increase in tension to compensate for a slight amount of stretching. Calfskin heads will require more attention.

The following information developed by Dr. Jay Collins offers a more complete explanation of snare drum tuning. The author of this fourth edition is a former Collins student.

When musicians speak of tuning an instrument one usually associates this term with the idea of an adjustment of the instrument's pitch. The snare drum, due to its very nature of being classified as a membranophone of indefinite pitch, is tuned by making adjustments based on other considerations. Basically, the snare drum tuning should involve the consideration of three things: (1) Sound, (2) Response, and (3) Sympathetic Vibrations. Within each of these basic areas other more detailed points must be considered. It will be helpful to consider these three basic areas individually.

Sound

We cannot expect to do a very adequate job of tuning the snare drum if we do not already have a preconceived notion of a good snare drum sound. After all, the sound of the snare drum is really the most important consideration to make from a musical point of view. The other two basic areas of snare drum tuning are primarily based on a consideration of ease of executions of parts for the player.

In past years the contribution of the snare drum to an instrumental organization has centered more around its rhythmic support for the music than its part in helping to make an over-all musical sound. More recently composers and conductors are making greater demands on all members of the instrumental group for rhythmic foundation and support. On the contrary, however, not enough consideration is being given by percussionists and conductors of these organizations to the sound of the snare drum.

Both players and conductors must examine their own situation and ask, "Are the snare drums contributing something to the sound of our music, detracting from it, or even masking some of it?" If the answer is "Yes!" to either of the last two parts of the question, it is probably as a result of using snare drums which have not been properly tuned.

If the snare drum sound is relatively low, or if the sound is loose and ringing or if it is a rattle sound, this will cause certain desirable musical sounds in the ensemble to be interfered with or lost entirely. This masking of sound by drums is one of the most frequently noticed percussion problems with most school instrumental ensembles. As directors and audience we have allowed ourselves to become accustomed to it.

We need to expect something different from our snare drums when we tune them. In general, the snare drum sound should be high in pitch, sharp and penetrating, and of short duration. This snare drum sound will allow for rhythmic punctuation of the over-all musical sound without interfering with it. It will also allow for a cleaner, more precise rendition of snare drum solo and counterrhythm parts.

Response

The response of the batter head when struck with the drum stick is a highly important point to consider when tuning the snare drum. It is possible to have the snare drum tuned so that the stick will bound back off the batter head without the sound being necessarily good. This is usually a result of a batter head which is adjusted too tightly to vibrate freely. Thus, the response of the batter head to the blow from the drum stick is directly related to the freedom with which the head may vibrate.

The batter head response should *not* be the same feeling as one might get when playing with drum sticks on a wooden or metal table. There must be more freedom for the head to vibrate. When this freedom of vibration exists to the proper degree, the air contained within the snare drum is displaced. We refer to this volume of air as the air column. The air column should be allowed to move as a complete unit of air. For this to occur, the snare head must be free enough to vibrate so that the air column may be displaced downward in a complete unit. If the snare head is too tight to allow this downward displacement of the air column, the air will be displaced in an irregular manner causing puffs of air to come out of the air vent of the drum and then other air to immediately enter and replace what is lost. If the drum is properly adjusted, there will be only slight air to leave the drum through the air vent as the air column is caused to be displaced as a unit—slightly downard, then upward, and then into normal position. The snare head must be loose enough to vibrate against the snares, but tight enough to send the air column immediately upward against the batter head.

Sympathetic Vibrations

It is obvious, therefore, that the response from the batter head is dependent upon the amount of freedom with which the head may vibrate while still being tight enough to give immediate response and help create a good high-pitched sound. In addition, however, the response is related to the manner in which both the snare and batter heads are allowed to vibrate in sympathy with themselves and each other.

We have long been the victims of an unsubstantiated belief that the batter head must always be adjusted tighter than the snare head. This we believed because it seemed reasonable to assume that the head to be struck should be braced for the abuse, and because of other reasons which we still find today in many drum instruction books that followed preconceived notions about snare drum tuning.

Much trial and error was necessary before the following conclusion could be made—the snare head must be adjusted slightly tighter than the batter head. After several years of tuning drums in this manner it was enlightening to find substantiation for this view from another percussionist in a drum publication. In Louis Bellson's *Introduction to Percussion, Vol. 1* (Hollywood: Try Publishing Co., 1964), he writes on page three: "The snare drum should have a snare drum sound. It should be a crisp, sharp sound. The bottom head, more recently, is tighter than the batter head."

Making the Adjustment

Before starting to tune a snare drum one must have the proper tools with which to work. In addition to a drum key a pair of sticks which are matched in size to the snare drum being tuned will be necessary. Also, a snare drum stand and possibly a screw driver will be needed.

With the drum on the stand in normal playing position turn the snare control lever off so that the snares do not sound. Adjust the batter head with the key evenly applying tension to each tension rod until the sticks will return immediately to a high position when allowed to fall to the head while being pivoted between the right thumb and index finger. Play a few rapid single strokes on the drum to see if the sticks respond quickly when they come into contact with the batter head. When satisfied with the batter response remove the drum from the stand. Check the snares to see if they are centered between the rim of the snare drum and between the opening for the snares within the counterhoop itself which is found on more recently constructed snare drums. If any adjustment is to be made it will probably be to move the snares closer to the side opposite the snare throw-off lever. It is very important that extra slack not be taken up with the snare adjustment screw to save using a screw driver to remove the slack or correct the position of the snares. When snare adjustments such as this are being made the drum should be placed snare head up on a flat surface and two people should work together with one holding the snare string and the other using the screw driver. Not all snare drums

require this particular type of adjustment, but the adjustment mechanisms of some certain drums will require either a small screw driver adjustment or an adjustment of knurled screws on both sides of the drum to center and tighten the snares.

With the snare drum on the flat surface place it on its side so that both heads are accessible. With the snares off tap the batter lightly with the drum stick while pressing one finger against the edge of the snare head. Repeat this procedure with the snare head and determine which head is the higher in pitch. If the batter head is higher (as is usually the case) tighten the snare head and repeat the testing procedure until the snare head is slightly higher in pitch than the batter head. If the snare head is higher loosen it until it is only slightly higher than the batter head. For more accuracy try to find the approximate pitch of the batter head and adjust the snare head to a major-second or a minor-third higher. Any more or less than this will start the heads toward becoming less responsive to each other.

Place the snare drum on the stand and turn the snares on. Loosen the snare adjustment screw until the snares rattle against the snare head. While striking the drum with the right stick, slowly adjust the snares tighter until the rattle ceases. Then turn the screw about another half turn tighter. Test the drum response and sound by playing single strokes and buzz rolls at all volume levels.

The drum should now be tested to meet various demands. It must produce a good sharp, high-pitched sound. There should not be much ringing in the sound although a slight ring is desirable (when away from the drum the ring is not noticed if it is only a slight ring). Drummers should be taught to use the tone control adjustment screws very sparingly, if at all. When the drum is properly tuned, it does not require any type of muffling such as cloth strips or tone control mufflers. The sticks should return from the drum quickly when allowed to fall to the drum while holding the stick on a pivot between the right thumb and index finger. The heads should now be vibrating sympathetically so as to allow a pliable feeling when playing a closed concert-style snare drum roll. If not, minor adjustments may be made by making the batter head slightly looser or tighter depending on the correction necessary. Other fine adjustments of the snare adjustment screw will be necessary if any head tension adjustment is made.

Once a snare drum has been properly tuned it is a simple matter to tune any remaining snare drums to match it. Merely turn off the snares of all snare drums including the one which has been tuned. Hold the snare head edge with one finger and tap the batter head of the tuned drum. Do the same with the untuned drum and adjust it until it matches the pitch of the tuned snare drum. Repeat this procedure with the snare heads and then make the snare

RECOMMENDED MODELS

Recommended snare drums for school use are summarized in the following table:

School Level	Types	Tension	Dimensions	Heads	Snares
Elementary	Concert or	Double	6½″ × 14″	Plastic	Wire
	Dance	Double	5″ × 14″	Plastic	Wire
	Field	Double	10″ × 14″	Plastic	Wire
Junior High	Concert	Double	6½″ × 14″	Plastic	Wire-gut
	Dance	Double	5″ × 14″	Plastic	Wire
	Field	Double	10″ × 14″	Plastic	Wire-gut, nylon
High School	Concert	Double	8″ × 15″ or 6½″ × 14″	Plastic	Wire-gut 18 strand
	Dance	Double	5″ × 14″	Plastic	Wire
	Field	Double	12″ × 15″	Plastic	Wire-gut, nylon
College- University	Concert	Double	8″ × 15″ or 6½″ × 14″	Plastic	Wire-gut 18 strand
	Dance	Double	5″ × 14″	Plastic	Wire
	Field	Double	12″ × 15″	Plastic	Wire-gut, nylon

adjustments described above. If the snare drums to be tuned are of different sizes they must be expected to have slightly different qualities of sound, but they may still be matched in response and feeling of head pliability. The 5″ × 14″ snare drum will give a better snare drum sound in concert instrumental and stage band work. The 6½″ × 14″ snare drum is good to have as a supplement to the above. It may be used for military, tenor or muffled drum effects and will serve as an extra snare drum when demanded by the music. Parade drums should be tuned as suggested above, but personal taste will determine the use of gut (or nylon) snares or wire snares.

SNARE DRUMSTICKS

Snare drumsticks should be selected for the particular drum with which they are to be used. In general, a shallow dance band type drum will respond best with comparatively light sticks and a deep field drum requires heavy sticks to bring out its best tones. Manufacturers have a rough system of classifying sticks by number and letter. Unfortunately leading manufacturers of sticks have never standardized the weights, lengths and shapes of sticks by uniform letter-number designations. Ludwig and Slingerland use the letters *A* for so-called orchestra sticks, *B* for band, and *S* for street (drum corps). Gretsch uses *D* for dance band sticks, *C* for concert (orchestra or band) and *P* for parade. The numbering is even more confusing as variables of shape, weight, and length are incorporated in the numbers assigned. The purchaser must acquaint himself with several of the more useful models, and use these as points of reference if further experimentation is needed.

Most drumsticks are made from straight grained white hickory wood. Rosewood sticks were once somewhat popular, but are rarely seen now. Sticks with nylon tips are available for approximately 50¢ extra per pair. These tips do have the advantages of being more durable, not chipping, and creating fewer nicks in drumheads.

However, it must be pointed out that some degree of sound brilliance is sacrificed when using sticks equipped with nylon tips.

Drumsticks should be personally selected, never ordered by mail. It is necessary to test each stick for straightness, which is easily done by rolling it along a smooth surface such as a glass countertop. Each pair should be matched for weight and balance, either by holding one in each hand or by actually weighing them on the small scale which many dealers have for this purpose.

It is not necessary for beginning students to buy a pair of the very heavy "practice" sticks. A better plan is to select a medium weight all-purpose stick that will be strong enough to use on the practice pad and will also be fairly well matched to the drum.

Many companies manufacture sticks for various purposes. The Vic Firth Model SD-1 (general purpose) or SD-2 (bolero) are examples of the variety of sticks available. Also acceptable are most of the mass produced 5B models, as these are usually well balanced, have a good taper and are of a comfortable weight for students.

Sticks for use with representative sizes of drums and for particular styles of music are suggested in the table and illustrations that follow:

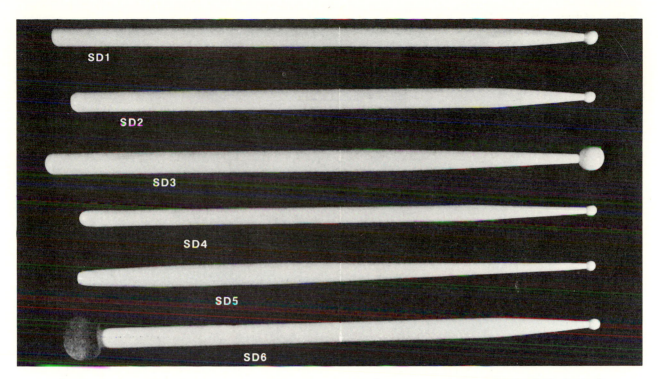

Snare drumsticks (designed by Vic Firth, principal percussionist for the Boston Symphony Orchestra). The snare drumsticks are hand turned from select maple identical to that used in the timpani sticks. They are all 'pitch-paired' and are finished with a catalytic varnish. The various models can be used for jazz, rock, soul, drum corps, marching band, chamber music, and symphonic work depending on the player's individual style and taste. Following are the specifications of the twelve models (weight is per stick):

General SD1

Length 16⅜", thickness ⅝", weight 2¼ oz., round tip. Good for all around orchestral work, rock, band, and ideal as a practice stick.

Bolero SD2

Length 15¾", thickness ⅝", 1¾ oz., round tip. Ideal for light playing, pianissimo rolls, and other delicate work.

Thunder Rock SD3

Length 16¾", thickness ¹¹⁄₁₆", weight 2½ oz., round tip. Large, heavy-beaded stick designed for tremendous rolls and loud, warlike playing. Equally suited for rock or drum corps.

Combo SD4

Length 15⅜", thickness ½", weight 1⅛ oz., round tip. Slim, small-beaded stick with a conventional balance. Light and fast in the hand. Good for a jazz quartet or chamber music.

Echo SD5

Length 15¾", ¹¹⁄₁₆" at the thickest point, weight 1⅝ oz., round tip. Designed for light and delicate playing that requires the extreme in finesse and control. Unusually long taper to the tip, as well as tapered to the butt. Cannot be used for loud playing. Great in Scheherazade.

Swizzle B SD6

Length 16¼", weight 2 oz., mounted on a Bolero shaft. A double-headed stick, the butt end capped with a head of medium-hard spun felt. It affords the player, by simply reversing them, a variety of sounds for cymbal rolls, tom toms, timbales, temple blocks, etc. and timpani. Good for chamber music and pit work.

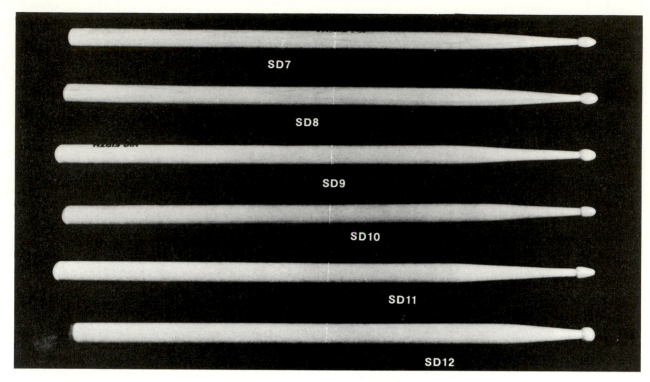

Whacker SD7
Length 16⅛″, thickness ¹⁹⁄₃₂″, weight 1¼ oz., nylon tip. Designed for the set drummer who desires a well balanced, top quality stick. It has great cutting power on all the drums as well as the cymbals.

Chopper SD8
Length 16¼″, thickness ¹⁹⁄₃₂″, weight 1¾ oz., nylon tip. Slightly longer and heavier than the Whacker. The tip is fuller and slightly more rounded. Great driving power.

Driver SD9
Length 16⅛″, thickness ¹⁹⁄₃₂″, weight 1¾, oz., oval tip. A big band stick with 'drive'. Has the weight for the 22″ ride cymbal.

Swinger SD10
Length 16″, thickness ¹⁹⁄₃₂″, weight 1¾ oz., oval tip. Another big band stick, slightly lighter than the Driver. Great for jazz.

Slammer SD11
Length 16¼″, thickness ⁹⁄₁₆″, weight 1¾ oz., 'arrowhead' tip. Tip is a bit unconventional, but it 'cuts' and 'pushes' with a minimum of effort.

Swizzle G SD12
Length 16⅝″, weight 2¼ oz. A double-headed stick with the identical felt head of Swizzle B, only mounted on an SD1 General shaft. Has extra weight and power.

PARTS OF THE INSTRUMENT

The diagram following illustrates the parts of the snare drum.

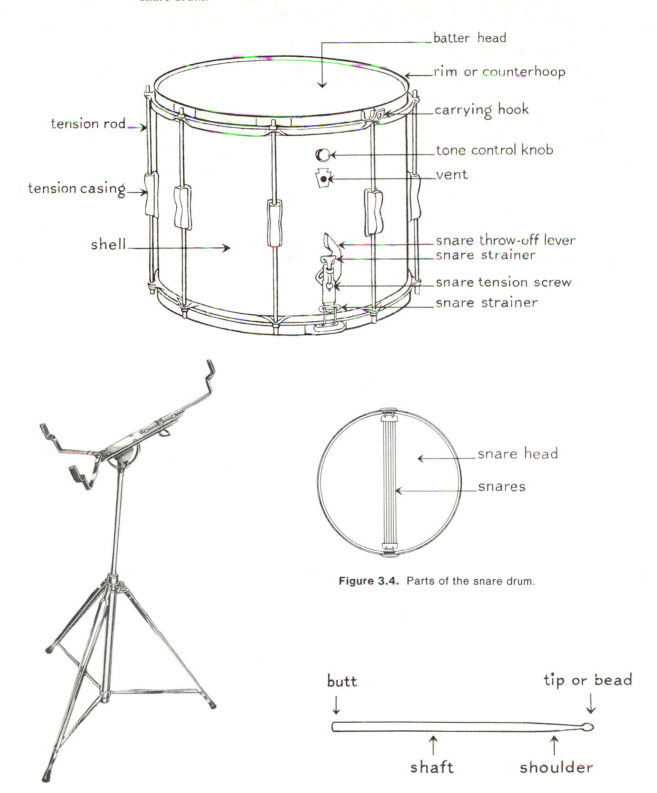

Figure 3.4. Parts of the snare drum.

Figure 3.5. Snare drum stand.

Figure 3.6. Parts of the snare drumstick.

Drum Type	Dimensions	Use	Sticks
Field	10″ × 14″	Marching band Concert band	Firth SD3 Firth SD1
Field	12″ × 15″	Drum corps or marching band Concert band	Ludwig 2S Firth SD1 or 3
Concert	6½″ × 14″	Orchestra Concert band	Firth SD1 Firth SD2
Concert	8″ × 15″	Orchestra Concert band	Firth SD2 Firth SD1
Dance	6½″ × 14″	Dance band	Firth SD10
Dance	5″ × 14″	Dance band or jazz combo	Firth SD9 or 10 Firth SD4

HOLDING THE STICKS

Until recent years, there was considered to be one correct way of holding snare drum sticks, that being the traditional grip. Now, there is a rather large group of percussionists advocating the use of the "matched grip"— that is, a grip whereby both hands grasp the sticks in a like manner using the right hand grip of the traditional method as a model for both hands. This "newer" method (it is really not a new method since it has been experimented with for some time. It was never officially recognized as a correct method of holding the sticks.) has definite advantages and should be considered seriously by all modern day percussionists. First of all, it alleviates the awkward and unnatural left hand grip and makes much more sense to the beginning student. Secondly, it facilitates the learning of the other percussion instruments since the matched grip for snare drum is quite akin to grips used with the mallet instruments and timpani.

The traditional grip has the obvious advantage over the matched grip in marching organizations which do not utilize the "hi-steppers." After all, this is why the traditional grip developed as it did. The snare drum was first a martial instrument. When it was introduced into the concert hall, its basic technique accompanied it there, including the slant of the drum, the traditional grip, and the rudimental approach to playing.

Since the traditional method will continue to be used and since the matched grip method utilizes, basically, the right hand technique of the traditional approach for both hands, it is felt best to proceed with a detailed discussion of the traditional grip.

Right Hand

The R stick is grasped in a rather natural manner, as one would grasp any stick of wood if it were handed to him, at a point ⅓ of the distance up from the butt end of the stick. The thumb nail should fall along the L side of the stick and point straight toward the tip. The other point of contact to form the R fulcrum is the flesh of the first joint of the R forefinger. See Figures 3.7 and 3.8.

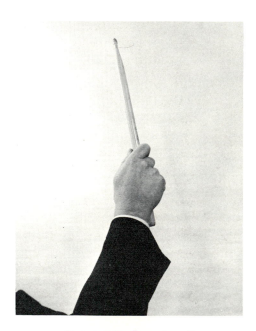

Figure 3.7. Top view, R.

The three remaining R fingers are curled loosely around the stick, maintaining always a *light* contact with the upper shaft of the stick. They do not tighten to a genuine grip, as this would prevent the stick's natural rebound. The butt end of the stick will protrude slightly from the right side of the wrist, in order to avoid its hitting the under-wrist. See Figure 3.7. In correct *ready* position the R wrist is *flat across the top*. The action of the wrist is forward and back. As an aid in establishing a correct concept of the R wrist action, ask the student to imagine that he is

Figure 3.8. Bottom view, R.

Figure 3.9

Figure 3.10

casting a fly rod as far as possible out into the water. He will recall that a whip-like action produces the desired result. Another useful teaching device is to simulate the action of cracking a whip. The entire arm, wrist and hand are involved. These or similar calisthenic exercises should be practiced in mid-air before proceeding to the practice of the R stroke on the pad or drum.

Left Hand

The L handhold and wrist action are not as "natural" as those of the R. It is recommended that the following sequence of steps be used when introducing the L handhold. The sequence of figures illustrates each concept. Each should be studied carefully.

Step One

Extend the L arm full length in front of the body, fingers and thumb forming a vertical plane with the floor, fingers together. See Figure 3.9.

Step Two

Grasp the stick by the tip with the right hand and insert it at the balancing point ⅓ the distance up from the butt end, between the thumb and the side of the palm, as far down into the webby crease as possible. Hold firmly at right angles to the palm. See Figure 3.10.

Step Three

The L wrist rotates in its action. Its *ready* position is approximately vertical. Start from the position shown in step two and rotate the wrist, *slowly at first,* around as far in either direction as the wrist will turn. Take care to hold the stick snugly enough to prevent its falling down to a position parallel with the palm. It must be maintained

at right angles to the L wrist. The value of this calisthenic lies in forcing the wrist to turn all the way in either direction. The action is similar to that used in turning a doorknob. The rotary action should be practiced in mid-air before the actual L handhold is introduced. See Figures 3.11, 3.12, and 3.13.

Figure 3.11

Figure 3.12

Figure 3.13

Step Four

With the stick still held securely in the web between thumb and palm, turn the ring and little fingers under until they almost reach the palm. These two fingers serve as a bouncing pad for the L stick. See Figure 3.14.

Figure 3.14

Step Five

Shift the direction of the thumb to a position pointing *down* the shaft toward the stick tip. It will bend at the joint slightly and may contact the top of the shaft for all or most of its length. See Figure 3.15.

Figure 3.15

Step Six

Curl the index and middle fingers *loosely* around the stick to maintain a *very light* contact with the top of the shaft when in *ready* position. (See Figure 3.16.) These fingers must give way, or open up, when the stick travels its normal course in making the full arm stroke. (See Figure 3.17.) There is a slight contact of the index finger at its first joint with the tip of the thumb, which will have to "break" on the back swing of the full stroke.

The principle danger in the L is that the stick will not be held firmly at its fulcrum by the thumb. *Never* should there be any space between the stick and the webby part

Figure 3.16

Figure 3.17

of the thumb joint. Students should be cautioned "never to see light" between the L stick and the base of the thumb joint.

Note: No concession is made to handedness in percussion technique. Left-handed students should hold the sticks in the same manner as those who are right-handed. This is logical, since both hands perform an equal service. Another factor is the impracticality of drumming left-handed in the marching band, at the drum set, or in any situation where players rotate on a certain set of instruments.

List of Common Faults—R and L Handholds

1. Stick not held at balancing point (⅓ distance from butt end).
2. R thumb pointing down instead of straight along shaft.
3. Forming R grip with second instead of index finger.
4. R wrist not flat but tilted over to the right.
5. L wrist not vertical but tilted over to the left.
6. L stick not held firmly enough at fulcrum.
7. Index and second fingers of L hand pressing down on stick shaft.
8. L wrist bent out away from body instead of extending straight from forearm.

PLAYING POSITION

Concert Snare Drum

The playing position for the concert snare drum utilizing the traditional grip is shown in Figure 3.18. The drum is set on the stand by the following procedure:

Figure 3.18. Playing position, concert snare drum.

1. Fit two sections of stand together, then raise top section to a position 8″ to 10″ below player's beltline. Set height adjustment screw. See Figure 3.19.
2. Spread three arms of stand to their holding positions. Pull adjustable arm out to maximum length. See Figure 3.20.
3. Turn stand so that the two nonadjustable arms are to the right, the adjustable arm pointing toward the player's left. Tighten angle adjustment screw. See Figure 3.21.
4. Place drum on stand with the snare throw-off lever *to the left*, next to, but not on the section of the arm that bends upward. See Figure 3.22.

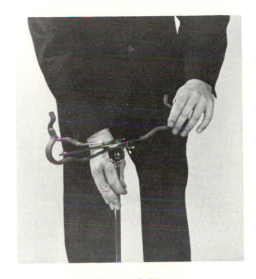

Figure 3.20

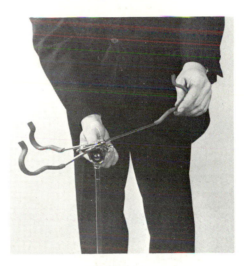

Figure 3.21

Figure 3.19

Figure 3.22

5. Push adjustable arm in until it grasps drum securely, then tighten set screw. See Figure 3.23.
6. Adjust angle of drum so that it tilts slightly toward the right. See Figure 3.24.

Figure 3.23

Figure 3.24

The instructor should demonstrate the foregoing procedure and then insist that these steps be faithfully adhered to whenever a drum is set on a stand. Students are often careless in this matter and many broken drumheads, cracked drum shells, and bent wire snares occur as a result.

The height and slant of concert snare drum may show a slight variation according to player preference, but a good rule is to have the drum 2 to 4 inches below belt height, and the right side about an inch lower than the left side. See Figure 3.17 for a good playing position. The music rack should be raised to the player's chest height.

Note: The snare drummer in the concert band and orchestra *always* stands while playing. The seated position for the dance band drummer will be dealt with in a later chapter.

Rest Position

Rest position is shown in Figure 3.25.

Rest position should be assumed during all rests of more than a measure of two duration. During tacet portions of the music the snare drummer should be seated.

Figure 3.25. Concert snare drum rest position.

Matched Grip Position

The position of the snare drum is altered slightly when the player utilizes the matched grip. Since the grip for both sticks is the same as the R hand grip of the traditional method, there is no need to tilt the snare drum. The drum should be level and parallel to the floor as in figure 3.26. The top of the drum should be 2 to 4 inches below belt height.

With the matched grip the muscular actions used in playing are the same in each hand, arm and wrist. This one factor alone will enable the player to progress more quickly and efficiently than with the traditional grip. A great many of the problems in teaching beginners emanate from the unnatural left hand position. This can result

Figure 3.26. Matched grip position.

in excessive teaching time being devoted to making corrections of the left hand. With the matched grip, special left hand problems are almost eliminated.

Muscular transference between the different percussion instruments is another point in favor of the matched grip. If the basic areas of percussion (snare drum, timpani, mallet-keyboard instruments, drum set, various multiple) are played using a similar grip (allowing of course, for minor variations in the different "schools" of technique), the student can progress more quickly toward the goal of becoming a well-rounded percussionist.

The matched grip adapts very well to the drum set, especially the now popular melodic tom-tom set-ups, and to the increasingly difficult solo multiple percussion repertoire. The traditional grip evolved as a result of the snare drum being carried originally and exclusively on a sling. With the advent of newer devices designed to carry the marching snare drum "level", there may be very little need of the traditional grip. Many drum corps now use the matched grip as a result of the newer carrying devices being available.

Inasmuch as today's percussionist is often expected to play a variety of instruments (and play them very well), the matched grip has tremendous advantage in versatility and flexibility when moving from one instrument to another. The author of the fourth edition GUIDE recommends that beginners be started with the matched grip.

Field Drum

Playing position for the field drum is shown in Figure 3.27.

Figure 3.27. Field drum playing position.

The steps for slinging the field drum are:

1. Place sling over right shoulder with latch in front.

Figure 3.28

2. Grasp the small hook with the left hand, bring it around to the front and fasten it through the eyelet.

Figure 3.29

3. Adjust the height by means of the adjusting device until the latch is about 2″ below belt height.

Figure 3.30

4. Pick up the drum with the left hand and snap the latch to the carrying hook (see Figures 3.28, 3.29, 3.30 and 3.31).

Figure 3.31

The field drum will hang at a pronounced slant over the left leg.

Rest position for the field drum is similar to that for the concert drum. During tacet portions of the music the drum may be unslung quietly and the player may be seated. Music racks should be chest high.

Check List for Mounting Drum and Playing Positions

1. Is drum too high? Too low?
2. Is angle of tilt correct?
3. Is snare throw-off to the player's left?
4. Are the arms of drum stand correctly spaced?
5. Is player standing at right angle to direction of drum's tilt?
6. Is player erect and alert?
7. Does player assume proper rest position during rests?

List of Common Faults

1. Arms of snare drum stand bent, causing snares to catch on set-screw.
2. Arms of stand not spread properly.
3. Adjustable arm pointing right instead of left.
4. Snare throw-off not to player's left.
5. Drum too low.
6. Drum tilted too low on the right side.
7. Field drum sling not attached to drum properly.
8. "Slouching."
9. Failure to adopt proper rest position.

PLAYING SPOT

The playing spot on the batter head of the snare drum is dependent on the sound desired. For maximum resonance the drum should be struck slightly off center. The exact center is a nodal point in the vibrational pattern of the drumhead. Blows struck at dead center are actually dead sounding. Consequently when an extremely dry tone is desired, drummers play at the center of the head. For very soft notes the portions of the head near the rim are used. In general, the softer notes are played near the edges and louder tones nearer the center. Both sticks *do not* have to strike within the area of a 25-cent piece, as is often said. So long as they remain equidistant from the rims they will produce like sounds. This separation of sticks allows the arms to hang at a uniform and comfortable angle, whereas if both sticks were kept close to one another in moving toward the rim, one of the player's arms would be drawn out of its natural relaxed position.

Figures 3.32, 3.33 and 3.34 show playing spots for loud, moderately loud, and soft tones. Notice the manner in which the sticks are separated.

The two sticks are held in playing position so that they form a right angle. Note that this angle is maintained whether the stick tips are close together or widely separated.

Figure 3.32. Snare drum playing spot, loud tone.

Figure 3.34. Snare drum playing spot, soft tone.

Common Faults

1. Less than a 45° angle between sticks.
2. One stick nearer the rim than the other, producing unlike tones.
3. Colliding stick tips, caused by attempting to play within too small an area.
4. Playing at or near center in soft passages.
5. Not varying the playing spots with varying dynamic levels.

STICKING

Stickwork, sometimes called *sticking* refers to the choices of right or left sticks within rhythm figures. Thus, for the rhythm figure

the stickwork designation is RRLRL. In beginning drum music the stickwork is usually given for each note. In actual scores stickwork indications are seldom given. An important part of a player's training is the development of a system of sticking which can be applied almost automatically in reading any rhythm figure. Much attention must be given to good stickwork habit formation from the outset, otherwise haphazard or incorrect sticking will eventually inhibit good sight reading, and hamper technique. An analogous situation would result if the pianist

Figure 3.33. Snare drum playing spot, moderately loud tone.

The beginning student should avoid extremes and use playing spots about one or two inches off center. Even while practicing on the pad it is recommended that the sticks be separated by at least 1½″ or 2″.

were unsure of his scale fingerings. Stickwork is one aspect of a percussionist's performance skill which should require little, if any, conscious effort. In order to achieve this semiautomatic level it is necessary to lay a firm foundation of consciously recognized correct responses from the very first lesson.

There are two generally used systems of stickwork. One might be termed the *strict alternation system* and the other the *right-lead system*.

According to the *alternation system* successive notes, no matter what their duration or grouping, are played from hand-to-hand. "Hand-to-hand" is drummer's parlance for strict alternation. Showing no particular preference for starting hand, once begun the music is played with the sticks "as they come." The previously mentioned rhythm figure

might be played either RLRLR or LRLRL.

The *right-lead system* of stickwork, as its name implies, uses the R as the starting hand for figures commencing on a strong beat. First beats in each measure (with certain exceptions in triple meter), and subsequent strong beats are played by the R. The L is used for weak beats and for notes of less than one unit's duration. Pickups with one or three notes start with a L, two or four-note pick-ups begin with a R. Long rolls and many of the short rolls begin and end with a R. The following examples of common measures of snare drum music will serve to illustrate the application of the right-lead system of stickwork: (Parentheses show where the sticking is optional)

$\frac{4}{4}$ Quarter Notes and Rests

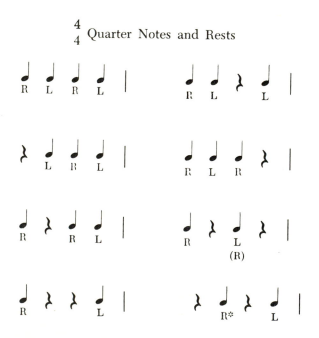

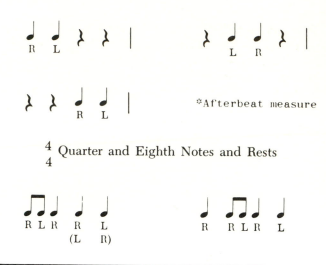

*Afterbeat measure

$\frac{4}{4}$ Quarter and Eighth Notes and Rests

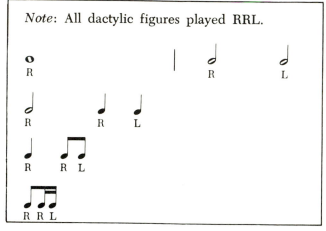

Two-quarter and C measures corresponding to the foregoing 4/4 measures would follow the same stickwork indications. Asterisks indicate exceptions, as in the afterbeat measure. The principal reason that alternate sticks are used in playing this very typical snare drum rhythm is that such a figure usually occurs in chains of many repeated measures. It would be somewhat ridiculous to play 8, 16, or more measures with only one hand, hence the practice of alternating afterbeats has become standardized:

3/4 Quarter Notes and Rests

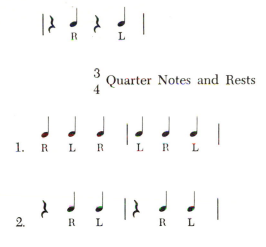

S.D. waltz rhythm always played as in example 2.

6/8 Most Common Figures

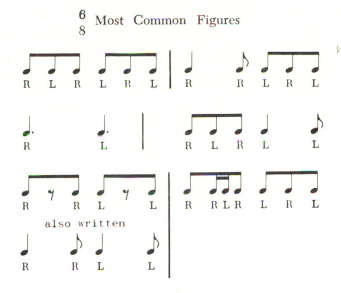

The author recommends the right-lead system in preference to the alternate sticking system for the following reasons:

1. It is used by the majority of fine percussionists.
2. Most of the best snare drum instruction methods employ it.
3. It is systematic and hence preferable to haphazard stick choice.
4. It facilitates sight reading because idiomatic figures, once learned, are always played the same way.
5. In reading unusual or complex figures the player has a working principle to guide choice of sticks.
6. It is advantageous in working at the drum set, where the R is basically concerned with the principally accented beats (cymbal notes, etc.) and the L is associated with the afterbeats.
7. A musically valid association is established between the R (strong beats, natural accents, first beats) and the L (pick-up notes, weak beats, fractional parts of beats, artificial accents, as in syncopation). Stickwork thus corresponds to the general principle of bowing a string instrument, wherein the first beat is usually played down bow, the next (weak) beat with an up bow. The R stick may be likened to the down bow, the L to the up bow.

Several points in connection with stickwork should be carefully noted. First, the addition of grace note combinations (called flams, drags, and ruffs in drummer's parlance) does *not* affect the basic sticking arrangement. For example,

Second, it is very important for the student to learn and consistently apply the proper stickwork for the idiomatic rhythm figures. Stated simply—always play like measures with the same sticking.

Third, care must be taken when using some of the beginning band and orchestra methods to see that the faulty stick indications are corrected. The authors of these books seem to have proceeded on the false assumption that snare drum stickwork is simply a matter of starting at the first note with either a R or L and taking turns with the sticks until the final note is reached. Particularly confusing to the student are those books which give two sets of stickings for every exercise. A second fallacy which seems to have gained currency among instrumental class method writers is that the L is the weak hand, and by starting everything with the L it will somehow gain strength. There exists no justification for this practice, any more than could the teaching of bowings exactly opposite to those actually used be justified for the beginning student on the theory that up bows are more difficult than down bows and need special emphasis. Finally, it should be noted that this system requires greater concentration from the beginning student, but ultimately, through its teaching of consistency and uniformity, it frees the student to direct his concentrative efforts toward all the other musical problems.

THE STROKE

The most fundamental of all drum techniques is the full arm stroke. In preparation for making the stroke, hold

Figure 3.35. Ready position.

the stick tips up about 1½″ above the practice pad. This is the starting point for all drum strokes and is called *ready position*. The full arm stroke on the drum is a three phase action: backswing; downswing; rebound (follow through). The sequence of figures illustrates the steps in making a R stroke.

On the backswing, the wrist initiates the action by humping up, leaving the tip of the stick lagging somewhat behind.

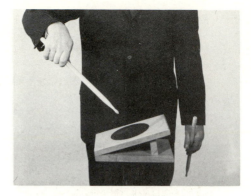

Figure 3.36. Wrist starts the action.

Figure 3.37. Lift arm.

Figure 3.38. Start of downswing.

Lift arm until elbow is nearly shoulder high.

The wrist starts down first, stick tip lags behind. Motion accelerates, reaching maximum velocity as stick strikes drumhead.

After impact, the stick's natural rebound then settles back to ready position and the R stroke is completed.

Figure 3.39. Rebound.

A useful teaching device is to have the student imagine that the stick tips are heavily weighted. This will aid in achieving a whip-like action of the arm, wrist and hand.

Common error. In practicing a series of R strokes, the stick is not allowed to settle back to ready position (1½'' above drumhead) before making the next stroke. Take much time between strokes. Practice a series of R strokes.

The L stroke is similar to the R except for the hand-hold and rotating wrist motion. Most students will find their first attempt to execute the L stroke clumsy and unsatisfactory. They will need encouragement and assurance that everyone has trouble with this awkward motion at first, but with daily practice it will soon seem as natural as the R. The sequence of Figures 3.40–3.44 illustrate the steps in making a L stroke utilizing the traditional grip.

Figure 3.40. Ready position.

On the backswing, the left wrist rotates first to the right slightly, leaving the tip of the stick lagging somewhat behind.

Lift arm until hand is nearly shoulder high.

Wrist rotates at top of backswing to the left, and initiates the downswing by a sudden rotation to the right.

After impact, stick's natural rebound then settles back to ready position and the L stroke is completed.

Figure 3.41. Backswing.

The index finger and thumb contact breaks at the top of the backswing, closing again during the rebound. The rotating motion of the wrist is the key to a good L stroke.

When using the matched grip, the L hand executes the full stroke in the same manner as the R hand.

Practice a series of L strokes slowly.

When both the R and L strokes have been practiced independently, begin their slow alternation, R then L. This alternation of full arm strokes is the foundation of drum technique. Space the strokes about two seconds apart. Check between each stroke for ways to improve. As in golf, one should take plenty of time between practice shots in

Figure 3.42. Lift arm.

Figure 3.43. Wrist starts downswing.

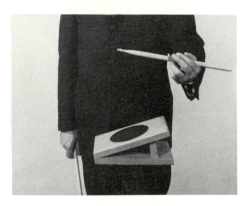

Figure 3.44. Rebound.

order to think of all factors and to correct mistakes. A helpful aid in eliminating useless die motions of the sticks is to think of a track, or a slot, about 2″ or 3″ wide, within which each stick must execute its backswing and down-swing.

Common Faults—R and L Strokes

1. Arm and wrist too rigid.
2. Waste motion caused by sticks "looping" outside the imaginary track.
3. Sticks not rebounding naturally.
4. Failure to allow sticks to settle back to ready position after rebound.
5. Failure to maintain correct grip on sticks.
6. Students' reluctance to exaggerate the arm motion. It should be pointed out to the student that this is an exaggeration (lifting elbow to shoulder level) and except in rare instances would the arms be raised to this level, examples being *sfz* attacks and performance with a marching band.

THE TAP

The tap is a single blow used to produce moderately light sounds on the snare drum. It differs from the stroke in that it is a *wrist* action, and does not involve the arms

to any appreciable extent. A large percentage of snare drum music is played using only alternated taps, the strokes being reserved for very heavy sounds and accents. Figures 3.45–3.47 illustrate the steps in making a R tap.

Figure 3.45. Ready position for the R tap.

Figure 3.46. Start of wrist action.

Figure 3.47. Start of downswing, R tap.

Starting from ready position, snap the wrist sharply, as in the stroke, but without raising the arm. This will produce a rather loud tap.

The arc travelled by the stick tip will be approximately 12″ to 14″. Play a series of R taps slowly, keeping stick arc and volume equal for all notes.

Figures 3.48–3.50 illustrate the steps in making a L tap, using the traditional grip.

To produce the same sound with the L stick, use the same 12″ to 14″ arc. Control is more difficult here, as the L handhold may still be in its awkward stage. Consequently, the arc of the stick tip will not usually be as regular as it should be, either in its length or straightness.

Figure 3.48. Ready position, L tap.

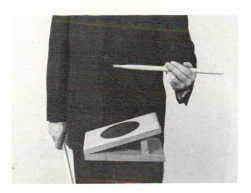

Figure 3.49. Start of downswing, L tap.

Figure 3.50. Rebound, L tap.

Students will need to be reminded frequently of the imaginary track within which each stick is to travel. Check also on the wrist actions. Remember—R wrist moves forward and back, L wrist rotates when using the traditional grip.

When using the matched grip, the L hand executes the tap in the same manner as the R hand. As in all percussion stroking, the taps require a whiplike stick motion with a natural rebound and follow through. Even though these motions will be smaller than those used in the full arm stroke, they are nonetheless necessary in order to avoid a stiff-wristed, crushed sound. Always remember that any percussion blow must get-on-and-get-off the struck surface to produce a good tone.

Practice a series of taps, R and L slowly.

When the loud taps (12 to 14 inch stick arcs) can be done fairly well, shorten the arcs in order to produce a softer tone. Less wrist motion will be required to do this, but more control is necessary and is obtained through the fine muscle and nerve coordination of the hands and fingers. The stick arc for *p* volume is about 2 inches.

Common Faults—R and L Taps

1. Wrist is too rigid.
2. Use of arm motion—only wrist motion is required.
3. Lack of stick control which causes buzz or unwanted sounds.
4. Failure to maintain correct grip on sticks.
5. Index finger of left hand failing to break contact with thumb, consequently preventing a correct arc to be traversed by the stick.

THE LONG ROLL

There are two basic ways of producing a sustained tone on percussion instruments. These are the *single stroke roll,* which is used on the timpani, bass drum, xylophone, marimba, bells, suspended cymbal, timbales, and occasionally the snare drum, and the *double stroke roll* which is the usual method of producing a long tone on the snare drum. The single stroke roll is made by rapidly alternating R and L blows on the playing surface of the instrument. The double stroke roll consists of rapidly alternating double strokes, RRLL etc., in which the first of each pair is a tap and the second a bounce. Since we are here dealing with snare drum techniques, only the double stroke roll will be considered in the following discussion.

Before introducing the stepwise procedures useful in teaching the snare drum roll, some general remarks should be given to clarify commonly used terminology and to enable the reader to gain an insight into the development of the roll as it is used in various styles of modern drumming. It often comes as somewhat of a surprise to nonpercussion playing laymen, musicians, and teachers to learn that today's all-around snare drummer actually uses an assortment of rolls which vary in duration, texture (degree of openness) and timbre. Factors which influence the type of roll are size of drum, style of music, volume desired, weight of sticks, thickness of drumhead, response of drum, and personal tastes.

The original sustaining tone of the military drum was very likely what we would now call an "open" roll, i.e., each individual tap-and-bounce sound could be distinguished by the ear. Before the introduction of the snare drum into the concert hall it was associated mainly with marching music, and this usage demanded loud, open rolls whose texture (timing of taps and bounces) conformed to the marching cadence. Wrist alternations were synchronzied with the footfalls of the marching drummer's feet.

With the advent of smaller and more responsive drums a change in the roll technique gradually evolved. The rolls became more closed and less "rhythmic" i.e., wrist motions were not synchronized with the pulse of the beat.

Although there is no proof, it is likely that the first drummers to use what is now called the "buzz" roll were the early dance and vaudeville drummers around the turn of the century. In this type of roll individual sounds are indistinguishable and the ideal is a continuous tone, very smooth in texture. It has been likened to the tearing of silk cloth. In the buzz roll more than two sounds are produced per wrist action.

Percussion instructors are divided into two rather distinct camps on the matter of how to teach the roll. One group sticks by the traditional approach of RRLL strokes *gradually* increased in speed through the taps on into the tap-and-bounce of the open roll, and finally attaining the speed of the closed roll. In this approach the student may not go at any rate faster than perfect evenness of timing and volume permit. The crucial point in the development of the roll using the traditional approach is the so-called "break" or "gear-shifting" point, when the acceleration rate becomes too fast to continue one sound per wrist motion and two-sounds-per-wrist-motion (tap and bounce) take over.

In the newer approach the student is not forced to spend weeks and months on roll development, but is provided with a double stroke roll at the outset, which he then perfects through practice until it becomes as controlled as that roll developed by the traditional method.

Good rolls have been developed by both methods. Generally the private teacher working with an able student will subscribe to the first method. The school instructor working with groups of students in a beginning band, orchestra or percussion class will find the second method most useful. Both methods of teaching the roll are outlined in this *Guide*. Following the teaching outlines there is a table summarizing advantages and disadvantages of each.

Steps in Learning the Roll, Traditional Method

The long roll is produced by alternating double strokes, RRLL etc. At first it should be played wide open, using two large strokes with each hand. It will be some weeks or months before the alternations can be speeded up (and stick arc cut down) through the taps, and on down into the open roll which is produced by a tap-and-bounce. At first this will not sound anything like a roll. Impatient students must be impressed with the fact that development of a fine roll is a long, continuous process. The criteria for determining the rapidity of alternations are 1. evenness and 2. equality of volume.

Practice the slow RRLL with no accented or predominant sounds. Equal stick arcs will help to maintain equal sounds. At beginning stages it is best to maintain a steady tempo. After the RRLL pattern has become fairly automatic, introduce the idea of gradual acceleration. Remind students that it is desirable to accelerate as much as possible *so long as perfect evenness of time and volume are maintained*. It is suggested that ten minutes of a 30 minute daily practice period be devoted to roll practice.

Speed up the alternation of the taps until reaching a point where it becomes necessary to "double up" and execute the RRLL by means of one tap followed by one bounce of the same stick. Now, instead of two wrist motions, only one is needed for each pair of sounds. This "shifting of gears" makes the closed roll possible. It is this shift from single taps to tap-and-bounce which is a hurdle requiring much practice and perseverance to surmount. To make the acceleration of sound up to, through, and on beyond this shift without disturbing the gradations of acceleration is the goal of practice.

If real control has been achieved, the reverse process, closed-to-open will be easily executed. Rudimental drum contests require the roll to be demonstrated in this fashion: open-to-close-to-open.

Steps in Learning the Roll, Newer Method

Beginning with the R alone, make a tap using about a 14″ arc. Next let the tap's natural rebound strike the pad (or drumhead) *once*. This will sound as "da-da" and consists of one tap plus one bounce, made with a single motion of the wrist. It will require considerable practice to achieve a single bounce sound which is controlled and is as loud as the tap which it follows.

When the R "da-da" can be done consistently, repeat the procedure with the L alone. Remember—try to make the bounce sound equal to the tap in each pair. Take plenty of time between practice tries. A slight downward pressure of fingers and hand on the top of the stick controls the rebound in order to get just *one* bounce.

When enough control is achieved and two fairly equal sounds are being consistently played with each hand, try synchronizing the wrist alternations to produce a continuous flow, RRLLRRLL, etc. Do not allow any gaps in the flow, even if all bounces are not sounding. There should never be any "holes" in the roll, even at this stage. A very useful teaching device to aid the student in gaining the right concept of wrist alternation speed is for the instructor to stand behind the student and grasp his hands and manipulate the student's wrist at the rate required for the open roll. See Figure 3.51.

Figure 3.51. Teacher guiding student's hands.

The closed roll is made by lowering the stick arcs and speeding up the wrist alternations.

A useful concept in teaching the roll by the newer method is "let the sticks do the work." The idea is to utilize the energy of the rebounding stick in making the controlled bounce. Timing is all-important. Diligent practice is required to perfect the long roll no matter how it is taught.

For those who wish to pursue the subject of the so-called buzz roll, an excellent article by George Lawrence Stone appears in his column in the January, 1961, issue of the *International Musician,* titled "Two Beat Rolls vs. the Buzz."

Common Faults—The Long Roll

1. Failure to maintan an even rate of acceleration in passing over the "break" (traditional approach).
2. Making more than one bounce sound following each tap (newer approach).
3. Failure to make the bounce sound equal to the tap.
4. Gaps in the long roll due to poor timing of wrist alternations.
5. Pressing or crushing sticks down into drumhead, resulting in scratchy texture of roll.
6. Stiffness of wrist action.
7. Inconsistent volume level between the two hands. The tendency is for one hand to predominate.

Note—for rolls of soft and medium volumes only finger, hand and wrist actions are required. In loud playing, the forearms, upper arms and shoulders are brought into play.

Notation of rolls is treated in a later section of this chapter under *Notation of Snare Drum Music.*

A useful device for aiding the intermediate or advanced snare drummer to improve his long roll is to practice pulsating in both binary and ternary patterns. The diagrams at the bottom of the next page illustrate this concept.

For a detailed treatment of roll texture, the reader is referred to pages 11–13 of *Beginning Snare Drum Method* by Paul Price, published by Morris.

Long Roll Taught By

Traditional Method

Cannot be used in playing drum music until perfected.

Best adapted for individual study.

Takes much patience; frustration occurs in conquering "the break."

Required in rudimental demonstrations.

Newer Method

Can be used when reading is introduced, although not yet perfected.

Best adapted for class study.

Sounds like a roll from the start. The challenge is to smooth it up, control degree of openness.

Traditional approach, open-to-closed-to-open would have to be developed later to demonstrate long roll "rudimentally."

THE SHORT ROLLS

The three short or stroke rolls most commonly used in snare drumming are the 5, 7, and 9 stroke rolls. They may be conceived as segments of the long roll, and their introduction should be delayed until the student has developed a fairly smooth and well controlled long roll. (The word "stroke" here refers to the number of times the tip of the stick strikes the drumhead during the execution of a given roll.) Idiomatically the short rolls are used in rudimental and orchestral snare drumming when notes of short value are indicated as rolls. The choice of stroke roll to be used in each case is governed primarily by the tempo of the music and secondarily by the style (rudimental, orchestral, jazz, etc.). In most rudimentally oriented instruction books and in rudimental solo literature, small numerals are often placed over rolled notes to indicate which of the short rolls is to be used.

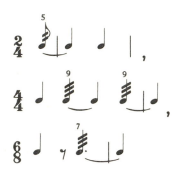

In all other music the choice of stroke roll is left to the performer.

More often than not the short rolls will be found to commence on weak beats, or fractional parts of a beat, and end with their final tap on a strong beat. Pick-ups to marching cadences are a good example.

In such weak-tied-to-strong-beat rolls the accent falls on the final single tap of the roll. When short rolls commence on a strong beat they are accented on their starting note, and are called *accented 5, 7, or 9 stroke rolls*. In accented stroke rolls, no emphasis is placed on the final single tap which then serves merely to conclude the alternate double strokes.

Much confusion about stroke rolls would be dispelled if percussion teaching would emphasize the salient point that *the short roll is merely a segment of a long roll adjusted to fill a certain time-slot*. Needless time is often spent learning and practicing, out of any musical context, 10, 11, 13, 15, 17, even 21 stroke rolls. The experienced percussionist knows that when the notation calls for a roll on a note of short duration he will start and end his roll to coincide with the beat, and only in retrospect will he be able to say whether he has used a 5, 7, 9, or 17 stroke roll. Only when interpreting a traditional rudimental passage will the drummer need to be particularly conscious of the exact number of strokes in the short rolls.

Despite the above remarks, all percussion students should practice the most commonly used of the stroke rolls as part of their early training. The 5, 7, and 9 stroke rolls are somewhat similar, but will be treated separately in the material which follows.

The 5 Stroke Rolls

The 5 stroke rolls consist of two groups of doubled notes and a final single tap.

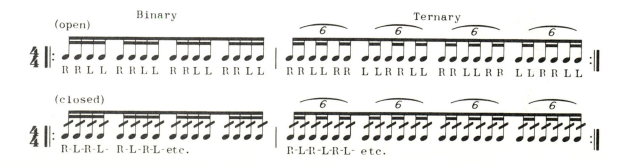

The foregoing examples show the breakdown of the 5 stroke rolls, but are not intended to illustrate actual notation as it would be found in drum music.

The accent here is on the final note. Three wrist motions are required in the 5 stroke roll.

In an open 5 stroke roll, the ear can distinguish the 5 sounds, but when the roll is closed the meshing of the sounds blurs the individual taps and bounces. In fact, a very closed 5 stroke roll will be of the same texture as the previously mentioned buzz roll in which there is no proof that each stick actually sounds only twice. The buzz texture is adaptable to the short rolls whenever the performer wishes to produce a sound of very fine texture. In order to clarify a confusing point of terminology, it should be pointed out that the so-called "press roll" or "crush roll" is not identical to the buzz roll. The press or crush roll is made by pressing both sticks on the drumhead simultaneously and allowing them to buzz for an instant or two. This method of production does not conform to that of a true roll, but it is nonetheless useful in certain cases such as the following, where there is not time enough to execute a legitimate 5 stroke roll:

Dance and jazz drummers have pioneered in the use of the press roll, and have even developed a technique of producing a roll with a single stick. For a more detailed treatment of this subject refer to Chapter 9, *Dance Band Drumming*.

Five stroke rolls occurring in series are usually alternated as:

A few examples of passages where the snare drummer would be likely to use a 5 stroke roll are:

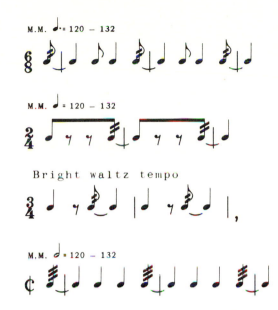

The accented 5 stroke roll has the same number of sounds and requires the same number of wrist motions (3) as the 5 stroke roll just described. The difference in execution is that the accented 5 stroke roll has an accent at its beginning and none on its final single tap. The difference in usage is that the accented 5 stroke roll is used when the rolled note starts on a primarily accented beat, or when an artificial accent is indicated.

Examples are here given which illustrate situations calling for the accented 5 stroke roll.

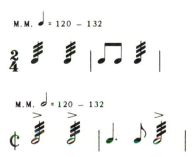

Vivo

Bright waltz tempo

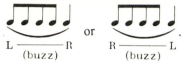

Common Faults—5 Stroke Rolls

1. Among beginning students, the most common fault is failure to use 3 wrist motions to make the 5 stroke roll. Many students, if not checked carefully, will play

which does not produce an authentic 5 stroke roll.

2. Placing an accent at the end of the roll when roll falls on the beat, i.e., choosing a roll which does not make musical sense.

The 7 Stroke Rolls

The 7 stroke roll consists of three groups of doubled notes and a final single tap.

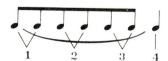

The foregoing examples show the breakdown of the 7 stroke rolls, but are not intended to illustrate the notation as it would be found in drum music.

The accent here is on the final note. Four wrist motions are required in the 7 stroke roll. Note carefully that the 7 stroke rolls do not end with the same stick with which they begin. In this they are unlike their companion short rolls, the 5 and 9.

As in the 5 stroke roll, when the 7 is played open all sounds will be distinguishable to the ear. Closed 7 stroke rolls will sound as a segment of the closed long roll. Remember that the degree of openness of any roll is dictated by tempo and style of the music. Seven stroke rolls occurring in a rudimental snare drum solo would be correctly played open.

Seven stroke rolls occurring in series are *not* alternated, for example:

Other examples of passages where the snare drummer would be likely to use 7 stroke rolls are:

Allegro

*When background beats (pulsations) are *ternary* a 7 stroke roll usually fits better than either a 5 or a 9. For this reason they are much used in 6/8, 9/8 and 12/8 time.

This figure illustrates the principle that tempo determines choice of stroke roll. Note same figure in sections on 5 and 9 stroke rolls.

If a 7 stroke roll starts on a strong or artificially accented beat, its accent is shifted from the final to the first note.

Accented 7 stroke rolls are not used as often as accented 5's or 9's. The following illustrate situations in which accented 7 stroke rolls might be used:

Vivo

Common Faults—7 Stroke Rolls

1. Poor timing of wrist alternation, which prevents roll from fitting nicely into its time-slot.

2. Accenting end of roll when roll commences on a strong beat.
3. Creating a feeling of decrescendo when performing accented 7 stroke rolls.

The 9 Stroke Rolls

The 9 stroke roll consists of four groups of doubled notes and a final single tap.

The foregoing examples show the breakdown of the 9 stroke rolls, but are not intended to illustrate actual notation as it would be found in drum music.

The accent here is on the final note. Five wrist motions are required in the 9 stroke roll.

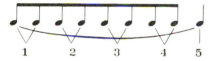

In an open 9 stroke roll all nine sounds will be distinguishable to the ear. A closed 9 stroke roll will have the same fine-grained texture as any other closed roll. Like the 5, the 9 stroke roll will fit best into time-slots which are pulsated binarily. For example:

Nine stroke rolls are usually alternated when they occur in series:

A few examples of passages in which the snare drummer would be likely to employ 9 stroke rolls are:

Adagio

See same figure in sections on 5 and 7 stroke rolls, noting tempo difference.

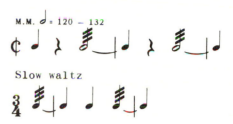

The accented 9 stroke roll has the same number of sounds and requires the same number of wrist motions (5) as the 9 stroke roll just described. The difference in execution is the shift of the accent from the final to the first note of the roll. The difference in usage is that the accented 9 stroke roll is used when the rolled note starts on a primarily accented beat, or when an artificial accent is indicated.

Examples are here given which illustrate situations calling for the use of accented 9 stroke rolls.

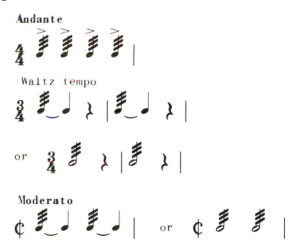

Common Faults—9 Stroke Rolls

1. Poor timing of wrist alternations, which prevents roll from fitting nicely into its time-slot.
2. Accenting end of roll in a situation where roll commences on a strong beat.
3. Creating a feeling of decrescendo when performing accented 9 stroke rolls.

R R L L L R R L L   R

A more specialized treatment of the notation of the short rolls will be found in the section on *Notation of Snare Drum Music*.

For a description of the so-called 3 stroke roll the reader is referred to *Beginning Snare Drum Method* by Paul Price, published by Morris, pages 52–53. This same book treats in some detail the 11, 13, and 15 stroke rolls.

THE FLAM

In addition to single strokes and double strokes (rolls) a third class of drum techniques consists of the "thickening" sounds. Their function is to add duration and volume to the single stroke. They are used principally on natural or artificially accented beats.

The most often used thickening stroke is called the *flam*. The flam consists of a soft grace note played almost simultaneously with, but ahead of, a loud stroke. It is notated as it sounds; one "little" and one "big" sound.

The sound should approximate the one syllable word "flam"—it should *not* sound like the two-syllable "fa-lam."

Flams can be learned by following the sequence of steps here outlined:

1. Place both sticks in ready position (1½″ above drumhead).

Figure 3.52. Ready position, R or L flam.

2. Leaving the L where it is, raise the R and make a regular full arm stroke, dropping the L in *just ahead of the R* stroke. *Do not* allow the grace note stick to rise appreciably—it should drop and make a single quiet sound which serves to thicken the main note.

Figure 3.53. R flam.

The two sounds are practically simultaneous, but never sounding exactly together. Practice a series of R flams slowly.

3. Reverse the roles of the two sticks to make a L flam. The R is now the grace note stick which drops in just ahead of the main L. Practice a series of L flams slowly.

4. When R and L flams can be executed satisfactorily, hand-to-hand flams should be practiced. A special trick is needed to get the natural rebound of the "big" stick down quickly to ready position in order for it to become the "little" stick for the alternate flam. Control the rebounding stick with a somewhat sudden tighter grip and thus force it to remain close to the drumhead. Do not force too stiffly, however, as some rebound is necessary and desirable. Drum parts seldom call for rapidly alternating flams, but they should

Figure 3.54. L flam.

be practiced hand-to-hand, at first open and then more closed. Practice a series of R and L flams, taking plenty of time between successive flams.

A useful teaching device is the the encouragement of the student to "make the big stick bigger and the little stick littler." This will help to avoid those "faker's flams" which are neither R nor L because both sticks are rising and falling in more or less equal arcs.

For loud flams use full arm strokes. When less volume is desired use lower stick arcs on the main notes. Very soft flams are made by using wrist taps on the main notes.

The grace note has no time value.

The grace note stick varies only slightly in its path for loud or soft flams.

Note: Stickwork remains the same when flams are called for as or single strokes, i.e., grace notes are not counted when determining sticking arrangement.

Common Faults—Flams

1. Grace note stick rises too much.
2. Grace note stick sounds too far ahead of main note. (*fa-lam* rather than *flam*.)
3. Both sticks striking head simultaneously defeating the purpose of the "flam" sound.
4. Grace note stick bounces, buzzes.
5. In alternating flams, both sticks rise equally.
6. Swinging arms from side to side.

THE DRAG

The second of the "thickening" strokes is called *the drag*. As in the case of the flam, the notation is a good visual symbol of the sound.

R Drag   L Drag

L L R   R R L

Two grace notes, made by the same stick, precede the main stroke. The grace notes drop in just ahead of the main note. In the open drag the three sounds are distinguishable to the ear, although felt by the player as a unit.

As in the flam, the "little" stick stays close to its ready position, and with a minimum of upward motion drops in just ahead of the main note. A controlled rebound follows the initial grace note tap. In hand-to-hand playing of the drags a tightening of the grip on the rebounding "big" stick is necessary because it must return very quickly to ready position in order to become the "little" stick for the alternate drag.

One problem that usually arises in the study of the drag is the tendency to fall into a rhythm pattern

of ♫ ♪ ♫ ♪ ♫ | etc. when practicing open drags. The drag itself has no rhythm, but sounds simply as a broad note. The soft grace notes supply the broadening sound *just barely* before the beat.

In the closed drag the two grace notes will be indistinguishable (as the individual taps and bounces of the finely closed roll) and will "drag" into the accented main note with a sound phonetically equivalent to "zzz-it."

Most students in learning to execute the drag need constant reminding that the stroke (main note) is louder and more important sounding than the grace notes which precede it. *It must also land squarely on the beat.* It should also be emphasized that the grace notes have no time value, are soft in volume, and that their time is "stolen" from the beat immediately preceding the drag.

Procedure for teaching and learning the *drag* should follow that outlined in the section on the flam.

For loud drags use full arm strokes. When less volume is desired use lower stick arcs on the main notes. Very soft drags are made by using wrist taps on the main notes.

Note: Stickwork remains the same when drags are called for as for single strokes, i.e., grace notes are not counted when determining sticking arrangement.

Common Faults—Drags

1. Drag not felt as a unit.
2. Grace notes too loud in relation to main note.
3. Grace notes assume a rhythmic significance.

(It should be noted that there is a discrepancy in terminology between the author's and the National Association of Rudimental Drummers' reference to the "drag" and "ruff" This is pointed out merely to assist the reader in avoiding confusion.)

THE RUFF

Ruffs are grace note combinations played with single alternate sticking. Ruffs serve as a means of thickening or broadening accented notes.

2 stroke ruff (flam)   3 stroke ruff

L R   R L   R L R   L R L

4 stroke ruff   5 stroke ruff

L R L R   R L R L   R L R L R   L R L R L

The 4 Stroke Ruff

In practice the 4 stroke ruff is most commonly used. A well known instance is Meacham's *American Patrol*, which contains an opening snare drum solo passage consisting entirely of 4 stroke ruffs. This solo, incidentally, is difficult to play because of the *pp* volume indicated.

The key to playing good 4 stroke ruffs is to make the three grace notes as quick and unimportant sounding as possible, "stealing" time from whatever note or rest precedes them, and aiming for the main note which must fall precisely on the beat. Ruffs are difficult to execute in rapid succession, but fortunately are not very often encountered in a series. A typical usage is the final chord of a march:

In learning the 4 stroke ruff, practice first the R ruff and then the L, slowly at first. Practice alternated ruffs only after good stick control has been achieved. The object of practice should be the exact control of the timing of the three grace notes so that the main note will fall squarely on the beat.

Practical playing techniques of professional percussionists often vary considerably from the pure rudimental tradition. The 4 stroke ruff is a case in point. Two commonly used substitute stickings are:

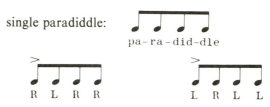

The foregoing substitute ruff stickings are used when 1) time does not permit the alternate sticking of the authentic ruff, and 2) when a more closed sound is desired than could be obtained using single sticking.

In practicing the first of these substitute ruffs

 be sure to make the

grace notes sound clearly as a true triplet. Avoid this

rhythm

The second of the substitute ruffs should sound like an extended drag. It may be practiced open, in which case fine stick control will be necessary to produce an even triplet with all notes sounding. As applied in performance, this extended drag is usually closed. Since the grace notes will then sound like a buzz no exact number of sounds can be distinguished by the ear.

As to the question of interpretation of the written figure ♫♩ , the performer's skill and good judgment will be determining factors in deciding whether to use the authentic 4 stroke ruff or one of its two possible substitutes.

THE PARADIDDLE SERIES—SINGLE, DOUBLE, TRIPLE PARADIDDLES

The word "paradiddle" is an onomatopoeic carryover from the rudimental era when such phonetic devices were used to teach drumming by rote. In the

single paradiddle:

pa – ra – did – dle

R L R R   L R L L

The paradiddle has no characteristic rhythm; it is merely a method of sticking which gives a slightly different sound than would the same group of notes played with normal alternated sticking. Paradiddles are a combination of single and double sticking, with a double pair of notes final in each.

The double paradiddle is a six note group:

R L R L R R   L R L R L L

The triple paradiddle is an eight note group:

R L R L R L R R   L R L R L R L L

The paradiddles are treated in this *Guide* as a technique for developing good stick control, and not as important rudiments of snare drumming. Indeed, they need never be used for interpreting band or orchestra drum parts. Rudimental solos, however, often specify paradiddle sticking for groups of sixteenth or eighth notes.

Each paradiddle set should be practiced in steady sequence, very slowly at first. It takes more than a little practice to play the paradiddles, and there is great stick-control value because of the ever-present challenges of speed and evenness. When practicing for speed make certain that the last two doubled notes are not crushed but sound as two distinct notes.

The accenting indicated in the examples shown above is only one of many possibilities. For example, the permutation of the single paradiddle would yield:

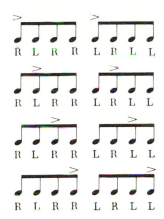

A good individual or class project is to write out and play the permutations of all three paradiddles. There is hardly a better stick control study. Many professionals use various treatments of the paradiddle series as warm-up and daily practice routines.

An interesting study in progressive meter change follows from the paradiddles when they are played l'istesso tempo. The 2/4, 3/4, 4/4 measure signatures result.

One of the chief musical values of paradiddles (aside from the fact they make fine flexibility studies for the percussionist) is the different sounds they produce for a given grouping of notes through their use of alternate and double sticking. The variations on the paradiddle sticking pattern, although, strictly speaking, themselves not paradiddles, are useful tools to utilize when attempting to blend phrasewise and match articulation with an ensemble. The following are examples of such variations and are good stick control studies:

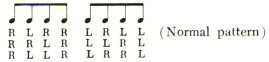

```
R  L  R  R     L  R  L  L     ( Normal  pattern )
R  R  L  R     L  L  R  L
R  L  L  R     L  R  R  L
```

The addition of flams to each of the accented notes in the foregoing example results in the so-called Flamadiddles. (See examples on page 62.)

In the interpretation of rudimental drum solos, the performer is obliged to use the paradiddles when they are designated in the score. For most players performing band and orchestra drum parts, alternate sticking will provide a more rhythmically secure sound; however, players should be mindful of the paradiddles' value in attempting to blend with an ensemble. Perhaps the paradiddles' chief inherent value to the modern day percussionist is as stick control builders.

THE RATAMACUE SERIES—SINGLE, DOUBLE, TRIPLE RATAMACUES

Similar to the paradiddle series, the ratamacues are a legacy from the rudimental tradition. The origin of the word is also onomatopoeic as applied to the single ratamacue:

The ratamacues are compounded of drags and triplets, with a final single stroke. The accenting is usually on each drag, but may also be withheld until the final single stroke. Thus:

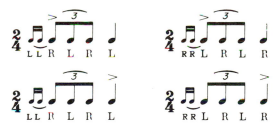

The single ratamacue is most logically written in 2/4 signature.

FLAMADIDDLES

Single Flamadiddle

Double Flamadiddle

Triple Flamadiddle

The double ratamacue has one additional drag, of the same hand, at the beginning:

The double ratamacue may also be accented on the final single stroke. It fits naturally into a 3/4 measure.

The extension of the ratamacue series provides the triple ratamacue:

It may be accented on the final single stroke also.

The possibility for playing a l'istesso tempo series of single, double, and triple ratamacues is similar to that illustrated in the section on paradiddles. Two-quarter, 3/4, 4/4 meters follow each other quite naturally to correspond to the number of beats in each ratamacue.

Practice each ratamacue slowly, with open drags, at first. There is no particular purpose to be served by running the ratamacue series for high speed. It is better thought of as an exercise for development of *clean* drags and *good* triplets. Bring out the accents wherever they are placed.

THE FLAMACUE

The flamacue is an additional example of the value of the ancient rudiments as technqiue builders. The flamacue as such is rarely met with in orchestra or band scores, however, it is often incorporated into rudimental drum solos. Its practice is recommended for the purpose of developing a fine degree of stick control. The flamacue is written:

In practicing the flamacues the trick is to displace the natural accent from the initial flam to a good solid accent on the single stroke which follows it. This will require slow practice at first. The flamacues should be practiced hand-to-hand. Note that the stickwork pattern is strict alternation.

Clean flams are called for in the flamacue, and watch particularly the final ♪ ♩ in the group.

Make it closed, and on time.

THE SINGLE STROKE ROLL

The single stroke roll is listed in the NARD* chart as among the 26 American drum rudiments, yet it is likely that the perfection of the very rapid and exciting single stroke roll is of fairly recent development among the drumming fraternity. Logically, the single stroke roll is but an extension of the alternate single strokes and taps which, it has already been pointed out, constitute the very fundamental technique of snare drumming.

Sustained single stroke rolls are rare in concert music, but short groups of ♫♫ 's are sometimes executed as single strokes by skilled drummers. An example for the orchestral literature is Rimsky-Korsakov's *Sheherazade*, fourth movement: (See illustration A at bottom of page 63.)

In dance music, jazz, and particularly Latin-American music the single stroke roll is used extensively for fills, endings, and timbale beats. A single stroke roll so rapid that it approaches the sound of an open double stroke roll is a basic part of the jazz drummer's repertoire.

*National Association of Rudimental Drummers.

The notation of the single stroke roll appears in the NARD rudiment chart as: (See illustration B at bottom of page.)

In practicing this rudiment it is well to start with slow full arm strokes, accelerating gradually and at the same time reducing the stick arcs on down through the wrist taps to the point where only the hand and finger movements activate the sticks. Practice should aim at attainment of maximum speed, therefore, proceed as far as possible, i.e., until the evenness and control break down. Follow this effort with a few seconds of rest in order to relax the arm, hand, and finger muscles, then start the procedure over again.

There is, of course, a physiological limit to the speed attainable and this limit will vary somewhat from one individual to another. Few students, however, approach their actual limit. Only with assidiuous practice can the single stroke roll be brought to a high degree of *controlled* speed. A useful psychological approach to practice is to think of *pushing ever beyond* the present rate, even though it may seem that from one day to the next no increase in speed has been achieved. Results of diligent practice can usually be noted more realistically on a week-to-week or month-to-month basis.

SPECIAL SNARE DRUM TECHNIQUES AND EFFECTS

Rim Shots. There are two generally used methods of producing rim shots on the snare drum. The first method employs both sticks. The rim shot is made by holding the L Stick so that the tip rests at or near the center of the drumhead and also makes contact with the rim midway down its shaft. This L stick is then struck sharply on the top of its shaft just below the L hand grip. See Figure 3.55.

Figure 3.55. Rim shot, crossed-stick method.

In addition to the crossed-stick method, there is a second way of making the explosive sound of the rim shot. It is simply to strike the drumhead and rim *simultaneously* with a single blow of the stick. Either stick can be used. See Figures 3.56 and 3.57. A fine control is needed to catch the rim and head simultaneously, as the slightest misjudgment in the angle and either the head or the rim will be struck and no rim shot will result. Dance band drummers usually favor this second method of making rim shots because it does not require the use of both sticks at the same time. For any rim shots which might be called for in a band or orchestra part, however, the first method is usually best because it is safer and there is nearly always plenty of time for its execution.

Rims, play on rims, or S.D. rim. The direction *rim* when marked on a snare drum part is not to be confused with rim shot. What is intended is the striking of the rim of the snare drum only. The sticks are held in regular snare drumming position, except that their angle is changed in order that the shoulders of the sticks strike the drum on its rim. The sound produced is rather brittle, "ticky," and nonresonant.

Single Stroke Roll Examples

A [P]

$\frac{2}{8}$ *f* repeat 4 times

B   R L R L R L R L R L R L etc.

On the shell. "On the shell" is like "on the rim," a direction to be taken quite literally. Execute any passages so marked on the shell of the drum with regular snare sticks.

Au bord. Au bord is a direction which, translated from the French means "at the edge" or "near the edge." For any passage marked *au bord,* play about one to two inches from the edge of the drumhead. This will produce a soft,

Figure 3.56. Rim shot, single R.

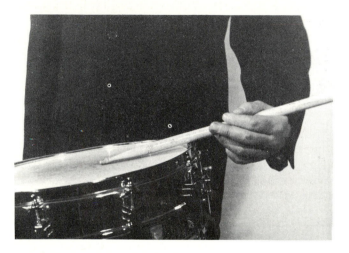

Figure 3.57. Rim shot, single L using traditional grip.

veiled tone. It is often used by the composer when he wishes the drum to convey the idea of sound coming from a long distance.

Senza cordes. Senza cordes means literally "without snares." To get the proper sound in passages so marked throw off the snares. On field drums with no lever mechanism for quick snare throw-off, a handkerchief or other small cloth can be inserted between snares and snare head to prevent the snares from vibrating.

Muffled drum. Muffled drum is the English equivalent of *senza cordes,* i.e., drum with snares disengaged. Muffled drum does *not* mean damp the drum tone with a cloth on the batter head. Muffled street drums are traditional in any marching done in a cemetery or at any service of a memorial nature.

Damping. There is some ambiguity of meaning in the term *damping* when applied to the snare drum. As the term is consistently used in this *Guide,* damping of the snare drum would indicate that the tone is to be stopped

instantaneously by sudden pressure of the finger tips on the batter head. In actual practice such a direction is never included in drum parts, staccato marks or "sec" being common ways of implying that the drum should be damped. If a direction is found to *damp drum* or "dampen drum," the player should place a handkerchief on the upper portion of the batter head. This will serve to cut down the resonance of the drum. If it seems desirable to cut the drum's natural resonance still further, place a wallet on the drumhead.

Wire or nylon brushes. The snare drummer in the band or orchestra will have occasion to use the brushes, either when called for in the score or when providing a modern sounding rhythm background for arrangements of pop tunes. The brushes are held in the same way that snare drumsticks are held. To get the full-sounding "swish" used by dance and jazz drummers, one brush is rotated on the drumhead while the rhythm figure is played with the opposite brush. One much-used beat is:

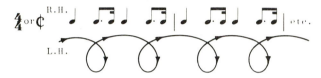

where the L brush is rotated clockwise twice per measure around the outer circumference of the head. The R brush keeps the basic jazz beat going, starting with the first count down at the lower portion of the head and moving across

the rotating L brush for the ♪. , back to its original position for the ♪ and staying there for the ♩ which starts the cycle over again.

For a more extensive discussion of brush techniques, see Chapter 9, *Dance Band Drumming.*

STYLE IN SNARE DRUMMING

Much of the misunderstanding surrounding styles employed in snare drumming stems from a tendency to overgeneralize certain playing techniques and concepts. An even more universal tendency prevails among snare drummers and instrumental instructors to attempt to completely categorize snare drumming and associate one style of playing exclusively with one performance medium.

As in the case of most deviations from traditional practice, that which is the common practice among the professional practitioners of a profession or skill becomes the "correct" or accepted manner to be passed on to those in the process of learning or attempting to perfect that particular skill. Common usage of words in a language

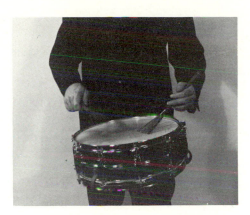

Figure 3.58. Using brushes on the snare drum (traditional grip).

dictate their meaning and cause any alterations which may come about in revising a dictionary. In just the same manner, generally accepted and employed practices in snare drumming styles should be followed and taught regardless of one's prior training which is often over-balanced on the traditional and militaristic rudimental style. This statement is by no means meant to cast aspersions toward a particular style of snare drumming, but is merely meant to indicate that more attention should be given to the fact that other methods of playing exist and are demanded even more today than ever before.

Style Categories

In identifying the snare drumming style categories it must first be immediately pointed out that the employment of one particular style category to be used most generally in a particular type of performance medium does not necessarily prohibit the performer from employing other styles of snare drumming. In fact, the medium itself has less to do with selection of styles to employ than does the type of music being rendered and the effect or sound desired from the snare drum.

Previously, and in some circles of snare drum traditionalists, it has been common practice to distinguish between two methods of snare drumming which are referred to as styles—*Open style* and *Closed style*. Sometimes this is supposed to mean the difference between drum corps and orchestral snare drumming. This style grouping is not completely accurate since many meanings, misunderstandings, and erroneous inferences may result from its use. Similarly, the use of the snare drum style terms—Rudimental Style and Concert Style as a basic snare drumming style categorization can be equally confusing and misleading. Specifically, the term rudimental means the first step or beginning in any skill, technique, or method. In snare drumming usage it is supposed to mean a style which is based fundamentally on commonly employed rudiments of snare drumming. This can also be

misleading since one might gather from this style grouping that snare drum rudiments are not used when employing the concert style.

It is therefore clear that a need exists to categorize snare drumming styles in terms of actual styles which are most commonly employed in all phases of drumming. It should be recognized that although one particular style may be employed more often than others in a particular performance medium, the selections of styles to employ is dependent upon the type of music being performed and upon the particular sound or effect to be produced by the snare drum.

Based on current practices in snare drumming it is this writer's opinion that the two general, most inclusive style categories should be termed *Parade Style* and *Concert Style*. In the case of any skill or profession it is important that its nomenclature be thoroughly understood.

Parade Style

Parade Style snare drumming means the snare drummer is using the system of alternating strokes from hand to hand or alternating patterns or rudiments. In this style it is not essential that a particular phrase or measure be started with the right hand. Instead the usual sticking patterns of traditional snare drum rudiments are followed almost without exception. The style is typified by the manner in which every stroke and rebound is clearly distinguishable and precisely and evenly spaced. The style of roll used is called the *Single Rebound* style which means that no more than one rebound from each stroke is permitted when playing a roll. In other words, as each hand moves toward the drum and returns two sounds are produced and *only* two. Many in the past have called this a double-stroke which is actully a misnomer since a stroke is considered to be one motion producing one sound. It should therefore follow that a double-stroke means two hand motions producing two sounds. Similarly a triple-stroke, etc.

To further clarify this snare drumming style category it might be helpful to mention some of the terms previously or currently used to describe it. Such terms are rudimental style, military style, open style, alternating style, band style, contest style, drum corps style, N.A.R.D. style, etc. It should also be understood that the matter of whether or not every single stroke and/or pattern is strictly alternated is dependent upon the requirements of the performance medium, the snare drummer's preference or ability, or upon other requirements or regulations.

Concert Style

In Concert Style snare drumming the snare drummer still alternates strokes and rhythm patterns, but with definite exceptions. These exceptions are based almost entirely upon consideration of the sound or effect to be produced and upon uniformity of the sound each time a phrase, measure or pattern is repeated. Any rudiment or pattern which creates accents not specified or implied in the music being rendered is omitted and substitute sticking combinations are used in its place. For example, in concert style, paradiddles are not normally used if a strict "machine-gun" effect is desired. Instead, rapidly alternating single strokes are employed. A series of triplets where the first of each group is to be accented would be more uniformly played as a succession of one right and two lefts rather than strictly alternating the strokes since there would be a tendency in the latter method of producing a different sound on the first stroke of every other triplet. Another example of the manner in which desired sound causes the snare drummer to depart from the strict alternation of strokes is in playing an eighth note followed by two sixteenths where the pattern is repeated. In this case and for the same reason given above in regard to the triplets, the sticking would be changed to right-right-left or right-left-left, however, the former sticking is usually preferred. This system of sticking is usually referred to as the "Straight System" since Edward B. Straight employed this method in the 1920s both in his well known drum method books and in his own teaching methods. Basically, all phrases and patterns are started with the right hand. With certain modifications according to individual tastes and demands, this system is used currently by percussionists in symphony orchestras, recording studios and discriminating concert organizations for more uniformity of sound.

The style of roll used is called the *Multiple Rebound* style which means that more than one rebound is usually produced from each stroke when playing a roll. This type of roll is used because there is more uniformity of sound in producing the roll regardless of the tempo and because it blends with sounds from other instruments in the orchestra or band. It is always played very closed without concern for the number of rebounds being produced from each hand motion with the drumstick. Other terms have been used to describe this snare drum roll. Some of them are closed roll, crush roll, multiple bounce roll, press roll, etc. The press roll is probably the next best term to use in identifying the multiple rebound roll since it is produced by a rapid and smooth alternation of each stick pressing (but not too firmly) into the drum head. The term multiple bounce actually means the same thing but is avoided whenever possible by this writer because of its usual use in some beginning drum books in which this type of roll is all the student ever learns. It is very important to realize that the roll referred to as the multiple rebound style roll is actually that portion of the traditional long roll played open-close-open when it is closed to the point at which more than one rebound is being produced from each stick.

In strict snare drumming contests and in drum and bugle corps competitions the snare drummer is never allowed to arrive at the point where more than one rebound per stick is being produced. It is this "completely closed" roll that is used in concert style snare drumming.

Another important consideration of concert style snare drumming is that since the sound is more important than the alternation of sticks in a strict, prescribed manner, the sticks are not raised in any "flashy" manner, but instead are kept close to the drum head and are raised only when the desired sound, such as various degrees of accent intensity, demands it.

Style Employment

Drum and bugle corps snare drumming demands the strict employment of the parade style. Parade style is used in most band marching situations as well as when the band or orchestra is performing a march intended for parade use. In band work, however, the parade style is not as strictly employed as in the case of drum and bugle corps drumming. For example, the band director may prefer to have the drummers use the multiple rebound roll at all times, etc. These exceptions depend upon the musical demands of each situation encountered. Chiefly, however, the concert style of snare drumming should be used when performing music commonly referred to as concert type music.

In playing marches in the parade style the snare drummer will probably end every roll with a single tap. For example a series of separated quarter note rolls would be played in strict parade style, (especially drum corps drummers) as if they were written as two tied eighth notes. In concert style, however, the snare drummer should never play the rolls in this manner. Instead a rule is followed to play rolls of any type strictly according to the duration required by the notational value. In this way the snare drum roll is permitted to blend with notes of like durational value played by the other instruments. The concert style is used in orchestral snare drumming except where it is necessary to produce alien sounds such as imitating parade snare drumming when the snare drum part calls for "military drum."

Although many snare drum rudiments may be used when using the concert style, they are not rendered in the strict alternating fashion common to parade style except when that particular effect is required by the music being performed such as in the case of a Sousa March being played by a symphony orchestra.

Other Drumming Styles

Although the two basic snare drum styles are the parade and concert styles, there are other practices in drumming which have caused drummers and composers to identify them to achieve specific sounds and effects. These are primarily based on a manipulation of the notated rhythmic patterns and may be played by combining rules and techniques of both basic snare drum styles. Some of these might be jazz style or dixieland style in which there is a deliberate syncopation of the written rhythm patterns and an emphasis of certain characteristic accents while using the concert style primarily. Drum set style might be another indication by the composer which means that several drummers are to use wire brushes on the snare drum. In this case the drummer is expected to know that the left brush is making a sweep across the drum head while the right hand alone plays the notated rhythm pattern.

Understanding styles of drumming is most important. It is unfortunate to hear a drummer play eighth notes in strict fashion if the composer has indicated that a syncopated style is to be used. It is just as unfortunate as well as annoying to hear a drummer give a free syncopated interpretation to eighth notes if a strict and literal rendition is intended.

The best method of gaining control and technique of the two basic as well as other drumming styles is to have experience in playing them in the organizations which employ them most frequently. A well rounded experience is essential in order to meet the demands of today's musical requirements unless the individual drummer never expects to perform in any but the one or two types of organizations in which he may have had some experience. A good percussionist is as capable of playing a demanding xylophone part in a symphony orchestra as he is a marchng drum beat, smooth concert snare drum roll, or the drum set rhythm for traditional or popular music dance rhythms. It is for this reason that many states are revising their percussion contest requirements to encourage good techniques in every field of percussion performance and to keep abreast of current demands and techniques of a contemporary percussion performance.

The major problem in orchestral snare drumming is attaining the control demanded to play *softly* enough without losing control. The most difficult kinds of passages are the soft, rapid series of single strokes or taps, and the *pp* roll, especially when these occur as solos. These two problem techniques should be practiced on the drum rather than on the practice pad. The goal of practice is: soft volume *and* precise rhythm.

Some composers have scored for *military drum* in symphonic orchestra compositions. Passages so marked should not be played on the small orchestra drum but on a gut-snared field drum mounted on a stand.

Dance band style is treated separately in Chapter 9, *Dance Band Drumming*.

SNARE DRUM NOTATION

Clef. When the snare drum part is printed on a staff the 3rd space of the F clef is used. If for some reason an-

other line or space is used, the part is marked *S.D.* In many contemporary works the various percussion instruments (non-pitch) are printed on single lines in order to save space. Some composers and percussionists are advocating the use of the neutral clef sign for the percussion instruments of indefinite pitch. Perhaps the use of the neutral clef is "splitting hairs," however, it does offer a way of cancelling the treble or bass clef signs when a percussion part changes from a pitched to an unpitched instrument. An example of each of the four usages is given following:

Roll Notation. There are several ways in which a roll can be indicated, by far the most common being the three slanted dashes through the note stem:

Note: the eighth note flag counts as one dash.

Occasionally in older music the trill sign is used to denote the long roll:

A third roll indication is four slanted dashes through the note stem. It is rarely seen nowadays. It is interpreted exactly as any other roll sign:

A fourth and newer method (however not widely used) of indicating not only a roll, but also that the composer desires the roll to be of the very closed, multibounce type is a symbol in the form of a "z" occurring over the note head or on the stem of the note:

Note well, however, that *not all* slanted dashes signify a roll. A single slanted dash indicates that the note is to be played as 8th notes:

A pair of dashes signifies that the note is to be divided into 16th notes:

The two foregoing abbreviations are easily misconstrued as rolls. A further note: the usual three-dash roll sign does not necessarily imply 32nd notes, although this would seem to be the logical inference. It simply means that the drum tone should be sustained by means of the roll technique for the duration of the note, and in the style dictated by the music.

An accent mark over a roll means to accent the attack:

The use of ties in connection with roll notation has great significance for the drummer. In the typical case a long roll will both begin and end *on the beat*—often ending on the next, or a later, strong beat. A tie connects the note (single tap) which is the end of the roll:

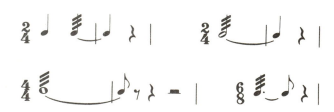

This concluding tap is accented naturally, or can be written with the accent sign >. It will nearly always be a R tap. It must fall cleanly on the beat. Much experience is necessary before the student will automatically adjust his wrist alternations to enable him to come out on the concluding single tap "right on the button."

If the long roll is written so that it does not end *on* the beat but extends up *to* the beat, no accent is made on the final single tap. The roll should ideally stop *just ahead* of the next beat. For students, a convenient and clean way of ending such rolls is to conclude on the final "and" count.

This is a nice point of interpretation. Common practice among professionals is to roll as close as possible to the next beat when playing in a slow tempo where a gap would be noticeable, and to end on the final beat, or half-beat, if the tempo is fast. The measure 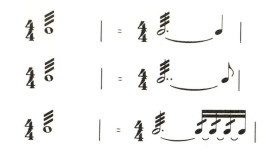 can be played in at least three ways dependent on the tempo:

Occasionally rolls are seemingly incorrectly written, that is, a tied-over sound would be better than a break in the rolls, and vice versa. For example:

As notated it is correct to break between each of the ♫ here, but if the ensemble has legato chords this would be better played:

Phrase with the ensemble in cases where rolls are ambiguously notated. Remember, the final arbiter is the ear.

Occasionally, "literal" or "measured" rolls are called for, i.e., the exact number of strokes as indicated by the note subdivided into 32nd notes. This is usually indicated by preceding the roll notation with one unit completely written out such as follows:

Grace Notes. Grace notes encountered in snare drum music are summarized in the following table:

1 grace note ... flam

... drag

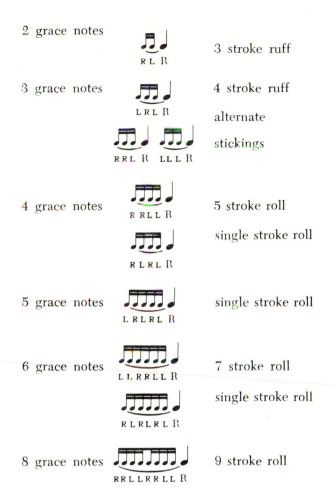

2 grace notes — 3 stroke ruff
R L R

3 grace notes — 4 stroke ruff
L R L R

alternate stickings
R R L R   L L L R

4 grace notes — 5 stroke roll
R R L L R

single stroke roll
R L R L R

5 grace notes — single stroke roll
L R L R L R

6 grace notes — 7 stroke roll
L L R R L L R

single stroke roll
R L R L R L R

8 grace notes — 9 stroke roll
R R L L R R L L R

Stroke Roll Designations. In rudimental drum literature, figures are often placed above short rolled notes to indicate which of the stroke rolls to use. Do not take these figures too literally! The correct choice of short roll *depends upon the tempo.* Obviously, at a slow rehearsal tempo the 7 or 9 stroke will be necessary to fill the time-slot occupied by a 5 stroke roll at a bright march tempo. Of course some adjustment in degree of openness can compensate for minor tempo variations. The point is that in the actual performance situation the choice of roll is a matter of individual judgment. The important thing is to fill the time-slot with sound.

Adding Flams. In some cases composers and arrangers leave the addition of flams to the discretion of the player, especially in marches where flams are most appropriate. In general, the part should be played *as written* until the wishes of the conductor can be determined.

Abbreviations Commonly Found in Snare Drum Music

5— 5 stroke roll
7— 7 " "
9— 9 " "
11—11 " "
13—13 " "
15—15 " "
17—17 " "
Br.—brushes
R—right
L—left
R.S.—rim shot
s.c.—senza cordes (without snares)
S.D., Sn. Dr., —snare drum
X—stick beat

For foreign language terms for the various types of snare drums see table, Chapter 2, page 16.

THE RUDIMENTS

The following is a listing of the 26 standard drum rudiments as adopted by the National Association of Rudimental Drummers. For those interested in the historical background of these rudiments, it is recommended that they read the article, "The Development of Drum Rudiments" by W. F. Ludwig available from Ludwig Industries, 1728 N. Damen Ave., Chicago, Ill., 60647.

The first 13 of the rudiments in the table are designated by the N.A.R.D. as "the thirteen essential rudiments" for their entrance examination. The notation and some of the stickwork have been edited to conform to the principles presented earlier in this book.

To the modern percussionist, the main values of these rudiments are as stick control and flexibility studies.

THE 26 STANDARD DRUM RUDIMENTS
(As adopted by the National Association of Rudimental Drummers)

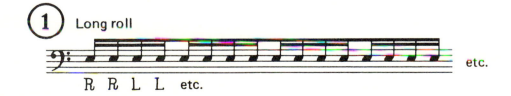

① Long roll — R R L L etc. — etc.

(2) 5 stroke roll

R R L L R   L L R R L

(3) 7 stroke roll

L L R R L L R   R R L L R R L

(4) Flam

L R   R L

(5) Flam Accent (#1)

L R L R   R L R L

(6) Flam Paradiddle

L R L R R   R L R L L

(7) Flamacue

L R L R L L R   L R L R L L R

(8) Ruff (Author uses the term "Drag" to denote this rudiment)

L L R   R R L

(9) Single Drag

R L L R   L R R L

(10) Double Drag

L L R L L R L   R R L R R L R

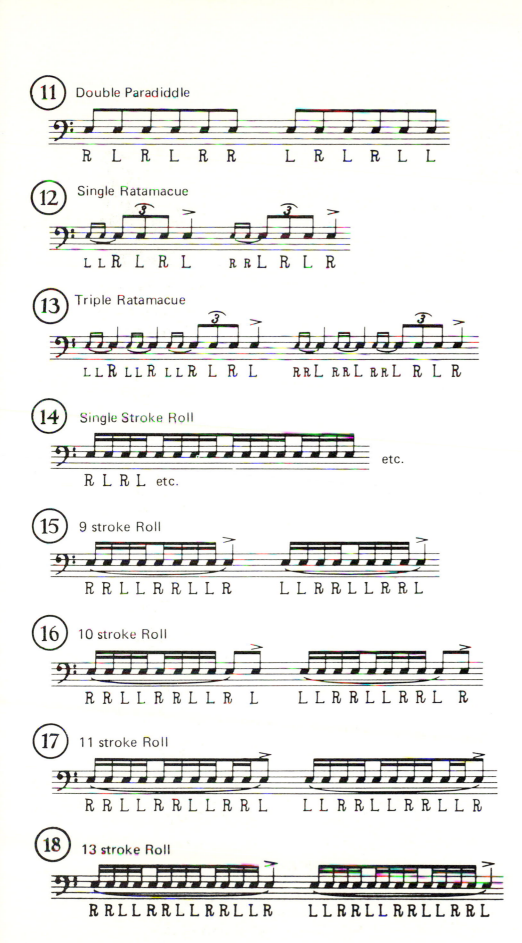

(11) Double Paradiddle

R L R L R R   L R L R L L

(12) Single Ratamacue

L L R L R L   R R L R L R

(13) Triple Ratamacue

L L R L L R L L R L R L   R R L R R L R R L R L R

(14) Single Stroke Roll

R L R L etc.   etc.

(15) 9 stroke Roll

R R L L R R L L R   L L R R L L R R L

(16) 10 stroke Roll

R R L L R R L L R L   L L R R L L R R L R

(17) 11 stroke Roll

R R L L R R L L R R L   L L R R L L R R L L R

(18) 13 stroke Roll

R R L L R R L L R R L L R   L L R R L L R R L L R R L

19 15 stroke Roll

R R L L R R L L R R L L R R L   L L R R L L R R L L R R L L R

20 Flam Tap

L R R   R L L

21 Single Paradiddle

R L R R   L R L L

22 Drag Paradiddle No. 1

R LL R L R R   L RR L R L L

23 Drag Paradiddle No. 2

R LL R LL R L R R   L RR L RR L R L L

24 Flam Paradiddle—diddle

L R L R R L L   R L R L L R R

25 Lesson 25 (Ratatap)

LL R L R   LL R L R

26 Double Ratamacue

LL R LL R L R L   RR L RR L R L R

CHAPTER 4

Bass Drum and Cymbals

GENERAL DESCRIPTION

The bass drum sound is a unique component of the total band, orchestra, marching band, and dance band sonority. With its lowest frequencies it puts a foundation on the ensemble. Both rhythmic and timbre functions characterize the bass drum. In metrical music like marches and dance-like pieces it can truly be considered the "heartbeat of the orchestra." Bass drumming is demanding in its musical, technical, and physical requisites. A bass drummer who takes his work seriously and plays with fine musicianship is that rare gem which most instrumental directors seek but seldom find. One reason for this situation is that, after having learned snare drum technique, the bass drum appears to the average student to be a bore. A selling job is often required in order to develop student interest in the bass drum. An instrumental director therefore must take care to show a full measure of regard for the importance of this instrument. He may easily find examples in almost any type of musical literature which demonstrate the importance of the bass drum. For example, in marches the band could function without the snare drums, but might flounder rhythmically without the solidifying pulse of the bass drum. The policy of rotating snare drum, bass drum, cymbals, and timpani assignments within the class or the percussion section of the orchestra and band will give all a chance to gain experience in bass drumming, and will enable the director to select the student showing particular aptitude for the important concert assignments.

There are several important points to be made in connection with the instrument itself before considering its playing techniques. First, the bass drum should be of a size appropriate to the ensemble. The following table summarizes the recommended dimensions for various types of instrumental ensembles:

Elementary school band or orchestra—14″ × 28″.

Complete concert band and symphony orchestra—
16″ × 32″—38″, or 18″ × 40″.

Marching band and drum corps—10″ × 28″.

However, it is noteworthy that many marching bands and drum corps are now using pitched bass drums, often four different sizes as follows: 14″ × 22″, 14″ × 24″, 14″ × 26″ and 14″ × 28″. Another possible combination is 14″ × 22″, 14″ × 26″, 14″ × 28″ and 16″ × 32″, although the latter and largest size may present problems for anything less than the most stout-hearted players! By using pitched bass drums there is an added dimension in sound color.

Dance band and combo—14″ × 22″ or 14″ × 20″. (Also available are 14″ × 24″ and 14″ × 26″ sizes.)

Figure 4.1. 14″ × 28″, single tension.

The bass drum should be of the double tension variety (each head can be tensioned separately). It should have two good quality heads made specifically for use on the bass drum. Although calfskin heads may still be preferred by certain top professional percussionists in symphony orchestras (usually with ideal or nearly ideal conditions of

Figure 4.2. Concert bass drum on rack, 16'' × 34'', double tension.

Figure 4.4. Scotch style bass drum, 10'' × 28''.

Figure 4.3. Concert bass drum mounted on an adjustable tilting bass drum stand.

Figure 4.5. Dance band bass drum, 14'' × 22''.

temperature and relative humidity), plastic heads are far more appropriate for all other applications. When the calfskin heads "shrink" in very dry conditions (especially on larger concert models), it becomes virtually impossible to achieve a characteristic bass drum sound that is low enough in pitch. Conversely, if the conditions are excessively humid, then the calfskin heads become "mushy" to the extent that rhythmic integrity is impossible.

A cradle or rack is necessary to bring the bass drum up to its playing position. All major drum manufacturers market a folding metal rack, but these are not entirely satisfactory because of the tendency of the heavy vibrations of the drum to rattle the braces of the rack. This type of rack, if used, should be padded with felt or other soft material in order to prevent distracting vibrations. A cradle made of wood cut to the exact specifications of the particular drum is a better mounting for the concert bass drum. Also available on the market is an adjustable tilting bass drum stand. (See Figure 4.3) This stand is highly recommended. It permits the performer to select the exact proper playing position for the drum to achieve maximum control and tonal effect. It facilitates executing rapid two stick parts and rolls. It also aids in positioning the bass drum for multipercussion playing. Even more desirable is the fully suspended concert bass drum stand which provides for optimum resonance of sound, has no metal-to-metal contact, is equipped with a complete tilting adjustment and locking mechanism and is mounted on wheels (with locks) for ease of transport. Web slings are necessary to carry the marching band bass drums, and are included in the purchase price quoted in the catalogs of the leading makers. The dance band bass drum requires a foot pedal equipped with a hard felt, cork, or wood beater.

TUNING BASS DRUMHEADS

The unsatisfactory sound of so many school bass drums is caused by *too much tension* on the heads. For concert playing, the bass drum should have a low, indiscernible pitch. Heads tuned too tightly will not produce the low partials that are necessary to give the drum its characteristic, resonant sound. On the other hand, if the tension is too loose, the drum will have a lifeless, slapping sound.

There are two approaches to tuning a concert bass drum. One is to tune both heads to the same low "pitch," the other being to tune the heads to separate "pitches." The latter method has the advantages of producing a sound of resonant quality with many overtones and quite indefinite in pitch. As an example of this method of tuning, let us consider the steps taken to tune a 34″ bass drum. With the left head completely muffled, tune the right head to a low E. Then muffle the right head and tune the left head to a low E♭. Obviously, the pitches will vary with different size drums i.e., lower pitches being used for larger drums and conversely, higher pitches being used for smaller drums; however, the minor second interval between the two heads should be maintained.

To ensure that bass drums utilizing calfskin heads in areas or periods of low humidity will be flexible enough to obtain the desired sound, tighten each tuning rod two or three half turns *after* each playing period. Then at the beginning of the next playing period loosen each tuning rod (an equal number of half turns) until a good low, resonant tone is obtained. The reverse of this process should be used in areas or periods of high humidity. This procedure will ensure enough slack flexibility in the heads so that a good tone can be produced in any kind of weather. Care should be taken to see that each tuning rod is turned an *equal number of half turns*. As with all drumheads, tension must be kept equal at all points around the perimeter of the head. If this rule is followed unfailingly from the time a new head is put on, the rims will remain equal at all points.

Marching band and drum corps bass drumheads, in contrast to those on concert band and orchestra instruments, should be fairly tight and since both heads are played upon, they should be tuned to the same pitch.

Dance band bass drums are usually tuned to produce a rather dead sound. The heads should not be tight, the exact amount of tension being a matter of personal preference. In addition to the tension, dance band bass drums require muffling devices. Nearly all bass drums made specifically for dance work come with a round disk-type muffler covered with soft felt which attaches by means of a clamp to the rim. It should be mounted so that it contacts the playing head. If the drum still has too much afterring, and most do, it has been found that one or two strips of flannel stretched across the inside of one or both of the heads eliminates most of the undesired ring. The step-by-step procedure for installing the flannel strips is:

1. With bass drumhead down on floor, remove the counterhoop (rim) and playing head.
2. Cut a strip of cloth about two or three inches wide, about six inches longer than the diameter of the drum.
3. Stretch the strip across the shell slightly to the right or left of the center line.
4. Fit the head over the shell so that it holds the cloth strip snug against its under side.
5. Remount the counterhoop and put a small amount of tension on each of the tuning rods.
6. Cut off the excess cloth which protrudes on each end.
7. Apply final tension.

Experimentation will show the number and placement of cloth strips necessary to get the characteristic dead tone associated with dance band bass drums.

A third device used by drummers to achieve a satisfactory tone is a patch of moleskin stuck onto the playing head at the spot where the foot pedal's beater strikes the drum. Moleskin is a soft felt-like fabric backed with adhesive plaster, and is obtainable in any drug store in small packages of 4 to 6 sheets. One sheet, which is approximately 3″ × 5″, is right for the purpose. Drummers today prefer to use a hard beater whose impact sound is softened by the moleskin patch rather than the fluffy lamb's-wool beaters which were once popular.

BASS DRUM NOTATION

The bass drum notes are most commonly written in the first or second space of the F clef, with their stems pointing down. In much of the standard band literature the snare drum, bass drum and cymbals are all scored on the same staff, as in the following examples:

In these examples the snare drum plays the upper notes and the bass drum and cymbals play the lower notes *in unison.* This is customary procedure for marches, dances, overtures, etc. In some of the newer band literature and in most orchestral scores the bass drum is written on a separate staff, often on a separate part. In such cases the staff or part is clearly marked *Bass drum, B.D., Bass Dr.,* or one of the foreign equivalents. (See table Chapter 2.) Occasionally the bass drum notes are written on a single line in the interest of saving space. It is customary for their stems to be pointed down, but there are many exceptions.

Rolls on the bass drum are indicated by the use of three slanted dashes through the note stem 𝄐 The trill sign is sometimes used, especially in older music 𝄎

In cases where the bass drum and cymbals play from the same notes, the composer or arranger indicates by the abbreviations *B.D.* and *cyms., cybs., cbs.,* or *cym.* when he wishes the bass drum or cymbals to play alone. After such note or notes, the abbreviation *Tog.* is used to indicate that the two instruments are to resume playing together. An example of such usage is:

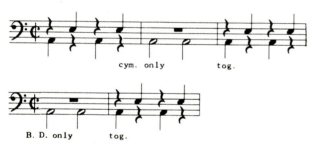

As a general rule bass drum notes are written with some regard for their actual duration. That is, if the composer wishes long booming tones he will use long value notes, as

If he desires a shorter, crisper or "deader" sound he will usually, if he is careful in such matters, write short value notes followed by rests, as

The player strikes and damps the drum in accordance with the style of writing. Staccato markings under bass drum notes mean to damp the tone very quickly.

THE PLAYING SPOT

No hard and fast rule can be adopted which will stipulate the correct playing spot on the bass drum. Variable factors are the size and shape of the drum itself, condition and characteristics of the heads, the atmospheric conditions of the moment, kind of beater used, style of the music, volume of tone desired, and so on. Most often one will find that the bass drum sounds best when struck at a point midway between the center and the rim. Most players find it convenient to locate the playing spot in the upper portion of the head when the drum is in playing position. Some very fine players are known to prefer the lower portion of the drum, however, allowing the arm to hang more or less straight down.

The drum is rarely struck at dead center, this being a nonresonant point on any circular vibrating surface. For certain effects, however, even this center spot is utilized. Trial-and-error experience is the only real help in determining the optimum playing spot on a particular drum in a particular passage of music.

HANDHOLDS AND BASIC STROKES

The handhold for the bass drum beater is made by grasping the beater about ⅓ of the way up from the butt end of the handle (where it feels balanced) with the right hand, thumb on top, fingers curled loosely around the stick. See Figure 4.8.

Figure 4.6. Upper playing spot.

Figure 4.7. Lower playing spot.

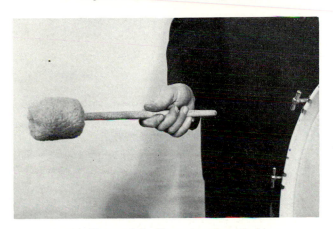

Figure 4.8. Bass drum handhold.

At least three major, and many minor, variations in the manner of making the stroke on the concert bass drum are in common use. The first can be described as a straight stroke style. To play in this manner one strikes the drum direct blows, varying the arc of the beater ball and the playing spot on the drumhead to obtain gradations of tone and volume. The wrist and arm are brought into play, with the wrist action providing the resiliency needed to produce a good tone. For the very loudest sounds, upper arm and shoulder muscles activate the stroke.

The second style of bass drum stroke is the glancing blow. Players who use this style employ the handhold as just described. Using a sharp wrist snap, the head is struck on the return or "up" phase of the ellipse described by the path of the beater ball. The playing spot is in the upper portion of the drumhead at a point near the player's chest. If a very hard tone is required the arm and shoulder muscles are brought into play. In playing regularly recurring beats, as in a march, the arcs described by the beater ball should be kept equal to ensure evenness of timing and volume. In rapid tempos equal *up and down* strokes are used by many players, each motion including a wrist snap which causes the beater ball to brush the head with a glancing blow.

A third style of bass drum stroke is made by allowing the arm to hang down at a natural angle while striking the drum with fairly direct blows, tending toward a "pulling up" motion on each stroke. The playing spot for this method of bass drumming lies in the lower portion of the head. See Figure 4.7.

The question arises as to which of the three styles should be adopted and taught. Among professional players in symphony orchestras the second method is rarely seen. The finest symphony players prefer either the first or third style, both of which are essentially *direct* blows. Percussionists with high school and college band training almost invariably use the glancing blow style, often incorporating fancy wrist flourishes into their strokes. Such motions are not only considered good showmanship, but their pendulum-like function is probably an aid in stabilizing the timing of the beats.

In the author's opinion the direct blow style is best, and should be taught both to band and orchestra percussion students. For one thing, it is basically a more natural action. Secondly, the notion that a bass drum should be struck a glancing blow to produce its proper sound is contrary to the accepted manner of striking nearly all of the other instruments of percussion. Thirdly, a glancing blow simply does not impart maximum vibration to a drumhead. It must be pointed out, however, that the resiliency of the blow (or stroke) to any percussion instrument is of the utmost importance. Once a stroke has been administered to an instrument, any lingering of the beater on the surface of the instrument impedes the free vibrating of that surface and drastically inhibits tone production. Hence, the use of the "glancing" approach is understandable when trying to teach the "resiliency concept" to a student.

The correct playing position for the bass drummer is shown in Figure 4.9.

Figure 4.9. Bass drum playing position.

Notice that the left hand is kept out over the head opposite to the batter head. In this position it is ready to contact the head in applying the light muffling action utilized when playing soft passages, and it is ready to apply the sudden inward pressure used to damp the drum after a short note or on a cut-off from the conductor. The slight left hand finger contact just mentioned helps to control the amount of ring to the tone of the drum, and should be used most of the time when playing at *pp,p,* or *mp* volumes. See Figure 4.10.

Figure 4.10. L hand muffling bass drumhead.

A completely different conception of bass drumming is evident in the so-called Scotch style of playing. College marching bands whose major duty is to provide football spectaculars usually feature one or more bass drums played in the Scotch manner. It is a flashy technique using two beaters made of hard felt equipped with leather thongs which loop around the player's wrist and fingers and thus may be twirled between strokes. For added flash, cross-over beats are possible in which the R beater strikes the left head and vice versa.

The dance band bass drum is played by means of a foot pedal. When the toe is depressed a spring arrangement pulls the beater ball forward, making contact with the drumhead. The pedal beater comes in handy in studio band work and is often utilized in the pit for musical shows, ballets, and light operas where one percussionist must play timpani, bells, xylophone, chimes, etc., and also double drums. In such situations there is always the problem of having too few hands, so that bass drum notes played by the foot make it possible to use both hands at the same time on the timpani, snare drum, cymbal, or even a mallet instrument. The term "double drums" was coined during the vaudeville pit orchestra era to refer to the then new set-up which permitted one man to play both snare and bass drums through the invention of the pedal. The term is now seldomly used.

THE BASS DRUM ROLL

The preferred method of executing a roll on the bass drum is with a matched pair of bass drum "roller" mallets, such as the Payson model, made of soft pile, hard felt inner core and hard maple handle. Unfortunately, a severe disservice to percussion was promulgated by composers, authors of orchestration texts and percussion books and a few nonpercussionist instrumental teachers, when timpani mallets are specified to roll on the bass drum. Timpani mallets are generally too small, too light and are simply ill-suited in the execution of bass drum rolls.

The roll is produced by making alternating *single* strokes, and in this respect is similar to the timpani roll. Care must be taken to adapt the speed of the roll to the size and tension of the head in order to elicit maximum resonance. If the roll is too rapid, the sound will be stifled, and if the roll is too slow, there will not be any semblance of a roll at all. With the use of a tilting stand and the drum in a horizontal position, the matched grip and style of playing will be conveniently utilized. The goal of practice should be control of the timing and the volume so that a smooth roll at any volume level is obtained.

Avoid using the double-ended mallet (which has a large felt head at one end and a small head at the other end) as it produces an uneven sounding roll.

DAMPING

The bass drum will continue to ring distractingly if it is not completely damped on both heads the instant the tone is to be stopped. To damp the bass drum the player must place the palm of the left hand and the wrist and finger tips of the right hand (the beater must still be held) quickly onto the centers of the heads and press inwards. Another method of damping which allows great control is to damp the right (playing) side of the bass drum with one's right knee, while damping the left side with the left hand in the manner mentioned above. For this method, the player rests his right foot on the drum rack or other convenient object. The drum should be damped at all cut-offs from the conductor, during rests, general pauses, and after notes marked *sec.,* or *secco,* staccato notes, and at the conclusion of long tones which are being allowed to sound for specific durations. The bass drum should *not* be damped after a note followed by a slur mark, as this is the usual method of indicating "let ring." Control of duration is not as precise when playing the bass drum by means of the foot pedal. About the only way to damp the tone in this case is to press the pedal very firmly on, or immediately after, the short note. The contact of the beater ball on the head will serve to damp the tone to some extent.

MISCELLANEOUS POINTS—BASS DRUM

1. A variety of mallets must be available to the player, including one large Payson model "sostenuto", a pair of Payson model "roller mallets", a pair of wooden and a pair of hard felt mallets. (See figure 4.11, from top to bottom). This array of mallets will handle most musical needs.

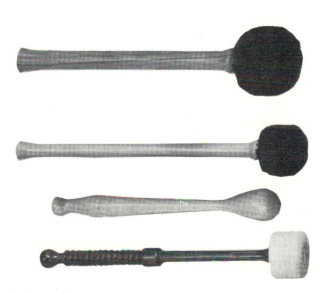

Figure 4.11. Various concert bass drum mallets.

2. The range of volume available on the bass drum is very great. Accenting thus may run the gamut from subtle, lightly accented tones to cannon booms and thunder peals. All accents printed in the part should be carefully observed by the bass drummer in order to extract the maximum musical effect from the sometimes monotonously regular patterns. Anyone who has ever heard a topnotch military band bass drummer will appreciate the skill in accenting by means of which the player literally creates his own part, furnishing a rhythmic drive to the band not obtainable by any other means. "If you hit the bass drum hard, it does not make any difference what the chord is above it; if you roll *fortissimo* on the bass drum, the rest of the orchestra [or other ensemble] can quit playing."[1] This is what Walter Piston once said to his orchestration class, and it accurately describes the tremendous power of the instrument and the care one must take in using it. Its response is a bit slower than other types of drums, but it is very effective in relatively slow-moving repeated notes as well as *secco* fast isolated strokes. It is effective in soft passages and adds tremendous weight to the percussion section in loud dynamic situations. The bass drum can also be used to evoke a feeling of impending doom with a *pianissimo* roll and in older symphonic literature it was often used to recall war or belligerent hostility.

3. Two Italian composers, Gasparo Spontini and Gioacchino Rossini, did a disservice to the musical conception of the use of percussion instruments. They popularized the cymbal attached to the bass drum, both instruments to be played by one player. Hector Berlioz formally denounced this crude practice in his famous text on orchestration.[2]

4. Do not be afraid that single notes marked *solo* will be too loud if played with full power. Exploit the "booms"—they are exciting and sometimes even dramatic.

5. In contemporary literature some bass drum parts require the drum be placed in a horizontal position and played with two mallets due to difficult and rapid rhythmic passages. Once again, there is an absolute need for a tilting stand.

CYMBALS

General Description

The clashing tone of the cymbals has been one of the most exciting timbre ingredients in music for many centuries. Oriental and near-eastern music featured cymbals long before the dawn of recorded history. It is a well known fact that the best producers of cymbals have been the Turkish artisans. Early in the Classic period of music,

Haydn and Mozart introduced these "Turkish Music" instruments into the symphony orchestra. The foremost makers of cymbals are the Zildjian family, whose father-to-son traditions include a secret formula for mixing the alloy from which the cymbals are made. The Zildjian family's products have dominated the world market since 1623. The family business split in 1929, one brother moving to the United States and the other remaining in Constantinople. It is supposed that the formula used by each is identical. The Avedis Zildjian Co. is the U.S. manufacturer. All Zildjian cymbals bear the imprint identifying them as K. Zildjian (the Turkish manufacturer) or Avedis Zildjian. In the paragraphs to follow much of the material has been drawn from an article "Sounding Brass and Cymbals" which originally appeared in *The Music Journal* and can be obtained from the A. Zildjian Co., Longwater Drive, Norwell, Mass. 02061, in pamphlet form. The author is Robert Zildjian.

Every cymbal of high quality contains virtually every tone, with attendant upper partials. The variation in tone among individual cymbals is due to the relative strengths of certain of the fundamental and partial tones in each. No single tone should dominate the sound of a cymbal. The only variance between different cymbals of a similar type lies in their *dominant* pitch and in their different reactions to sympathetic vibrations. The response of some cymbals is faster than others of the same category. This means that one cymbal reaches full vibration sooner than another. There is no such thing as a cymbal tuned to a C, or D, etc. (The tuned antique cymbals, or crotales, are an exception.) The only difference, pitchwise, is that some cymbals produce a generally high aggregate sound, others being medium or lower in relation.

Cymbals to be used as a pair clashed together should be selected to *blend* with each other, not to *match* in general pitch. The complimentary sounds produced by two carefully matched cymbals is spoken of as a "marriage." Thin cymbals are usually lower in pitch than medium or medium heavy. There are exceptions, however, which may account for the common misconception that the opposite holds true. The quickness with which the cymbal reaches full vibration ("speaks") is dependent upon the amount of metal in the cymbal, therefore thin and small cymbals are usually the fastest.

The most popular sizes of cymbals for elementary and junior high school bands and orchestras are 14″, 15″, 16″, and 13″ in that order. This may serve as a rule of thumb when purchasing cymbals for such groups. The most common mistake made by persons responsible for the purchase of school instruments is to buy cymbals which are too small and too heavy. The author therefore recommends 16″ diameter cymbals which are *thin* or *medium thin* for general use in elementary band and orchestra.

Heavy cymbals are more martial and solemn in tone without the brilliant upper overtones, and are preferred for use in drum and bugle corps.

For the high school, college and professional concert band and orchestra a pair of *medium* or *medium thin* 18″ concert or symphonic cymbals are standard equipment, paired to obtain a compatible blend of tone. The trend today is toward *medium thin* to obtain the lightness and brilliance of the so-called "French" tone. In addition to a pair of 18″ cymbals, the high school or college band and orchestra should have one pair of matching band cymbals 16″ to 18″, one pair of large, medium thin cymbals 20″ to 22″, plus two or three smaller cymbals for suspended cymbal use. These should probably include a 14″ thin, 17″ thin, and 18″ medium cymbal. This basic list will cover the requirements of the repertoire of most musical organizations.

There are two other types of cymbals which have certain specialized uses. The first of these are called antique cymbals, or crotales. They are small, thick cymbals which come in pairs ranging from 2″ to 5″ in diameter. They have definite pitches through a chromatic two octave range. The sounds produced are of great clarity and have an ethereal beauty. The edges are struck together to obtain their characteristic tone. Certain Impressionistic Period works, notably Debussy's *Afternoon of a Faun,* specify antique cymbals, as do several of the experimental compositions of contemporary composers. The second type of small cymbals are the so-called finger cymbals. These are small untuned cymbals about 2 inches in diameter, much thinner than the antique cymbals. The manner of playing is the same as for the antique cymbals. Finger cymbals can be mounted on springy wire handles which can be squeezed together to contact the faces of the pair of cymbals. They are then called metal castanets by the manufacturer. Figure 4.12 shows each of these types and several pairs of antique cymbals.

The assortment of cymbals for the dance band drum set which has been developed by Zildjian are designated as Bounce, Bounce-ride, Ride, Crash, Be-Bop, Fast, Splash, Sizzle and Swish. A Bounce, Bounce-ride, or Ride is used for open stick work in playing the basic jazz beat ♩ ♫♩ ♫ . These types come in weights running from medium heavy down to extra thin. A Crash cymbal is used for single note crashes and is not made for prolonged riding. The preferred weight for the crash cymbal is thin. The so-call Be-Bop cymbals are specially tapered to build up a heavy sustained tone when played with the single stick ride rhythm. Drummers usually prefer a large diameter, 19″, 20″, or even 24″ for this purpose. The Sizzle cymbal has rivets placed around the outer edge

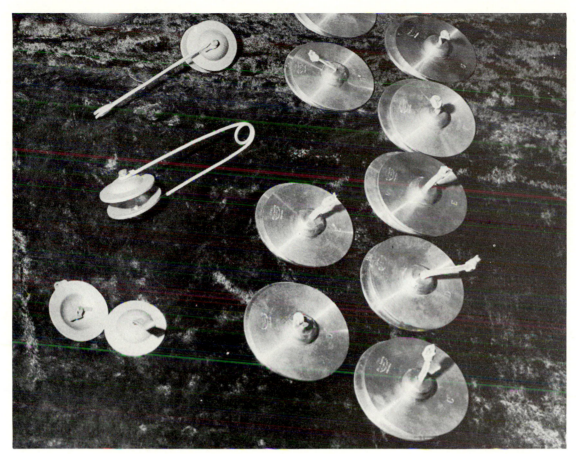

Courtesy A. Zildjian Co.

Figure 4.12. Metal castanets, upper left. Finger cymbals, lower left. Antique cymbals at right.

which vibrate when the cymbal is struck, and are useful in jazz work as a change of sound from the ride cymbal in sustained rhythm. Swish cymbals are similar, but their edges are turned up, which imparts a "pangy" Chinese sound. Dixieland jazz drummers are the chief users of the Swish type of cymbal. The paired Hi-Hat (also called sock, or hi-sock) cymbals are mounted on a stand and operated with the left foot. They ching together on the afterbeats in dance and jazz music. They should be of medium thin or thin weight, and the preferred sizes are 14″ and 15″.

Cymbals are somewhat delicate, especially the thin, paper-thin, and extra-thin weights. They are easily cracked and bent at the edges, so they should be handled with care. Cymbals should never be thrown into a "trap box" or bin, and they should never be left lying on the floor where a false step might ruin them. If cymbals are to be trans-ported often they should be carried in the mackintosh zipper bags made for the purpose. Cymbals should never be buffed on a wheel, as the heat generated by the friction can remove the temper from certain areas of the cymbal's surface, causing them to go dead. To clean cymbals, use a low- or non-abrasive cleaner such as Bon Ami or Copper Clean.

To remove small cracks at or near the edge of a cymbal, drill a small hole about ¼″ in diameter slightly beyond the end of the crack. Hacksaw a V shaped piece out which includes the portion containing the crack. Saw right up to the drilled hole, and smooth off the sawed edges.

Wooden handles should not be used for the pair of cymbals. They are usually too rigid and they kill a good deal of the brilliance in the cymbals. Leather or rawhide straps are the best holders for the band and orchestra cymbals. Avoid the fluffy lamb's wool pads which are used to protect the knuckles of the player. Less of the tone is stifled by using felt pads, which can be cut out of any fairly heavy felt. The steps in tying the cymbal strap knot are as follows:

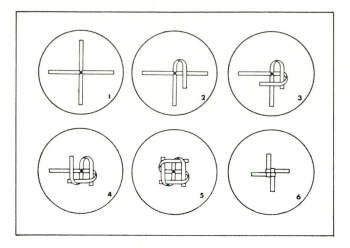

Figure 4.13. Tying cymbal strap.

Note: The knot itself should be tight, but not the bind of the strap through the cymbal. The straps should feel somewhat loose in order to allow maximum vibration. The knot always should be checked prior to playing.

CYMBAL NOTATION

When cymbals are played as a pair, one clashed against the other, the Italian word *piatti* (literally, *plates*) is used to describe both the cymbals and the style of playing them. Piatti is a useful term because it differentiates the pair of cymbals clashed together from a single cymbal struck with a stick or other beater.

In much standard band literature, and some orchestral music of the lighter variety, the cymbals play in unison with the bass drum. Sometimes the part will be so marked, but often the percussionist must assume that such was the composer's intention. As can be seen in the following illustrations, the cymbals play from the notes written in the first or second space of the F clef. The note stems point down. In this type of scoring for cymbals and bass drum, when either is to be played alone, the part will be marked "Cyms. only," (cyms) or "Bass drum only" (B.D. only, B.D., etc.). This may apply to a single note, a phrase,

strain of a march, movement or entire composition. After a note, phrase, or strain indicated for either B.D. or cymbals *alone,* the abbreviation *Tog.* (together) is used if the composer wishes both the B.D. and cymbals to play the succeeding notes together. A diamond-shaped or X-shaped notehead is often used for solo cymbal notes, as:

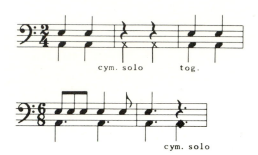

Modern notation is getting away from this by assigning a definite line or space to the cymbal part and using normal noteheads. Unless otherwise specified, cymbal parts are played piatti style. *Suspended cymbal, susp. cym., one cym.,* etc., are directions indicating the use of a single cymbal mounted on a floor stand and struck with a drumstick, mallet or timpani stick. Also, any roll or trill sign on the cymbal part indicates the use of the single cymbal played with sticks or mallets.

Roll signs for cymbal notes are conventionally the three slanted dashes through the note stem, or the trill sign.

It is possible to approximate a sustained roll-like sound using the pair of cymbals, but it is not a very satisfactory effect. When the composer deliberately specifies this style of roll he uses such directions as "rub cymbals together," "clashed cymbal roll." This type of roll is made by rotating the pair of cymbals in opposite directions while allowing their edges to be in light contact.

A tie or slur mark after a cymbal note means to let the cymbal or cymbals ring beyond their indicated value. If an unlimited after-ring is desired, the direction "let ring" or L.V.—let vibrate is given in the part.

A variety of sticks, mallets and other implements can be used to obtain interesting sounds on the suspended cymbal. If there is no indication in the part to the contrary, the suspended cymbal is struck with yarn or cord-wound marimba or vibraphone mallets. Timpani mallets do *not* serve well on the suspended cymbal, although many cymbal parts still denote "a suspended cymbal struck with a timpani stick." These instructions are not to be taken too literally, as the composer had no better method available at the time. A major problem with using timpani mallets on suspended cymbals is that most timpani mallets produce too nebulous an attack to be of any musical value.

A very large suspended cymbal properly struck with low register marimba mallets, such as the Musser M-12 model, can produce wonderful sounds that are not unlike a small gong. If a score calls for "xylophone mallet on suspended cymbal," considerable discretion must be used to avoid damaging the cymbal. As a result of the development of synthetic bar material for xylophones, there are many more very hard xylophone mallets available, perhaps *not* what was originally intended by the composer. The indication "wood stick" or "with SD stick" means to strike the cymbal with a drumstick. Commonly found foreign language directions are: "avec baguette de bois" (with wood stick), "avec baguette d'eponge" (literally, with sponge-headed stick, however, notes so marked should be played with soft felt timpani sticks).

Other beaters which are called for on the suspended cymbal are the wire brush, xylophone mallet, triangle beater, and even a fingernail file (Milhaud's *Aubade*)! When such exotic beaters are indicated the score will be clearly marked to show the notes which are to be struck with the particular beater.

Abbreviations Commonly Found in Cymbal Music

piatti—the pair of clashed cymbals
cym, cymb, cyb, cymbs, cb, cbs—cymbal, or cymbals
susp. cym.—suspended cymbal
secco, or sec.—dry, short
chk.—choke (damp)
X—cymbal note (older form of notation)
L.V.—let vibrate

BASIC STROKES

To play the pair of clashed cymbals requires considerable physical strength as well as good musical sense. The cymbal straps are grasped in the manner illustrated in Figures 4.14 to 4.18. Note that the hands *do not go through* the loops of the straps. Young players will invariably put their hands through and wrap the loops tightly around their wrists. Such a manner of holding is actually quite clumsy and is too tight to allow the cymbals to vibrate fully. However, for reasons of security in maintaining the grasp and for the purpose of twirling the cymbals, the hands may go through the loops for marching.

To play steady beat passages, as in a march, the cymbals are held out in front of the player's chest. They are

Figure 4.14. Ready position.

Figure 4.15. Start of stroke.

Figure 4.16. Finish of stroke.

struck one against the other with their outer edges *almost,* but not exactly, coinciding to produce the sound on the beat. If there is an exact coincidence of the two cymbals, a suction will result which embarassingly holds the pair of cymbals together and produces nothing but a dull "plop." To avoid this locking, make sure that the cymbals ease into contact, leading edge first.

Experienced percussionists do not usually move both arms alternately up and down, as would perhaps seem natural. Instead, their cymbal stroke is made by holding the left cymbal in fairly stationary position, slanted with the top edge toward the left, and bringing the right cymbal alternately into up and down contacts against it. In passages where the notes are widely spaced, or for single notes, the same position is used, but all the strokes are "down," or, more exactly, "down and out." Figures 4.14, 4.15, and 4.16 show the ready position for such a cymbal stroke and the position of the cymbals just after impact.

Gradations in volume are obtained both by changing the velocity of the moving cymbals and by the amount of edge placed in contact. For the very softest cymbal tones, it is possible to barely "ching" the top edges of the pair together. If the player will take the pains to practice, he can learn to control the cymbal contacts to the point where pianissimo notes can be played using the entire circumference of the cymbals. This is really a much better sound than the aforementioned top edge contact, but it takes fine neuromuscular control and an intimate knowledge of the particular properties of the pair of cymbals being used. To increase the volume, the right cymbal is moved faster and travels a longer path. For loud single crashes, the right clashes with considerable speed at impact. The left cymbal, rather than remaining stationary as it does for soft notes, draws in and away at impact, so as to separate the cymbals.

For widely spaced notes or solo single crashes the player must give careful thought to the volume and duration appropriate to the passage. For a long and prominent after-ring the cymbals should be brought up and faced toward the conductor by turning the wrists. The extending of the arms up to a position about head high and slightly in front of the player will accomplish the best results. This is sometimes called the *flare stroke,* and is useful for projecting the tone in solo crashes. To start the flare stroke, drop both cymbals to a position slightly in front of either thigh, bringing the cymbals into contact with a rapid upward sweep, and follow through by turning the wrists so that the cymbals face the conductor. The trajectory of each cymbal is similar for the left and right in the flare stroke. Figures 4.17, 4.18 and 4.19 show the ready, impact, and final positions of the flare stroke.

Another type of stroke can be called, for want of a better name, the *separation* stroke. This type of stroke is made by placing the edges of the pair of cymbals into contact silently prior to the time the note is to be played. To sound the cymbals, move them in opposite directions. The contact of their edges will produce an ethereal "ching" as the cymbals are separated. The effect is rarely called for, although it is truly beautiful in sound. The volume in the separation stroke is controlled by the speed of the motion used.

Figure 4.17. Ready position, flare stroke.

Figure 4.18. Impact.

Figure 4.19. Finish of flare stroke.

TECHNIQUES OF PLAYING THE SUSPENDED CYMBAL

One cymbal used alone is an indispensable part of the percussion equipment in band or orchestra. Many scores call for suspended cymbal, although nowadays the old style hook-like arm arrangement has been replaced by the dance drummer's cymbal floor stand. What is required, in any case, is a good quality crash cymbal mounted on a floor stand about waist high.

Figure 4.20. Suspended cymbal struck with snare drumstick.

For single note crashes on the suspended cymbal using a snare drumstick, strike the edge of the cymbal sharply at about a 45° angle. For a less harsh impact, percussionists in symphony orchestras often strike the suspended cymbal on its top surface with a yarn-covered vibraphone or marimba mallet. Figure 4.21 shows the suspended cymbal played with a xylophone mallet. Always have the left hand free to choke the cymbal after a crash. Do not choke, or damp, the cymbal if the note has a slur mark after it or is marked "let ring." Damping is accomplished simply by grasping the edge of the cymbal firmly. With both drumstick and mallet beaters much variation in tone and volume can be obtained. Experience is the best guide in obtaining the musically appropriate sound in a given passage.

Figure 4.21. Suspended cymbal struck with xylophone mallet.

Another style of suspended cymbal playing is sometimes called for, namely, the striking with the tip of the drumstick on top of the cymbal. This is similar to the bounce or ride cymbal technique of the jazz player, except that the rhythm figures will vary. The sound is completely different from that of the crash. It is useful in very light passages. See Figure 4.22. A number of sounds can be obtained, depending upon which part of the surface is struck. A "ting" sound can be produced by striking the suspended cymbal on the dome section, using either the tip or shoulder of the drumstick or a triangle beater.

Figure 4.22. Suspended cymbal struck with tip of drumstick.

One additional little used but interesting manner of playing the suspended cymbal is to drag a metal object such as a triangle beater or key across the cymbal's surface from the dome out to the edge. See figure 4.23. This imparts a "zing" sound.

Figure 4.23. Suspended cymbal played with triangle beater.

THE CYMBAL ROLL

The roll is often called for in cymbal parts. For this reason the suspended cymbal must be considered standard equipment. The single stroke roll is used. The cymbal is struck rapidly alternating blows on its top surface with yarn marimba sticks or mallets. In order not to knock over the cymbal stand when playing a loud roll, place the two mallets at opposite sides of the cymbal. Occasionally cymbal rolls are marked to be played "with S.D. sticks" or simply "wood sticks." In this case snare drumsticks held in the usual manner are used to make a double stroke roll on the surface of the cymbal. This will cause the higher frequencies in the cymbal tone to predominate, producing a more "tinkly" sound than does the mallet technique.

Figure 4.24. Suspended cymbal roll with mallets.

Figure 4.25. Suspended cymbal roll with snare drumsticks.

A variety of drumsticks, timpani sticks, and vibraphone—marimba—xylophone mallets should be at the disposal of the cymbal player.

A hint regarding the mounting of the suspended cymbal: do not let the wing nut be screwed down tight, as it is imperative that the cymbal be riding as freely as possible. Any slight bind or pressure is likely to damp out the high frequencies which give cymbals their brilliance.

DAMPING

To damp the cymbals when played piatti style, the player has merely to draw in the vibrating cymbals to make contact with his clothing at the front of his shoulders. This stops the sound instantaneously. See Figure 4.26.

It behooves the cymbal player to use care in observing the notation of his part. If a short value is used, or staccato

Figure 4.26. Damping the pair of cymbals.

marks are present, very quick damping is called for. If the note is of a long value, allow the cymbals to ring at least for the duration of the note before damping.

The suspended cymbal is damped by grasping it firmly with the left hand.

The cymbal part may sometimes show a slur or tie extending over a rest, such as—

This means to let the cymbal or pair of cymbals ring somewhat beyond the value of the note. If the composer or arranger desires the cymbals to ring indefinitely, the direction "let ring" or L.V.—let vibrate is printed over or under the note.

Figure 4.27. Stand for crash cymbals.

Finally, a suitable table or rack must be provided so that the hand cymbals will have a resting place that is convenient to the performer for quick changes, and which will also provide space for necessary mallets and/or other percussion equipment. See Figure 4.27.

This table or rack should be directly in front of the performer and (in the case of working with a right-handed bass drummer) directly to the right of the bass drum. This is so because, most often, the bass drummer and cymbal player are working together, often reading from the same part. In this way the cymbal player's rack or table may be shared with his colleague who will want to use it to have a convenient place to lay his bass drum mallets. The rack or table must be well-padded so that there will be absolutely no noise when the cymbals, mallets or other traps are placed upon it. Carpeting material is usually found to be most satisfactory for this purpose.

Most professional cymbal artists use an adequately large, specially padded table. Some performers, however, prefer the slotted rack. This is nothing more than a narrow upright box that has been divided in half, providing two slots for standing the individual cymbals on their edges. The inside surfaces of these slots are padded and the entire affair is secured to a very sturdy floor stand. Sometimes a tray is provided on each side of the box for mallets, etc. A cymbal rack of this type is not at all difficult to construct from discarded scraps of lumber and the base of an old heavy music stand.

Notes

1. Samuel Adler, *The Study of Orchestration* (New York: W. W. Norton & Co., Inc., 1982), pp. 356–357.
2. Hector Berlioz and Richard Strauss, *Treatise on Instrumentation,* Translated by Theodore Front. (New York: E. F. Kalmus, 1948), p. 391.

CHAPTER 5

The Mallet-played Instruments

GENERAL DESCRIPTION OF THE XYLOPHONE, MARIMBA, VIBRAPHONE, BELLS, BELL-LYRA (GLOCKENSPIEL) AND CHIMES

The Xylophone. The prototype xylophone was a crude set of tuned wooden bars laid flat upon a bed of straw developed around 1500 in Europe and called the strohfiedel (German for "strawfiddle"). Its primitive ancestors probably date back many centuries to African and Javanese origins. One J. Gusikow was the first virtuoso of the strohfiedel, and in 1830 aroused the interest of Mendelssohn. It was not until nearly fifty years later, however, that the xylophone was actually introduced into the symphony orchestra by Saint-Saëns in his famous *Danse Macabre.*

As an improvement over the bed of straw, the bars were later mounted on a wood frame and this frame laid on a table. The next development was a floor stand to accommodate the frame and bars. Tubular metal resonators are often added to the modern instrument, but they are not always present, and indeed, are not necessary for production of a true xylophone tone. The characteristic sound of the xylophone is hard, brittle, and incisive. Its tone quality derives from the thick rosewood (or synthetic) bars and the hardness of the mallets used to strike these bars. The xylophone has a thin tone and lacks carrying power when soft rubber or yarn-wound mallets are employed. The bars are laid out in the keyboard arrangement corresponding to the keys of the piano, with the lower bank of bars containing the natural tones and the upper bank the chromatics. For convenience of execution the upper bars extend slightly over the lower ones.

A good size of xylophone for school use is a three octave c' to c''' model, with or without a floor stand and resonators. Many xylophones are made with a 3½ octave range, f to c''', and of course these added notes are a convenience in eliminating the need for frequent octava sopra transpositions in the low register. A fibre carrying case is a good investment if the instrument is subject to a good deal of portage.

As an absolute minimum, a heavy-duty vinyl cover, designed to fit over the keyboard, should be available to protect the xylophone when it is not in use.

Courtesy G. C. Jenkins Co.

Figure 5.1. Xylophone.

Figure 5.2. shows the bars of the standard 3½ octave xylophone and their corresponding written pitches. The xylophone sounds one octave higher than written.

The xylophone requires hard mallets. At least two pairs would be needed for all-around use, one of medium hard rubber and the other of very hard rubber or plastic. Good xylophone mallets are hard to find, and should be selected personally at a drum shop rather than ordered from a catalog, as it is nearly impossible to know in advance what a mallet will sound like from the pictures and meager descriptions furnished in the manufacturers' catalogs. The handles of most xylophone mallets are made of rattan, plastic, or a combination of fiberglass and rubber or plastic. In recent years, several makers have been quite successful in the use of woods other than rattan.

Although the xylophone was originally treated as a "coloristic" instrument often relegated to doubling piccolo and high register flute parts in the score, recent years have seen the emergence of several substantial solo works written expressly for the xylophone. Among these may be included: *Sonata* by Pitfield, *Concertino* by Mayuzumi and *Fantasy on Japanese Wood Prints* by Hovhaness. The xy-

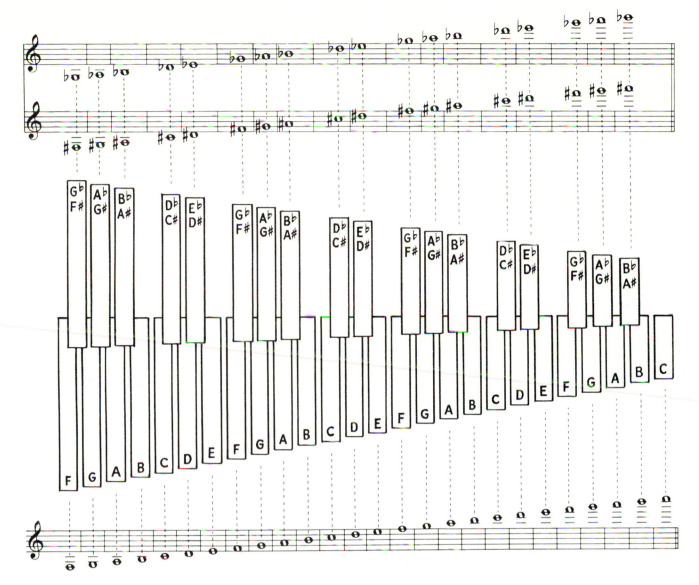

Figure 5.2. Xylophone keyboard.

Figure 5.3. Marimba.

lophone, however, does *not* lend itself to solo playing as well as the marimba.

The Marimba. The marimba is essentially a xylophone equipped with resonators to increase the volume and resonance of the bars. There is some evidence that the marimba dates back to primitive cultures both in Africa and Central America, where gourds mounted beneath the bars were found to amplify and mellow the natural sound of the hardwood. While the xylophone may or may not have resonators, the marimba always has them. There is one other essential difference in that the marimba bars are cut somewhat wider and thinner than xylophone bars to make them more elastic, thus imparting a more resonant sound. The keyboard layout is the same for both the marimba and xylophone, although as a rule the marimba will have one or more octaves more than the typical xy-

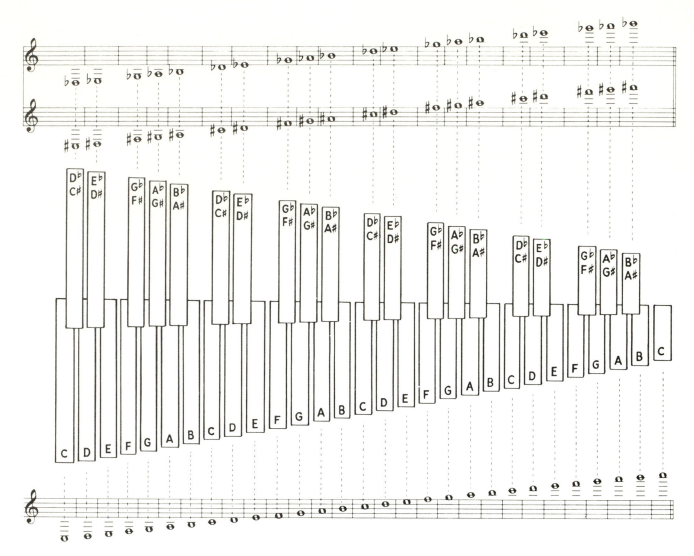

Figure 5.4. Marimba keyboard.

lophone. The additional notes of the marimba are dictated by the solo demands of the instrument and the four-mallet style often used in solo playing. The marimba is particularly effective in its lower register. Two, three or four note chords struck singly or tremolo sound rich, mellow and organ-like. In its upper register the marimba sounds about like a xylophone, perhaps a little mellower. The marimba is not often scored for in band and orchestra music, as it does not have a quality which penetrates as does the xylophone. The marimba therefore has become essentially a solo instrument. Marimba ensembles are fairly popular also. A good marimba for school purposes should include the fourth octave (c′ down to c), making the total range c to c′′′. It is noteworthy that at least one manufacturer, Ludwig/Musser, has introduced a marimba (M-350, symphonic grand) with an extended lower range, down to F, a fifth below the C shown in Figure 5.4. Another Musser model, the M-250, extends down to A, a third below the C shown in Figure 5.4. Ludwig/Musser,

as well as other manufacturers, also produce various types of bass marimbas. The Musser M-400 is an amplified bass marimba that sounds like an acoustic or electric bass. However, the M-400 must be plugged into an amplifier. A complete array of new bass sounds is now available by using various types of mallets. Further sound possibilities are available with the use of tone modification devices. The M-400 extends the marimba range yet even lower than that of the M-350 model. The marimba should be mounted on a stand with casters for mobility in solo use. Figure 5.4 shows the bars of the 4 octave marimba and their corresponding written (actual) pitches. In the 1960's the marimba gained stature as a result of the serious concert efforts of Vida Chenoweth and, more recently, other marimba virtuosi such as Jack Conner, Leigh Howard Stevens, Gordon Stout and Bill Molenhof, to mention but a few notable performers on the instrument. Paul Creston has written a delightful and challenging *Concertino for Marimba and Orchestra,* and Robert Kurka composed a marimba concerto before his untimely death. James Basta, Darius Milhaud, Gen Parchman and Peter Tanner have also written very substantial solo works for the marimba. Until the late 1950's and early 1960's, these works listed and a few more isolated works along with transcriptions or arrangements of works written for other instruments comprised the entire repertoire for the marimba. However, this is rapidly changing with demanding works being written by Diemer, Sifler, DePonte and several Japanese composers such as Miyoshi, Miki, Ishii, Noda and others.

The marimba should never be played with the very hard, uncovered rubber mallets used on the xylophone. Not only will the rich mellow sound of the rosewood marimba be lost thereby, but the very hard rubber mallets can dent and throw out of tune a marimba bar. The only exception to this rule may occur when a marimba with synthetic bars (Musser calls their bar material 'Kelon' and Deagan refers to theirs as 'Klyperon') is used. In this case hard mallets may be used, especially if xylophone parts must be played on the marimba. Three or four pairs of medium and soft uncovered rubber mallets and five or six pairs of yarn covered marimba mallets are essential basic items. The serious student marimbist and the professional may own twenty or more pairs of mallets ranging from very soft to very hard rubber and yarn.

The Vibraphone (Vibraharp). The vibraphone, sometimes called vibraharp, is the most recent development in the mallet-played instrument group. Its two most prominent distinguishing characteristics are its electrically driven fans mounted at the top of each resonator to impart alternating loud and soft pulsations of the tones, and its damper pedal mechanism. With its rotating fan-like blades it gives the illusion of a vibrato in its tone quality, but the "vibrato" is of intensity only, not pitch. The bars are made of aluminum alloy, whose metallic tone further distinguishes the vibraphone from the wood-barred instruments. As can be seen in Figure 5.5, the upper bank of bars does not extend out over the lower, as in the xylophone or marimba. The reason that this is so is in order that the upper ends of the natural bars can lie in such a way as to contact the felt damper bar, while the lower ends of the chromatic bars contact the same damper felt. The "vibra" mechanism is not always used, many of the modern jazz players preferring the cool sound of the straight tone. In concert band and orchestra scores directions such as "motor on," "motor off" "vibré" and "non vibré" indicate to the player when to use each effect. A small switch mounted near the upper end of the instrument turns the motor on and off. When the motor is off, strict attention should be paid to the fans in order to determine whether or not they are in a "closed" or "open" position in relation to the bars and resonators. They should be in an "open" position and can be manually turned to that position if they already are not so aligned. Most

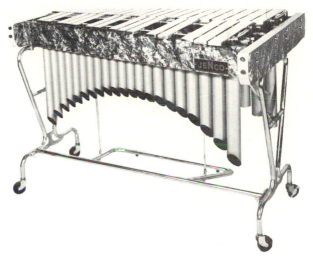

Figure 5.5. Vibraphone.

models also have a device for controlling the rate of speed of the fans. Amplification, at an added cost, also is available for newer models.

The most popular size of vibraphone is three octaves, f to f'''. This is the recommended instrument for all purposes. Figure 5.6 indicates the written (actual) pitches of the standard three octave vibraphone bars.

The usual mallets used on the vibraphone are the yarn-covered type. The core of these mallets is of rubber, the handles of rattan, plastic, fiberglass or moderately flexible wood dowel. The relative hardness of the rubber core is what determines the tonal quality of the mallet. Most models are available in soft, medium and hard strengths and virtually every gradation in-between. Sometimes medium hard unwound rubber mallets work very very well on the vibraphone in certain situations where a more pointed attack is desired, rather than the somewhat nebulous attack sound of softer yarn mallets. Fortunately, recent years have seen the emergence of an endless array of vibraphone mallets designed to please everyone and be suitable for any musical situation. One of these mallet types consists of cord style yarn which is wrapped around a solid, specially formulated and shaped rubber core. This style of mallet is frequently a favorite with outstanding vibists because it is possible to produce good tone with a minimum of effort. Of course, the best policy is to try out a set of mallets on a vibraphone before purchasing them. The player should have at least five or six sets at his disposal.

The moving parts of the vibraphone should be kept lubricated with a light oil such as 3-in-1 or perhaps even better, one of the newer, non-greasy types of silicone lubricants. Also, the instrument should be kept covered when not in use to prevent accumulation of dust around the moving parts. It is an excellent idea to keep an extra rub-

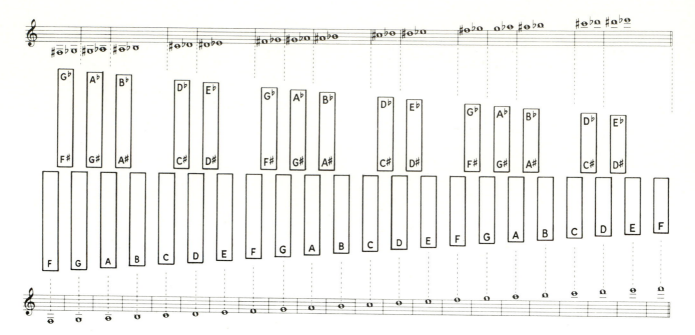

Figure 5.6. Vibraphone keyboard.

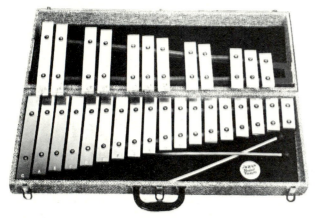

Courtesy G. C. Jenkins Co.

Figure 5.7. Orchestra bells.

ber belt on hand, as these items frequently break or get misplaced. Even under the best of conditions, rubber pulley belts will gradually deteriorate and require replacement. The bars can be maintained with a quality metal polish that is relatively mild and non-abrasive. Always be sure to remove any polish residue with a clean, soft cloth.

Bells. The small bells used in the band and orchestra are variously referred to as orchestra bells, glockenspiel, and campanelli, though orchestra bells may be the most correct term. The set of bells consists of steel bars mounted in the keyboard fashion, usually attached to wooden rails, padded, and equipped with rubber insulated sound posts, mounted directly within the carrying case. The cover can

be detached and the bells placed upon an adjustable floor stand designed for this purpose. A very satisfactory alternative to the conventional bell stand is to use a heavy-duty folding restaurant tray stand. The sound of the bells is clear and yet "tinkly", and they are quite penetrating when played with metal bell hammers. The bells are usually the most often used of the mallet-played instruments in school music scores. Some of the bell parts are fairly simple technically, though in recent years more complicated parts have been written for the instrument. Only in an emergency should a nonpercussionist, such as a pianist or other instrumentalist, be pressed into service to cover a bell part. All members of the band and orchestra percussion sections should become acquainted with the bells and learn to perform simple bell parts, at the very least.

With regard to size, the bells are probably the most consistent of the mallet percussion instruments. With the exceptions of the Parsifal Bells developed specifically for the Wagnerian orchestra and some older three-octave models, they are now almost exclusively of one size: 2½ octaves from g to c''' (written pitch). They sound two octaves higher than written, though many composers, arrangers and orchestrators do not realize this. Figure 5.8 indicates the written pitches of the bars on a three-octave set of bells.

For the orchestra bells, the small solid brass tipped mallets work quite well. Other useful and appropriate bell mallets include very hard rubber, plastic, acrylic and wood. Some of the rubber and plastic types of bell mallets are good for softer passages but quite a bit of contact "click"

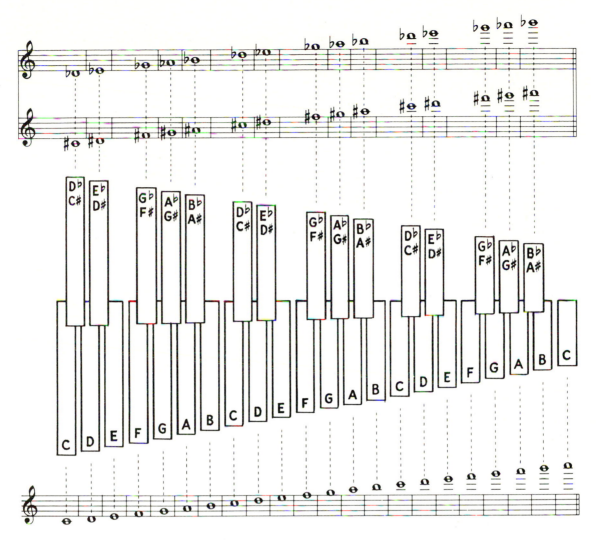

Figure 5.8. Orchestra bells keyboard.

is usually audible upon impact. Wood mallets such as the Musser M-15, can produce a very subtle, delicate and almost ethereal quality of tone on the orchestra bells.

The resonance of orchestra bells may be increased by winding nylon string between all of the pegs or soundposts so that the bars will rest on the string and not on the felt or rubber bushings.

Sometimes orchestra bells are scored in a range that just simply does not blend with the orchestration. The player may have to experiment with different octaves to find the best balance.

Bell-lyra. The bell-lyra, often called glockenspiel, is a now virtually out-moded marching version of the orchestra bells. This instrument has now been generally replaced by horizontally carried marching bells, thus allowing the player to use two mallets, perform parts that are far more intricate and play parts that make more musical "sense". The major difficulty in playing the older

type of bell-lyra lies in accustoming oneself with the outward-running keyboard. The keyboard of the bell-lyra is shown in Figure 5.10. Note that the two octaves span a to a″, sounding two octaves higher than written.

Courtesy G. C. Jenkins Co.

Figure 5.9. Bell-lyra.

Chimes. The chimes, sometimes called tubular chimes, are indispensable items in the concert band or symphony

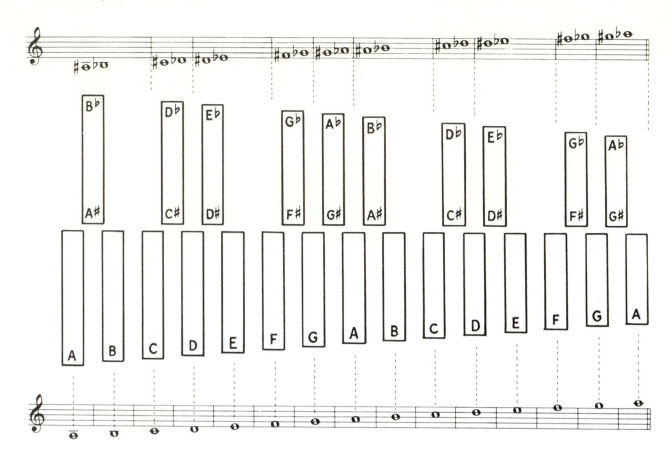

Figure 5.10. Bell-lyra keyboard.

orchestra. The tone quality of the chimes resembles that of the carillon bells associated with church music. Their tone is sombre yet stirring, and is therefore often used by composers to suggest religious and patriotic moods. An example of the former usage is Puccini's one act opera *Suor Angelica.* Ravel employed the chimes effectively in his orchestration of the *Great Gate of Kiev* from Mussorgsky's *Pictures at an Exhibition.*

Today, chimes are commercially, available in two sizes from c′ to f′′, and from C′ to G′′. They sound as written.

Chimes have a unique overtone series that differs from the overtone structure of all other musical instruments. This, primarily, accounts for the great amount of controversy to be found concerning the transposition of this instrument. In order to simulate the out-of-tune sound of bells, the chime tone contains many frequencies, particularly at the moment it is struck. These various frequencies or overtones rapidly decay leaving three main pitches. For example, if c′ is struck, we hear both a predominant c′ and c′′ along with a rather strong out-of-tune sixth below. Due to this peculiarity, we experience much confusion concerning the transposition of this instrument. The chimes should be considered a nontransposing instrument.

The standard chime mallet is constructed with laminated wood or rolled rawhide mounted on a tapered hardwood handle. In recent years, Ludwig/Musser and Slingerland/Deagan have introduced dual head chime mallets with the option of interchangeable mallet tips mounted on a durable metal shaft with molded rubber grip. The Deagan chime mallet kit is noteworthy in that it has available *three* distinctly different screw-in tips- plastic, nylon and fibre- for mellow, medium and bright response. Although this type of chime mallet is somewhat more expensive than the traditional rolled rawhide type, it is well worth the extra cost to have three different degrees of mallet hardness available. Although many chime parts can be played with one mallet, two matched mallets should be readily available, as some intricate passages cannot be performed with one mallet. A chime rack is indispensable. The type with padded holes through which the tubes pass is best, since this device prevents the tubes from swaying under impact of the mallet and clanging with adjacent tubes. The best modern instruments have a damper pedal similar in action to that of the vibraphone. This allows the added advantage to the player, as it frees one hand from the duty of damping nonchordal tones individually. Two-mallet technique is thus greatly facilitated. The best models of chimes have tubes which measure 1½ inches in diameter, a chime rack heavy enough to support the weight of so many metal tubes with some measure of stability, wheels with brakes on the frame (or rack) and a thick vinyl or canvas cover to protect the instrument when it is not in use. Figure 5.11 shows a one and one-half octave set of chimes with damper pedal, the recommended model for school, college, and professional use.

Courtesy G. C. Jenkins Co.

Figure 5.11. Chimes.

COMMON CHARACTERISTICS AND DISTINCTIVE FEATURES OF THE MALLET-PLAYED INSTRUMENTS

With the exception of the tubular chimes, the mallet-played instruments are essentially vibrating wood or metal plates. The acoustical properties of vibrating plates need to be known to the player of these instruments. The most resonant point of the bar is its center. Nodal points are nonresonant areas which are located at approximately the points where the bars attach to the frame. Half way between the nodal points and the ends of each bar are located resonant spots which are useful playing spots. See Figure 5.12. In playing chromatic passages on the mallet instruments, the natural notes should be struck at the center of the bar for maximum resonance while the playing spot on the chromatic bars will be located half way between the near end of the bar and the point at which it attaches to the frame. By utilizing these nearer playing spots, much unnecessary motion is eliminated. However, if the tempo is not very fast, then the bars are best struck in the center for maximum tone and resonance.

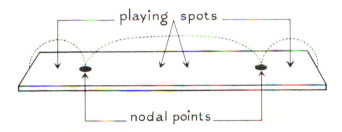

Figure 5.12. Playing spots, xylophone, marimba, vibraphone, or bell bar.

The basic handhold is the same for all the mallet instruments when played with two mallets. Each is grasped in the same way as the R snare drumstick, at a point slightly more than ⅓ of the way down from the end of the handle. Ready position for the mallets is about 1 to 1½ inches above the bars. The L mallet should strike above the R if both are on the same bar. If both mallets are playing successive notes on one of the chromatic bars, the left will play at the center and the right at the playing spot at the near end of the bar. To produce a good tone the mallets must strike the bars with a resilient blow. A rather sharp forward snap of the wrist activates the stroke for both R and L. The arms are involved only in notes of the very greatest volume or in long skips up or down. Figures 5.13 to 5.15 show various playing positions for the pair of mallets.

The major technical problem in playing the mallet instruments is the development of a kinesthetic sense of intervallic relationships. The mallets must travel through space and land accurately on the correct bar and proper playing spot. Sample sequential studies for the development of interval accuracy follow. They may be practiced on the xylophone, marimba, vibraphone, or bells.

Another facet of the interval problem is the difficulty encountered when changing from one instrument to another. An instrument with wide bars, considerably separated, will require longer reaches than an instrument with narrow bars and close spacing. This difficulty is not as

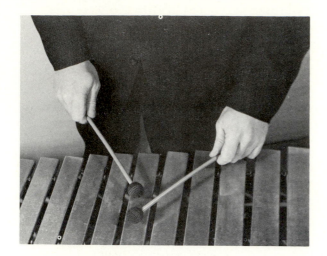

Figure 5.13. R and L on natural bar.

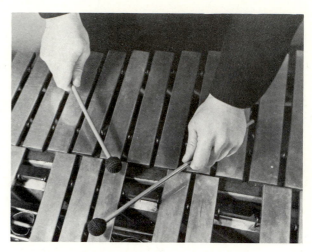

Figure 5.15. R and L on chromatic bar.

Figure 5.14. R on chromatic bar, L on natural bar.

great as one might suppose, however, for the reason that the ear plays a large role in the kinesthetic process as it relates to pitch and distance in these instruments. A skillful player needs only a few seconds of warm-up orientation to change rapidly from one instrument to another.

In teaching the techniques of the mallet instruments, the instructor should insist upon a minimum motion of the mallet. Recall that the ready position for each stroke is 1 to 1½ inches above the bar. The mallet head will then travel upward slightly before striking. The mallet should not be held up 6, 8, or 12 inches above the keyboard prior to the stroke. It is a useful concept to think of the mallet arriving at its destination of an inch or so above the bar as long as possible in advance of the sounding of the note. If this concept is developed through slow practice of intervals, it will facilitate accurate technique later in the playing of rapid passages.

1. Scalewise melodic movement

Study #6 illustrates how cross-overs may be avoided by using *successive* rather than *alternate* sticking. <u>A percussionist never should hesitate to mark sticking, particularly on mallet parts.</u>

Practice Study #10 without rolls at first, thus:

etc.

A problem inherent to the mallet instruments, and which can become quite critical if not corrected at the outset of instruction, is that of the use of the eyes. Performers on mallet instruments must develop split or peripheral vision so as to encompass the keyboard, the music, and the conductor. Any beginning mallet player will have a strong tendency to look at the keyboard as he plays. If this is not corrected, it will result in his failing to watch the conductor and greatly impede his reading ability. Peripheral vision, rather than direct eye contact with the keyboard, should be developed. Then, the constant shifting of the eyes from music to keyboard will not be necessary.

The xylophone, marimba and vibraphone are played from a standing position. In order to keep the mallets directly in front of the body where they are most easily controlled it is necessary to shift the body weight from one foot to the other when changing registers of the keyboard. The three and four octave instruments are so long that a step or two to one side or the other is often required to maintain a balanced playing position. The player should not stand erect, but lean slightly toward the keyboard. The bells can be played from a sitting position if it is more convenient to place them on a low table or stand. For the usual small set of bells no appreciable shifting of body weight is necessary. The chimes are played from an erect standing position.

The distinctive tone qualities which characterize the various mallet instruments have already been mentioned. Because of these distinctive tonal features each of the instruments has become identified with certain typical idioms. Composers and arrangers do well to develop a firsthand knowledge of the best idiomatic usage for each of the mallet-played instruments.

The xylophone is at its best in dry, brittle, percussive melodic lines. It should not be overworked in any one composition, as its tone is monotonous if too long continued. Two-note chords, called "double stops," are commonly found. The tone can be sustained by means of a roll, which is a rapidly alternated series of single strokes. High velocity passages of chromatic or diatonic scales and arpeggiated figures are quite playable on the xylophone. Because the vibrations of the bars are of very short duration, the xylophone tones do not blur or build up any appreciable clang.

The marimba is very similar to the xylophone in its technical demands. When played two-mallet style the same velocity is possible. Rolls are executed in the same manner also. The major difference is one of idiom. The marimba bars are more resonant than those of the xylophone, but their tone is less penetrating. Consequently, the instrument is not as useful in the orchestra or band. Because of the longer vibration time of the marimba bars, however, it is ideally suited to legato melodic lines and hence well suited to solo playing. Double stops and three and four mallet chords sound good on the marimba, particularly in its lower register. The technique for holding three or four mallets will be described in the section on playing techniques. To sustain chords beyond their normal single stroke duration a tremolo is used, in which the mallets which play the chord tones are alternated in rapid sequence. Solo literature, both transcriptions of solos originally written for other instruments and pieces composed specifically for the marimba, make extensive use of the tremolo.

The vibraphone has the ability to sustain its tones without the use of a roll or tremolo by means of its free-ringing metal bars and pedal control. The motor-driven vibrato mechanism gives the tone a warm quality that is very beautiful when played alone and also blends well with other instruments. The vibraphone has a greater dynamic range than the other mallet-played instruments. These advantages have made the vibraphone a favorite instrument in the popular music fields, especially in small combo jazz. When the vibraphone first made its appearance in the large studio-type radio orchestras of the 1920's and 1930's, it was usually confined to arpeggios and four-mallet chordal passages, coloristic effects, etc. Since that time the trend has been toward a more melodic style. In concert music the vibraphone is used in a variety of ways. Single bell-tone octaves, short melodic lines, and chordal passages are all common. Arrangers of "pops concert" symphonic scores seem to be particularly fond of the lush tones of the vibraphone.

The orchestra bells are at their best on single tones, octaves, and arpeggios. They do not sound good in rapid passages or scale-wise progressions because of the clashes produced by the after-rings of the bars. Slow moving melodic lines are possible, but the player must damp certain tones carefully if he is to avoid unpleasant clashes. Rolls are not often used, as the bell bars continue to vibrate for the value of all but the longest of notes.

MALLET TECHNIQUE

In teaching the mallet instruments one should start with the basic single stroke, which is common to all of the instruments in the group with the exception of the chimes. For a description of the basic single stroke refer back to the paragraphs on Common Characteristics and Distinctive Features of the Mallet-Played Instruments. Note the position of the hands and wrists in Figures 5.13 to 5.15. The single stroke on the chimes is made by tapping the top end of the tube, contacting the "cap" section with the mallet at an angle as shown in Figure 5.16. For most chime notes, a light wrist action is sufficient to produce a good tone. The forearm is brought into play when it is necessary to produce a very loud chime tone. When playing slower passages where utmost resonance is desired, a slight "rolling" of the mallet head upward at the moment of contact is helpful. This motion involves a quick lifting of the wrist.

The single stroke roll used on these instruments requires much practice in order to achieve the speed necessary for a smooth tone. Slow and even alternate R and L strokes on a single bar prepare the wrist for the later stages of roll development. For control play a series of quarter notes, progressing thence to eighths, sixteenths, and thirty-seconds. The arcs of the mallet heads become shorter as the rate of speed is increased. Gradations of volume are governed by the length of the arcs and the force of the wrist snaps.

Figure 5.16. Chime stroke.

Legato playing of rolled note intervals is facilitated if the R mallet is moved to the new bar first when the skip is upward, and the L mallet moved first when skipping downward.

In the tremolo the roll technique is simply split between two notes. Unless the player has developed a rapid single stroke roll on a single bar, this division of the reiterated sounds between two bars is likely to sound rather spotty. On the marimba, particularly in its lower register, the tremolo need not be as rapid as on the xylophone for the reason that the vibration times of the bars are greater, and thus the mallet contacts do not have to renew the vibrations as often to produce a continuous tone.

The handholds for playing with three and four mallets are illustrated in Figures 5.17 to 5.20. Notice that the handles of the *highest* and *lowest* mallets go *over* the other two handles as they are held by the thumb and fingers of each hand. The handles remain in contact at this crossover or pivot point. The central problem in four-mallet technique is the adjustment of the width of the angle formed between each pair of mallets so that the desired bars will be struck. This angle adjustment is made principally by the thumb, index, and little fingers of each hand.

To increase the angle of the mallets, slide the thumb forward along the shaft of the inner mallet, at the same time applying pressure with the side of the index finger to the other mallet and pulling the little and ring fingers forward. The position of the outer mallet will remain relatively unchanged. The most difficult playing angle is the very narrow one needed to reach minor and major seconds.

Figure 5.17. Two mallets R, one mallet L.

Figure 5.18. One mallet R, two mallets L.

Figure 5.19. Four-mallet handholds, top-view.

Figure 5.20. Small interval R, large interval L.

Another method of holding three or four mallets is known as the "Musser" grip. This method of holding two mallets in one hand does not cross the sticks and provides access to wide intervals and somewhat more independency of each mallet. Although this method has been around for some time, its advantages rapidly are becoming more obvious as the literature for the marimba becomes more demanding.

Independency of hands and individual mallets required by contemporary literature makes the "Musser" grip desirable. Compositions requiring extended one-handed rolls, extremely wide double-stop intervals and rapid passages involving great skips characterize many of today's compositions.

Some of the obvious advantages of the "Musser" grip over the regular or traditional grip such as eliminating the problem of the interval of a second, providing a wider spread between two mallets of the same hand, and individualization of each mallet justify utilizing this grip when attempting the more difficult literature.

To sustain long tones in the four-mallet style it is necessary to tremolo the notes on the marimba, but not on the vibraphone. The marimba tremolo is made by holding the mallets in a rather loose grip and rocking the wrists in a left-to-right motion while at the same time maintaining the up-and-down alternations. The mallets will then contact the bars in the order L outer, L inner, R inner, R outer. The rate of speed of the tremolo must be great enough to produce the illusion of a sustained tone on each of the bars. This individual contact method of making the tremolo is preferred over the sometimes heard "two and two" style, in which each pair of mallets contacts the bars as a unit. It is a smoother and more musical effect when

skillfully performed. It requires much practice to bring under perfect control.

Stickwork. Stickwork, sometimes referred to as hammering, is essentially the same for all of the mallet-played instruments. Normal usage can be stated as a policy: in an ascending scalewise passage, begin with the L and alternate; in a descending scalewise passage, begin with the R and alternate. In chordal contexts and arpeggios, use the L for the lowest tone and proceed upward with alternate mallets—start with the R in similar descending figures. In other words, use the L on lowest notes and the R on the high extremes in any given passage. In between the extremes, alternate mallets are used more often than not. There are certain contours of melodic line which are more easily executed by using successive sticking, i.e., RR, LL. Examples of passages in which alternate and successive stickings are called for are given on page 98. These examples are intended to illustrate *typical* stickwork problems. By applying the principles illustrated in these and the studies on pages 96 to 102, one can develop a systematic approach to mallet playing which will be adequate for all but the most unusual sticking problems.

Damping. Damping is never necessary on the xylophone, seldom on the marimba, and is taken care of on the vibraphone by the damper pedal. The bells (glockenspiel) require damping by the finger tips in order to avoid unpleasant clashes of tones. To aid in phrasing, finger damping is utilized also on the vibraphone. In simple passages where the notes do not succeed each other rapidly it usually is possible to play the notes with one mallet and damp with the opposite hand. When two mallets are required the damping must be done while the mallets are being held in the hands. A light contact with the extended middle finger on the surface of the bar to be damped is

Figure 5.21. Damping, bells.

sufficient to kill the tone. If it is necessary to damp suddenly after a sequence of bell notes which are still ringing, run the finger tips of each hand quickly in toward the center of the keyboard making sure that each sounding bar is contacted en route. Another quicker method to damp a series of tones, suddenly, is to place the arms on the keyboard using the L arm on the natural keys and the R arm on the chromatic keys. Do not damp bell tones too soon. Let them ring freely at least for the duration of the written value. It is noteworthy that Ludwig/Musser now offers, as an extra cost option, a model of orchestra bells with a hand-operated damper mechanism.

Damping on the chimes is accomplished by grasping the vibrating tube firmly with the hand at a point a foot or so below the top end. Not all chime tones should be damped, as often the intention of the composer is to let the chimes build up a clang in the fashion of steeple bells. In many cases the player and conductor must determine whether or not to damp the chime notes. Sets of chimes equipped with a damper pedal simplify the problems of duration of chime notes. The damper pedal when pushed down causes a felt covered damper to contact the tubes.

MISCELLANEOUS POINTS— MALLET INSTRUMENTS

Solo passages for the mallet instruments contained in band or orchestra scores should be memorized. Knowing such excerpts from memory will enable the player to keep a close eye on the conductor. An excellent source of excerpts from standard literature is contained in Goldenberg's *Modern School for the Xylophone, Marimba and Vibraphone,* published by Chappell. This same method book also contains copious technical study material presented in graded sequence. It is one of the best volumes of its kind now on the market, and should be in the hands of every student and player of the mallet instruments.

Out-of-tune xylophone and marimba bars must be sent back to the factory for tuning. If they are too far out of tune to be retuned, replacement bars may be necessary. Do not attempt to remove or add wood or other material to an out-of-tune bar in the hope of putting it back into tune. This is a job for the expert.

Frequently the written part for bells, xylophone or other instrument will exceed the range of the instrument at hand. In this case it is necessary to transpose some of the tones an octave up or down in order to bring them into the range of the instrument. Often it is better to transpose a whole phrase or entire passage than to make awkward skips which distort the melodic line. The player should try to keep the passage in question generally high or low, depending on musical judgment to ascertain what sounds best in the particular context. Bell parts frequently sound better when played an octave lower than written, probably because the composer or arranger was unaware that the bells sound two octaves higher than written.

It is a good idea to keep the bars of the xylophone, marimba, and vibraphone covered with fibre board or heavy cloth cut to fit over the keyboard. If a heavy-duty vinyl cover is not supplied with a mallet instrument at the time of purchase, then the appropriate cover, designed to fit the specific instrument, should be purchased as soon as possible. There is hardly anything more damaging to a mallet instrument than "finger-nail glissandi" encouraged by leaving the instrument uncovered. If the instruments are going to be moved with any regularity, then it is essential that the correct fitting fibre cases be purchased in addition to the vinyl drop covers. The expense of cases will more than pay for itself over the long run and make instruments more compact and easily transported also.

Although rolls are often notated with three slanted slashes through the note stem ♪ , or by a trill sign placed above the note, both of these notations can easily be confusing to the player. The note with three slashes could be interpreted as a measured tremolo of thirty-second notes, which would be too slow at certain tempi to sound like a roll. A trill sign is also a weak notation when a roll is intended because a trill literally means to execute the given note with the diatonic second adjacent to it. Therefore, unless a trill is actually intended, this is a poor sign to use when a roll is desired. Much of the confusion can be easily avoided if the roll is notated with *four* slashes through the stem of the note, ♪ , if in fact a roll is desired.

The *Xylorimba* is an obsolescent hybrid instrument which was designed to combine the mellow tone quality of the marimba with the penetrating sound of the xylophone. In the three and one-half octave instrument, no longer manufactured, only the lowest octave and half sounds like an authentic marimba. The remainder of the bars have a distinctly xylophone quality. Boulez' masterpiece *Le Marteau Sans Maître,* written in 1954, calls for a xylorimba.

When the nature of the passage will permit, hold the music in the left hand while playing the chimes with one mallet. There is no convenient place to put a music rack for the chimes, as the tubes obscure the player's view.

CHAPTER 6

Timpani (kettledrums)

HISTORICAL DEVELOPMENT

The kettledrums as we now know them are the product of many centuries of gradual development. They form one of the two main lines of membrane-covered drum development, these two lines being drums with bowl-shaped sound reflecting shells and those with hollow cylindrical shells. According to Sietz[1] the origin of the kettledrum dates back at least to Old Testament Hebrew times. The size and shape of the Hebrew kettledrum is not known, nor do we know whether it was used singly or paired. The ancient Greeks were known to have employed a form of kettledrum in celebrations and rituals. During the Middle Ages, European contact with the Near East resulted in the introduction into Europe of a small-sized version of the timpani called the *naggareh,* or *naggareth.* These kettledrums later became known in France as *nacaires* and in England as *nakers.* They were used in pairs, either carried at the waist of the player or mounted on either side of a horse's shoulders, and became a symbol of affluence and aristocracy. These relatively small kettledrums were known in Europe as early as the thirteenth century.

The direct forerunners of our modern timpani date from 1457, according to both Sietz[1] and White.[2] In this year certain ambassadors of King Ladislaus of Hungary were sent to France to seek the hand of the daughter of King Charles VII. Included in the entourage were "drumes lyke bigge ketels, caryed one on each syde of ye horse's necke." These large drums were played by the performers with an affected grace of style which was to have a great influence on the manner of kettledrumming throughout Europe during the 16th and 17th centuries. In Germany about the beginning of the sixteenth century the name "tympana" was given to the large kettledrum. In 1542 King Henry VIII of England procured a pair of these large kettledrums from Vienna for use of his cavalry. White cites 1735 as the publication date of the first instruction book, called "Heroic and Musical Art of the Trumpet and Kettledrum." Emphasis was on the "heroics," or elegance of playing posture and manner of striking the drum.

In seventeenth century Germany there were some significant departures made in the construction of the kettledrums which allowed for their later adoption into the orchestra. For one thing, the heads were mounted on hoops and held down by means of metal counterhoops which had several screws placed around their circumference. Clumsy as this first tuning arrangement must have been, it marked the beginning of a truly musical usage of the kettledrums. Early in the nineteenth century handles were added to the tuning screws and their number reduced to six or eight, making tuning quicker and easier. The size of the pair became standardized at this time to approximately the present dimensions of 25″ for the small kettle and 28″ for the large kettle. Illustrations of the time depict timpanists using wooden or ivory-tipped sticks shaped like malls.

Michael Praetorius authorized timpani in certain numbers of the *Polyhymnia Caduceutrix and Panegyrica* (1619). An early instance of a clearly labeled, written out part for timpani appeared in a mass (Saltzburger Festmesse) for fifty-three voices in 1628 by Orazio Benevoli. Written for the dedication of Salzburg Cathedral, Benevoli specified that the drums be tuned in fourths.

In these early works the kettledrums usually played with an ensemble of trumpets. A common arrangement was to have the three upper parts played by trumpets and the fourth part interchangeable, or doubled, between the fourth trumpet and the timpani. This usage set the trend for scoring kettledrum parts during the Classic period. White credits Lully with the first serious orchestral score including timpani, the opera *Thesée* produced in Paris in 1692. The culminating phase of the Baroque period saw both Bach and Handel scoring generously and skillfully for the timpani. These masters followed the established principle of tonic-dominant tuning, and used the drums chiefly in conjunction with the trumpets and horns.

Beethoven was the first composer to assign a more independent role to the timpani, even to the extent of writing solo passages of great dramatic impact. He was also the first composer to depart from the strict fourth or fifth interval tunings. In *Fidelio* Beethoven requires the timpani to be tuned to a diminished fifth, and in the Finale of the Eighth Symphony and the Scherzo of the Ninth they are tuned one octave apart.

Both Wagner and Berlioz in the nineteenth century extended the tonal and technical demands on the kettledrums. Both scored occasionally for two sets of timpani to be played by two players. Berlioz can be credited with the development of a variety of beaters for the timpani, and his parts often call for sponge-headed sticks, which he invented for the purpose of obtaining a soft and mellow tone quality. Berlioz' *Symphonie Fantastique* calls for the timpani to be muffled with pieces of cloth placed on the heads—the first use of *coperti*.

During the first half of the twentieth century, both the ranges and technical demands upon timpani were increased considerably. The limits of the range are now *great* C to small B♭ and even beyond, especially when a fifth drum of 20″ diameter is used. This drum can easily reach c¹ and d¹. Vic Firth, timpanist for the Boston Symphony Orchestra, has a set of 15 and 14 inch piccolo timpani which are capable of reaching high d¹ and f♯¹ respectively with a clear resonant sound.

Considering that the traditionally standard pair of timpani, with diameters of 25 and 28 or 26 and 29 inches, will produce all of the notes found within the octave F-f, the timpanist still requires a minimum of four drums. The need is dependent upon the simple matter of tone and to meet the requirements of range. It is important to understand that the quality of tone at the extreme upper or lower range of any timpano is poor; the best sounding notes are produced from the mid-range to the top of the range. For maximum resonance, notes which exceed the middle register of any size drum are best played on the next smaller size in the set.

The very lowest note on any timpano should be avoided if at all possible because optimal resonance and beauty of tone are simply not possible. The bottom note on a timpano is comparable to an open string of an orchestral stringed instrument and should be avoided unless specifically designated.

Although a number of sources persist in advocating the 25 and 28 inch sizes as the standard pair, this is no longer true, having been generally replaced with the 26 and 29 inch diameters. These two sizes seem to provide greater tonal body throughout the compass of each drum, especially at the extreme ends of the range on each drum. Professional timpanists generally concur that the 26 and 29 inch combination will produce a much improved tone quality.

The practical range of each timpano is at least a perfect fifth, and this corresponds to the bowl diameter. The ranges of the five sizes recommended by the present author of this *Guide* are as follows:

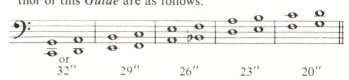

The range of each drum may be extended slightly in either direction, especially when plastic heads are used. The resulting tones, however, will not have the same quality as the notes within the confines of the designated ranges.

The purpose of adding more timpani to the basic pair is to extend their range, to give a greater flexibility in the choice of timpani for the required pitches, and to reduce the number of tuning changes within a composition. A set of four timpani has become essential to perform much of the music written for advanced high school level performance and certainly in most college, university and professional situations. The rapidity with which tuning changes must be effected makes it necessary for the modern symphony orchestra timpanist to use machine-tuned timpani of the pedal, master-key, chain, or rotary types. A description of the commonly used types of timpani, together with recommended sizes, types, and set-ups for various purposes, follows in succeeding paragraphs.

TYPES OF TIMPANI

The simplest and least expensive type of kettledrum is the so-called hand-tuned or hand-screw model. The essential features of the hand-tuned timpani remain relatively unchanged from the kettledrums of the seventeenth and eighteenth centuries. Tension on the head is adjusted by means of the six screw handles around the perimeter of the bowl. When the handles are turned to the right the counterhoop is lowered, thus stretching the head taut and raising the pitch. The pitch of the head is lowered by turning the handles in the opposite direction. A tripod base is used to set the drum up high enough for convenient playing position. Some models have lightweight metal standard bases which are permanently attached to the bottom of the bowl. With the slightly modernized version of hand-tuned timpani, tuning is accomplished by turning a master hand crank, conveniently mounted near the playing surface, which connects to a single screw tuning mechanism. There is some advantage in that all tuning lugs are turned simultaneously by the master tuning crank. However, this model is not nearly as flexible, as is the now more standardized pedal tuned model.

Few hand-tuned models are being manufactured today as a result of the demand for timpani which can be tuned more rapidly. It is because of the time required to make a change of tuning (six handles must be turned on each change) and the fact that the player must stop play-

Figure 6.1. Hand-tuned timpani.

Figure 6.2. Pedal-tuned timpani.

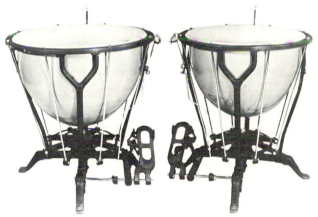

Figure 6.3. Dresden-type timpani.

ing in order to adjust the handles that the hand-tuned kettledrum is now obsolescent. They do make good training instruments, however, and can be used in elementary school bands and orchestras where the timpani parts rarely call for rapid changes of tuning.

The most popular type of machine drums (timpani which tune by means other than hand screws) are pedal tuned. There are several varieties of the pedal mechanism, but their common characteristic is a foot pedal which attaches to a vertical rod within the bowl of the drum and is connected to a "spider" of six or eight cables which run to equidistant points on the counterhoop. When the toe portion of the pedal is depressed it lowers the rod inside the bowl, which in turn pulls down the cables which connect to the counterhoop and raises the pitch by applying tension to the head. When the toe portion is raised and the heel is depressed, the reverse process takes place and the pitch of the head is lowered. Pedal-tuned timpani are the most convenient for most players' general use. Their great advantage over any other type is that they can be tuned while both of the timpanist's hands are engaged in playing. For instance, if a long roll is begun which sounds out of tune to the timpanist, he can continue to roll while correcting the intonation by means of the foot pedal. The pedal device is also the fastest type of mechanism so far invented for tuning. The chief disadvantage of older model pedal-tuned kettledrums is that some of the natural resonance of the bowl is lost with the addition of the internal spider mechanism and with the attachment of the heavy metal base. This has been corrected in the newer models with external tensioning systems.

The Dresden type of pedal timpani were developed in Germany and are now also manufactured in the United States. This type combines the tone quality of the best hand-tuned kettles with the convenience of the pedal mechanism. It does this by having all of its moving parts on the outside of the bowl and its bowl supported from the top edges by heavy braces, which allow it to vibrate maximally. The shape of the bowl, being more deep and elliptical than most other types, gives the Dresden timpani a purity and richness of tone unmatched by any other.

Another advantage of the Dresden-type drum is its saw-toothed ratchet pedal mechanism which eliminates the problem of slippage sometimes encountered with the ordinary spring balanced pedal. This very advantage can also become a disadvantage, however, as it is necessary to kick out a heel clutch when making a change in the Dresden pedal setting, and this makes tuning slower by a second or two. The main drawbacks to the Dresden timpani are their high cost and their great weight. They are not practical for other than permanent location use. They are manufactured in this country in the following sizes: 52 cm. (approximately 20.5''), 58 cm. (22.88''), 64 cm. (25.19''), 72 cm. (28.38''), and 78 cm. (30.75'').

Another type of machine-tuned kettledrums is the so-called rotary timpani. The basic principle of this type is that the bowl rests on a large screw, and when the kettle is rotated clockwise an internal spider mechanism pulls downward and thus applies tension to the head, raising its pitch. When the kettle is rotated counterclockwise the reverse action lowers the pitch. Usually two hands are needed to accomplish the tuning, especially in the upper register

Figure 6.4. Standard rotary timpani.

where the tension is great. This, plus the fact that the best playing spot on the head will not always be available, make the rotary timpani considerably less popular than the pedal models. One manufacturer has recently come out with a rotary timpano made specifically for school use which has tuning indicators around the counterhoop which can be preset to show how far to rotate the kettle for each tone. This simple device works well when plastic heads are used, as they are not subject to variation in pitch caused by changing atmospheric conditions.

Courtesy G. C. Jenkins Co.

Figure 6.5. Rotary timpani with tuning indicators.

Several other types of machine timpani are in use, but are not often seen in this country. One such model, which is now being custom made for symphony timpanists by Saul Goodman formerly of the New York Philharmonic Orchestra, makes use of a bicycle-type chain which runs around the perimeter of the bowl and connects with a sprocket at each of the tuning points. When a master key is turned the entire chain moves, causing equal pressure to be exerted on the head at each tuning point. This type of drum has a good tone quality, as there is no internal mechanism or standard base to stifle the resonance.

Persons charged with the responsibility of purchasing timpani for various musical organizations must make a choice from among the several types of timpani, and there are usually questions as to the type of head, new vs. reconditioned drums, etc. The following table is included to serve as a guide in making such decisions. The table should be considered as *suggestion* rather than outright recommendation, as the factors of cost, availability, portability, and personal preference of the player must be taken into consideration when spending the large amount of money required to purchase a set of timpani.

Type of Ensemble	*Recommended Timpani*
Elementary School band and orchestra	Pair of pedal timpani, 26″ and 29″ diameters, plastic heads, tuning gauges, copper bowls preferred, fiberglass acceptable.
Junior High School band and orchestra	As above, with third drum added, preferably a 32″, fourth drum should then be 23″.
High School band, orchestra, percussion ensemble	Four pedal timpani, 23″, 26″, 29″, 32″, copper bowls, fully suspended, plastic heads, tuning gauges (perhaps).
College/University band, orchestra, percussion ensemble	Set of *five* pedal timpani, Dresden or similar type, same sizes as high school plus 20″, plastic heads, copper bowls, fully suspended.
Professional band	Set of four (or five) pedal timpani, as for college/university.
Symphony, opera orchestra, professional chamber group	Set of four or five Dresden, copper bowls, plastic or calfskin heads, fully suspended.
Pit orchestra	Two or more pedal timpani, copper bowls, plastic heads, a model which allows base to detach from bowl, a great aid in portability for the touring ensemble or company.

TIMPANI HEADS

Heads for the kettledrums traditionally have been made from the hides of young calves. Within recent times, a synthetic material has been developed and perfected which solves the problems caused by the calfskin heads' susceptibility to changes in the relative humidity of the air. Although these plastic heads initially had some serious drawbacks, they are now of such quality as to be considered almost the norm. Due to their ease of installing, stability of tuning, and durability these plastic heads are strongly recommended and, today, are more widely used than the older calfskin heads. Plastic heads are also less expensive and are far more widely available than are calfskin heads.

Another point to consider is that since it is impossible to control the evenness of texture and thickness of calfskin heads, they vary in sound production from point to point on the head. This is not a problem with plastic heads.

Even though in a few cases some professional timpanists still argue in favor of calfskin, it generally is accepted that the plastic heads are much more ideal for usage in all educational and outdoor situations.

No matter which type of head is used, the tension must be kept equal at all points around the circumference of the head if a clear tone is to be obtained. *Tuning handles should always be turned an equal amount at each change.* The manner of putting each segment of the head into tune (tuning the head with itself) will be treated in detail in the section of timpani tuning.

One final note concerns mounting timpani heads. Calfskin heads should always be purchased already mounted on the flesh hoops. To mount a calfskin head on the kettle, dampen the head on both sides with clear cool water up to, but not under, the flesh hoop. Allow the head to dry somewhat until it is limp, wiping off spots of excess water with a towel. Next, place the head on the kettle in such a position that the light strip which runs down the center of the head (the backbone portion) runs between two opposite tuning handles. As the newly mounted head begins to dry, place the metal counterhoop in position, thread the handles, and begin to apply tension at each point. The drums must be watched carefully throughout the procedure lest the drying take place too rapidly. The tuning handles should be turned gradually an equal number of half-turns until the head is dry and produces a good tone on a note in its middle register. *Do not* play on the timpano for several hours after the head has been mounted. It is best to wait until the next day before using the drum.

With a timpano head that has gone dead, or becomes so false that it cannot be tuned accurately, it will usually pay to try to rejuvenate it by the "wetting down" process just outlined for mounting a new head. One variation of the process when wetting down a used head is to let the head dry thoroughly off the drum after the initial wetting, then repeat the entire process. If a head does not sound good after it has been wet down, it should be replaced. Plastic heads are mounted dry and are not ever "wet down." One thing to watch when mounting plastic heads is to see that the top edge of the bowl is smooth and absolutely free from nubs or scratches, as these can tear the head easily. Tallow or lanolin applied to this top edge of the bowl prior to mounting the head will ensure that no portion of the head will bind, and it will also eliminate

annoying squeaks as the head stretches over the top of the bowl.

PARTS OF THE TIMPANI

Figure 6.6 shows the detail of the timpani bowl, head, hoop, and collar assembly.

The main parts of the timpani are shown in Figure 6.7. Not all models will include all parts illustrated, but the main features of the model here shown are common to all models.

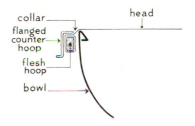

Figure 6.6. Detail of timpani head assembly.

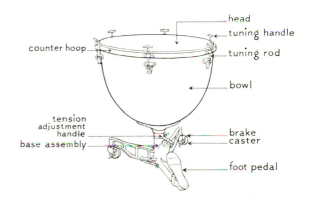

Figure 6.7. Parts of the timpani.

TIMPANI STICKS

The importance of the timpani sticks in tone producton is considerably greater than is commonly supposed. By the use of various materials for the beater ball, handle, and inner core, timpani sticks can be made to give a variety of tone qualities. The timpanist needs an assortment of sticks if he is to do musical justice to the parts written for his instruments.

The historical development of the timpani stick is an interesting but little known story. Prior to Hector Berlioz (1803–1869) the kettledrummer was limited to two basic materials for his sticks—wood and ivory. The shape of these sticks was that of a mall, and they must have been somewhat heavier than the sticks used today. It is hard to imagine that all through the Baroque, Rococo, and Classic periods, when so much progress was made in the construction of the instruments themselves and in the musical resources of the parts written for them, the sticks should have remained in such a crude stage of development. Such was the case, and it remained for Berlioz to begin the experimentation which has led to our present day models. Berlioz first tried leather covers over the ends of his sticks but was not satisfied. As he indicates in his famous treatise on orchestration, "they produce a sound less startling than the preceding (wood sticks), but they are very dry nevertheless." He later experimented with other materials, including mushrooms! Eventually Berlioz settled upon sponge-covered sticks as being the best that could be produced, as he claimed that such sticks could produce a musical, rather than a purely noisy, tone. He described the tone elicited by the sponge sticks as grave and velvety, and indeed they may have seemed so to one accustomed only to the sounds of wood or leather sticks. Berlioz' timpani parts frequently call for "baguettes d'éponge" (sponge sticks), which is correctly interpreted by the modern timpanist as meaning soft felt-covered sticks, not available in Berlioz' time. Felt was eventually found to be the most satisfactory covering material, probably by German timpanists in their never-ending search for the ideal stick.

Most of the better modern timpani sticks are made with straight grained hickory handles and their cork or wood cores are covered with a high quality of damper felt. The handles are about 13½″ or 14″ long and are about ½″ in diameter at the butt end, tapering down slightly to about 5/16″ at the point where the ball is attached.

The choice of sticks is a highly personal matter, and there is a bewildering number of commercially made sticks from which to choose. The main concern of the teacher should be to see that his students avoid the extremes often issued for use in the schools. The very hard solid felt beater ball should be avoided, as it is not a generally useful stick. The other type of stick to avoid is the very fluffy lamb's wool variety, which is entirely too "mushy" to produce an acceptable tone. The fact that these latter sticks are relatively inexpensive is not a sufficient reason for issuing them for use by young students. An elastic type handle is not recommended. A rigid handle assists production of the best tone and a clear, concise pulsation. One gets about what one pays for in a commercial timpani stick, and the least one should expect to pay for a pair of sticks at the current prices is $12.00 to $20.00. A good all-purpose stick for school use is one of medium hardness, such as the Firth model T1 shown in Figure 6.8. In speaking of high quality sticks for timpani, it would be amiss not to mention the Vic Firth line of mallets. Vic Firth is the solo timpanist and principal percussionist for the Boston Symphony Orchestra and the timpani mallets he designed are based on many years of experience, experimentation and the expertise gleaned from performing as one of the world's great artists. Vic Firth timpani sticks are hand turned from selected rock maple. The core and shank are turned from

one piece of wood. This eliminates the possibility of the ball coming unglued or a washer or thread breaking or cross-threading. The felt is sewn on the stick in such a way as to eliminate the seam. This means that any area of the stick can strike the timpano head without concern for a seam which could mar the sound of the instrument. It also extends the life of the stick, as the entire felt surface can be played upon. The sticks are finished with an extremely hard catalytic varnish. There are six distinctly different models of sticks, each designed for a specific purpose.

In addition to the Vic Firth timpani mallets mentioned above, there are other high quality mallets designed or made by Saul Goodman (the former timpanist and principal percussionist for the New York Philharmonic), Fred Hinger, Richard Holmes, Cloyd Duff, Al Payson, Andrew Feldman and others. For timpanists who desire to purchase any of these brands of mallets (or the replacement covers for them) at discounted prices, the following address is provided: Lonestar Percussion, 10610 Control Place, Dallas, Texas 75238. This address will prove especially helpful to instrumental directors and aspiring timpanists who wish to obtain top quality mallets but who do not live in or near a larger metropolitan area occupied by a well-stocked percussion specialty shop.

The timpanist should have at least six pair of mallets handy at all times, in order to be prepared for the ever increasing demands being placed upon timpanists. The opening meaures of Richard Strauss' *Don Juan* employ wood sticks for an electrifying effect on the timpani. Stravinsky's *Firebird, Infernal Dance of the Roi Katschei* features a timpani ostinato played with wood sticks.

Some professional orchestral timpanists own no less than twenty different pair of mallets and certain players even have favorite mallets for certain composers' works. Timpani mallets require a certain amount of care if they are to render good service. The player should have a stick "tote bag" which is specifically designed to carry mallets in a safe and orderly manner, as carriers of this type have several separated compartments. Perhaps even better might be an attaché case or another type of stick/mallet case designed for this purpose. In addition to carrying timpani mallets, such cases are useful to carry all manner of sticks, beaters, triangles and other small accessories, and can also accommodate scores, books and ensemble music.

There are several reasons, some are psychological, for having each percussionist own their mallets. The investment in one's own gear will certainly encourage greater seriousness of purpose, mallets have a way of receiving better care when they are student-owned and there is a psychological plus when even the younger players carry a stick bag or case; it causes them to feel equal to students who carry trumpet, clarinet, etc. cases. Younger students

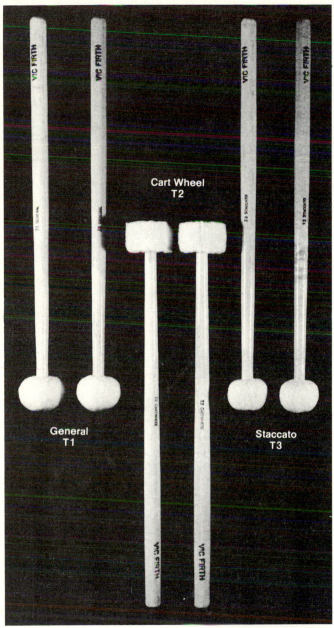

Courtesy Vic Firth

General Timpani Stick/T1

An all-around stick for general playing. It is soft enough to produce a beautiful, full sound for the classical repertoire, and is firm enough for the attacks and rhythmic clarity necessary in the contemporary repertoire.

Cart Wheel Timpani Stick/T2

This stick is the softest of all the Vic Firth models. It is intended for soft velvet-like rolls, legato strokes, and is ideally suited for obtaining maximum richness of sound. The core of the stick is a medium-hard felt that is covered with a layer of very soft felt. The core is not flat, but it is slightly convex to allow the stick to produce a beautiful, round sound. It attaches to the stick from the handle end and not from the playing end. The ball cap and shank are turned from one piece of wood. This cap prevents the ball from flying off the stick and eliminates the need for any wood threading or washers. As well as the end cap, the felt is cut to a press fit and is doubly secured with an epoxy cement. For sustained solo rolls, especially in pianissimo, this stick produces the most beautiful sounds possible.

Staccato Timpani Stick/T3

This stick is designed for producing clear rhythmic articulation. The ball of this stick is slightly smaller, and the felt slightly harder than the General Timpani stick, thus producing a more pointed articulate sound. The stick is useful for rhythmic definition in the classical repertoire, and an absolute necessity for rhythmic projection in the contemporary repertoire.

Figure 6.8. General purpose, cartwheel and staccato timpani mallets (l to r).

especially must be encouraged to keep their mallets clean and in good repair at all times, as mallets are indeed a vital link in the process of tone production.

Felt used to cover timpani sticks tends to rough up and form into small nodes. If these fluffy spots are not removed periodically they can affect the tone quality. To trim the excess felt from a beater ball or disc, use a small pair of scissors. Hold the stick in the left hand, rotate slowly while trimming *evenly* around the entire surface of the covering.

In the interest of economy, the timpanist who is willing to persevere with a needle, thread and scissors may wish to recover worn-out sticks. Only a high grade of piano damper felt should be used, the ½″ thickness being carefully split into two equal thicknesses. Use the *inner* side of the split felt for the outer covering. Dental floss makes the best thread, as it is strong and durable and fine enough for the purpose. Sew with a whipstitch in the manner used for the original stitching.

Seamless timpani mallets are the most useful and should be employed as much as possible. However, in the unfortunate situation of being forced to cope with the seam, the suggestions below will prove quite helpful.

Timpani sticks should always be held so that the seam of the stitching is on the up side so as not to contact the drumhead, as the seam will produce an inferior tone. As

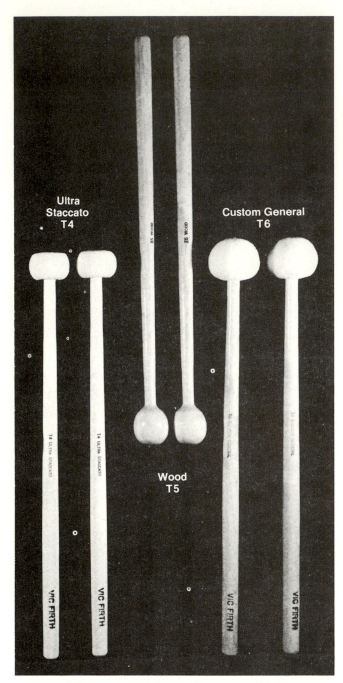

Ultra
Staccato
T4

Custom General
T6

Wood
T5

Courtesy Vic Firth

Ultra Staccato Timpani Stick/T4
A new concept in timpani sticks, this stick produces the
clearest, most articulate sound possible next to the all wood
timpani stick. The ball of the stick is made of a high grade,
Spanish finished felt. Because it is extremely hard, its shape is
obtained by actually spinning it as you would a piece of wood.
The ball cap and shank are turned from one piece of wood.
The ball attaches to the stick not from the playing end, but
from the handle end. The cap prevents the ball from flying off
the stick and eliminates the need for any wood threading or
washers. As well as the end cap, the felt is cut to a press fit
and is doubly secured with an epoxy cement. This stick is
ideally suited for staccato rhythmic projection on timpani,
however, it could also be used on various drums in chamber
and percussion ensembles, as well as for tenor drums in
marching bands and drum corps.

Wood Timpani Stick/T5
This is a 'special effects' stick requested by both classical and
contemporary composers. It produces a hard, clattering sound
that adds rhythmic 'bite' and definition to the sound of the
instrument.

Custom General Timpani Stick/T6
This stick is similar in shape to the General Timpani stick
except that it is slightly larger and heavier all around. It
produces a marvelous, big sound and is capable of powerful
attacks. It must be used with discretion for it to be most
effective, otherwise it becomes overpowering. Only a player
with strong, well-developed hands should employ these (ex.
Brahms, Wagner, Bruckner, Mahler)

Figure 6.9. Ultra staccato, wood and custom general timpani mallets (l to r).

an aid to keeping the sticks in the proper position, mark
a line or cross in heavy pencil on the handle of the stick
near the ball to indicate where the seam is located. This
pencil mark should be visible to the player at all times to
insure against striking the seams.

If the threaded end of the stick protrudes beyond the
washer used to hold the beater ball or disc in place by
more than a quarter inch or so, it should be sawed off.

Dents, and even small tears, often are inflicted on the timpani head by an excess length of wood protruding beyond
the ball.

PLAYING SPOT

The usual playing spot on the timpani head is shown
in Figure 6.10.

Figure 6.10. Playing spots.

The playing spot should be located between an adjacent pair of tuning handles, in order to avoid entangling the sticks with the handles. Many newer models have either collapsible or removable tuning handles which avoids this problem altogether. Key tension rods that do not protrude above the level of the head will also avoid the problem. However, the timpani tuning key will have to be available and handy in order to make any necessary adjustments.

When using calfskin heads, the exact spot on the surface of each head which sounds most resonant has to be determined by experimentation and is subject to a great deal of variation, changing from time to time even on the same head. This is generally not true of plastic heads and, of course, is a definite advantage of these heads. Some types of kettledrums cannot be rotated to bring this optimum playing area into position convenient for playing. This holds true for the Dresden type, some models of standard pedal timpani, and rotary timpani. Hand-tuned and most models of pedal timpani can be placed so that the optimum playing spot is in a good position. To provide the best sound, once this general good playing area has been located, the heads should be struck in an area not closer than two inches nor further than five inches from the rim. Played too close to the rim, a head will produce a "pinging" sound. As you approach the center, the deader the sound becomes. If struck in the center, there will be practically no vibration and the pitch will hardly be discernible.

SET-UPS FOR TWO, THREE AND FOUR KETTLES

The pair of timpani is placed so that the high (small) kettle is at the right of the low (large) one. The pedals are placed at an angle so that they can be easily reached by the R and L feet respectively. As the player stands or sits in playing position, no tuning handle should lie directly in the path to be traveled by either stick.

Figure 6.11. Placement of the pair of timpani.

Figure 6.12. Placement of three timpani.

Figure 6.13. Placement of four timpani.

When three kettles are used it ordinarily will be most convenient to use one large and two small timpani, but there are exceptions to this. Place the kettle that sounds best on the extreme high tones on the right, the second small kettle in the center, and the large drum on the left. By arranging the three kettles in a semicircle, the pedals and playing surfaces can be kept within easy reach of the player.

When four timpani are needed, they should be arranged in the form of a half-circle in order to bring the pedals and the playing surfaces of all drums within reach of the timpanist. The kettles should be set close together, but not so close that one will actually contact another. Unfortunately, the four available timpani will not always constitute a matched set of four different sizes. In this case, the two center drums should be the best of the four, as the bulk of the playing will likely be done on these inside kettles. The two outside drums, particularly if they are of the hand-tuned type, often can be preset to the highest and lowest tones of the composition and used for only these tones. This practice cannot always be followed, however, particularly in certain modern works which demand a large number of tuning changes throughout the entire register.

PLAYING POSITIONS

Most players prefer to stand while playing the timpani. The correct standing position is shown in Figures 6.14 and 6.15. Note that the player leans somewhat forward. An erect standing position does not permit adequate leverage and balance. The taller the player the more he will have to lean forward to maintain this balance.

Figure 6.15. Playing position, side view.

Figure 6.16. Seated playing position.

Figure 6.14. Playing position, front view.

A timpani stool is required in certain situations, particularly when the part calls for two simultaneous changes of tuning necessitating the use of both feet on the pedals at the same time. In other compositions there may occur only sporadic single notes for the timpani, and a stool is a help in reducing the fatigue which comes from standing during long rests. Few timpanists play everything, or nearly everything, from a seated position. If a stool is used

Figure 6.17. Timpani on tripods tilted for standing playing position.

it should be high enough to bring the seat portion up to the same level as the rim of the kettledrums. Some players use a stool and play from a seated position in music which

Figure 6.18. Timpani on tripods, seated position.

Figure 6.19. German handhold.

Figure 6.20. French handhold.

is not technically demanding, but leave the stool for a standing position which will permit better leverage when the going gets rough.

The types of kettledrums which are mounted on detachable tripods can be titled to bring them into a position for either standing or sitting. However, these are rather obsolete models and are rapidly disappearing.

TIMPANI STICK HANDHOLDS

There are two contrasting schools of timpani technique each of which employs its own style of holding the sticks. It should be said, however, that there is a great deal of latitude within each of the two main schools. For convenience in referring to these two main styles we can designate them as "French" and "German," although to do so may not be entirely accurate. The German school holds its sticks "overhand," in the manner of the R snare drumstick. The forearm and wrist are held comparatively straight. The French style involves grasping the timpani stick with the thumb on top of the stick, fingers curled loosely around the underside. This method depends largely on suppleness of wrist and finger action. Soft volume rolls are made by alternately squeezing and releasing the fingers as they curl around the handle of the stick. A number of American players have adopted a style of holding the sticks and making the timpani stroke which is a cross between the two extremes. It is recommended that the beginning student learn the German handhold first, as this is used by a majority of players for most notes of moderate and loud volumes. The French handhold is useful when making a very soft roll, but this is a later refinement in technique which does not concern the beginner.

In teaching the German handhold the following stepwise procedure is recommended:

1. Grasp each stick at a point about ⅓ of the way up from the butt end with the thumb running parallel to the stick and opposed by the first joint of the forefinger. The strength of the grip on the stick is controlled almost entirely by the thumb and forefinger.
2. Curl the second, ring, and little fingers loosely around the stick. The little finger should not touch the wood. These fingers serve to guide the stick, and activate certain very small motions of the stick. They remain in light contact with the stick by opening up, or giving way, as the stick makes its backswing prior to a loud stroke.
3. Practice throwing the wrists forward and back while holding the sticks in the foregoing manner, simulating the action which will be used later to make the stroke on the timpani.

THE BASIC SINGLE STROKE

The first class or individual exercises for the timpani stroke can be done on practice pads or any drumhead. It is not absolutely necessary to have the timpani to play on at first, although it would be desirable. Using the so-called German handhold, the first study should be the alternating of slow strokes. Both the R and the L work alike. Raise the arm in a relaxed manner, elbow first, followed by the wrist, and finally the hand. The ball of the stick should lag behind. This "up-phase" of the stroke is done slowly, but starting at the top of the downswing the velocity of the beater ball increases rapidly until it reaches its maximum speed and force at impact. Figures 6.21, 6.22 and 6.23 show the path of the arm, hand and stick in making a full stroke with the R. The L is identical. The natural rebound from the timpani head should be absolutely free. Any continued downward pressure on the head will cause a muffling of the tone. *Tone* is ever the watchword in timpani playing! A useful concept is to think of *drawing the tone out of the drum* rather than pounding it in. Only by making a resilient stroke and allowing a free rebound of the sticks can this concept be realized.

It must be realized that the above procedure uses exaggerated and excessive motions in order to teach the concepts and movements involved to the beginning student. These motions must be refined and considerably reduced as the student progresses. The wrist's snap-like action is the key to good timpani strokes whether they be loud or soft.

Figure 6.21. Backswing.

Figure 6.22. Start of downswing.

Figure 6.23. Impact.

STICKWORK

The general rule for stickwork in timpani playing is: when alternating between the high and low drum, use the R on the high drum and the L on the low. In passages which stay on one or the other kettles, alternate sticking also may be used. In actual practice, however, there is a wide variation in the stickwork employed in similar situations by different players. Many timpanists prefer to use a great deal of repetition of the same stick when playing certain kinds of figures on one drum, for example, in a series of triplets at slow tempo, where all notes are of equal volume.

It is felt that a more even tone and volume production can be maintained in this manner. This approach is, perhaps, better left to the professional rather than the beginner. In rapid tempi also, doubling of sticks will be easier to execute than cross-sticking. For example:

sticking. For example:

The cross-sticking given in the foregoing example would be needlessly awkward. The timpanist occasionally will run across situations which demand that one stick be crossed over the other, but when there is an alternative it should be used.

The following examples illustrate recommended and alternate stickwork in a variety of typical timpani passages.

1. In D, A

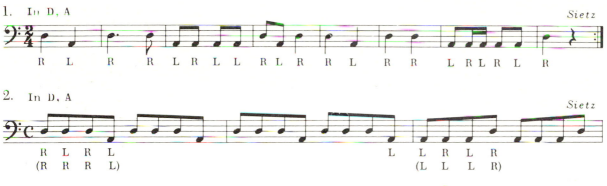

2. In D, A

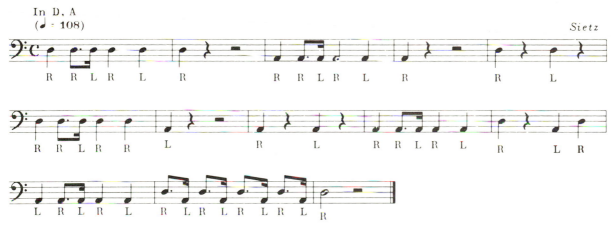

3. Sietz' original stick indications are in parentheses in Study #2. Unless the tempo be very fast, the alternated sticking is just as good.

   In D, A
   (♩ = 108)

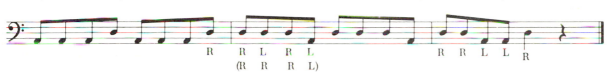

4. The bracketed figures must be perceived as units to avoid cross-overs in Study #4.

   In D, A
   Slowly (♩ = 104)

Hochzeitmarch from Midsummer Nights Dream Music

5. In C, G

rit.

6. In C, F
   Allegro

7. In A, E

Symphony No. 7

   Vivace

Beethoven

8. In E, B
   Allegro

DAMPING

The timpanist must know how to damp the ringing tone of the timpani which, if allowed to vibrate, will sustain for a surprisingly long time. Damping is done with the hand opposite the one which plays the note to be damped. A firm downward pressure near the center of the

Figure 6.24. Damping with opposite hand.

timpani head is required, as shown in Figure 6.24. A circular motion around the center of the head with the extended fingertips of the hand will also serve to damp the tone of the timpani.

Only on staccato, sharply accented, or *sfz* notes should the tone be damped very suddenly. Usually it is best to allow the tone to ring at least for the duration of the note's written value. In some cases the tone should be left to vibrate freely regardless of its written value, for example:

This and similar passages require the timpanist to exercise his best musical judgment. Experience with a variety of literature is necessary to bring maturity of interpretation. A good policy for the beginning kettledrummer would be to damp:

1. those notes which seem to clash with the succeeding harmony;

Figure 6.25. Damping with same hand.

2. those notes which precede general rests or pauses;
3. fermatas and final notes at the conductor's cut-off.

In fast moving passages when there is not time to damp with the opposite hand, an alternative is to damp with the hand which holds the stick. Contact the head with the tips of the fingers. Do not let any part of the stick touch the head. This method of damping is shown in Figure 6.25.

The word "coperto" (pl. "coperti") means to muffle the head of the kettledrum by covering a segment of it with a piece of soft cloth such as felt or baize. American scores usually use the indication "muffle" or "muffle with a cloth" to mean the same thing. The effect of such muffling is a deadening of the natural tone of the timpani. The piece of cloth should be placed on the head at a point opposite to the playing spot. The degree to which the tone is muffled is dependent upon the size and weight of the fabric used for the purpose, and where the fabric is placed (center, edge, etc.).

Figure 6.26. Timpani coperto.

The timpano mute, though no more than a minor adjunct to timpani performance, is a necessary part of the player's equipment. Unfortunately, few college-level timpanists use mutes, and very few high school students use them. The reason for this may be that, until recently, commercially made timpani mutes were simply not available. However, in recent years, major symphony orchestra percussionists such as Vic Firth (Boston Symphony) and Al Payson (Chicago Symphony) have designed and made available timpani mutes which are far easier to use than the plain cloth mentioned earlier. Figure 6.27 shows a Firth timpano mute.

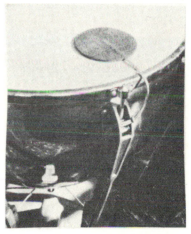

Courtesy Vic Firth

Figure 6.27. Firth timpano mute.

The mute serves a dual purpose: that of a damper, as well as that of a mute. The terms damp and muffle may be considered to be synonymous in that the intention is to place the finger-tips on a resonating head to stop the tone. This prevents the head of the drum from ringing through the rests. To damp means to completely stop the vibration of the membrane. To mute means to partially damp the head while it is being played, in other words, to serve the same function as a violin mute or trumpet mute. The mute is most often used as a damper to prevent a drumhead from vibrating sympathetically with other sounds. This is done during a rehearsal or concert on a drum which is not being used for an extended period of time. For compositions in which timpani are tacet, all the drums should be damped; otherwise, the sympathetic vibrations might be audible (and distracting) to other players in close proximity. Under certain circumstances, these sympathetic vibrations might be audible to the audience and result in an indistinct "hum" being a source of distraction and possible annoyance to the audience.

The Italian term *muta* (sometimes confused with mute) is the indication for a change of tuning in the orchestral parts for timpani. For instance, *muta* in G/d means that two timpani should be tuned in G and in d.

THE TIMPANI ROLL

The timpani roll is produced by a rapid alternation of single strokes. In this respect it resembles the roll of the xylophone and marimba. The objective is to produce a steady tone, with a very minimum of stick sound (impact of beater-ball and head). The under-lying physical principle of the timpani roll is: *the head is set in motion by the initial impact of the stick on the head, and then this vibration is reinforced at the same point in its vibrational path by succeeding impacts.* Stated another way, the sticks' impacts must be *in phase* with the rate of vibration of the timpani head. From a practical standpoint, what this means is that the rate of roll alternation must be more rapid for high tones than for low ones. The steady and even flow of tone exemplified in the roll of the expert timpanist is made possible only by great care in the timing of the alternating strokes. If there is too rapid a rate of alternations a choked tone will result; with too slow a rate there will be "holes" in the sound.

Rolls on the kettledrum require a little accenting on the first stroke in order to establish the tone precisely on the beat. If the roll is tied over and/or ends *on* a beat, a definitive final stroke is also required. Both sticks must traverse equal arcs in order to produce sounds of equal volume. Arm, wrist, and hand muscles should be relaxed and supple. The concept to be kept uppermost in mind is "draw the tone out of the drum." A feeling of freedom of rebound goes hand in hand with the development of a feeling for proper roll speed. "Let the sticks do the work" is a useful idea in timpani playing as well as in snare drumming.

For rolls at *p* or *pp* volume, use the French handhold previously described. The alternating stick motions are activated by the squeezing and releasing of the fingers as they curl under the handles. See Figure 6.28. A lighter touch for very soft rolls is more possible through this method than is usually possible with the so-called German style, although individual preference may govern the eventual choice.

In the case of a crescendo roll, starting at *p* or *pp* level, the player can begin the roll with the thumb-on-top finger roll, and as the volume is increased switch gradually to the overhand (German) position. The latter is naturally a more powerful position and better adapted to loud playing.

In the decrescendo, it will be found somewhat awkward to switch from the overhand to the thumb-on-top handhold without perceptibly interrupting the flow of the alternations. The student should practice the decrescendo roll using the German position "all the way down."

Figure 6.29. Timpani roll, **mf** volume.

Legato rolls are very common in timpani music. When a slur mark is used to connect rolls of different pitch, a special trick will help the player to effect a smooth connection when moving from one kettle to another, as in the figure:

The trick is simply to move one stick to the next kettle on the beat while the other stick remains to finish out the tone. The lead stick, when moving from the high to the low drum, will be the L. When moving from the low to

Figure 6.28. Timpani roll, **pp** volume.

Figure 6.30. Timpani, **f** volume.

the high kettle the R stick goes first. The lead stick starts the tone with its initial blow and thus gives the illusion that the roll has already begun, when actually it takes about half a second before the second stick can be brought into position and the true alternations of the roll begin. Legato rolls are encountered so often in timpani parts that it will repay the student to master the technique just described through careful practice.

Another roll commonly found in timpani parts is the forte-piano (fp) roll such as:

This is so often played incorrectly and it is a very simple matter to execute properly. The secret is to let the drum do the work for you. Don't fight it as so many timpanists do. To produce this roll properly, strike the drum with a strong stroke. Permit the vibrations created to die away until the sound reaches the degree of softness desired. When this point is reached, resume rolling again to maintain the desired level of softness (or gradually crescend as in example two above).

TUNING THE TIMPANI

It can be stated without fear of contradiction that tuning is the most difficult aspect of timpani playing. No matter what type of kettledrum is used, securing good intonation will be the timpanist's major problem. Several factors are involved. First of all, the kettledrum tone is not a pure tone, but a complex one from an acoustical standpoint. The complexity of the overtone structure varies from one kettle to another, from one point to another on the surface of one head, and from low to high notes on the same kettle. One difficulty lies in the ease with which timpani heads vibrate sympathetically to a variety of frequencies. Notes which sound in tune to the timpanist when played with the other instruments often sound out of tune on a solo entrance. Another factor, probably unrecognized in most cases, is the acoustical property of the stage, hall or rehearsal room. Sometimes a place which is "dead" acoustically will make accurate tuning all but impossible, to the great consternation of the timpanist. The resonance of timpani bowls is another factor, since some notes will be more easily obtainable than others due to the shape of the bowls. Under certain conditions a needed note may seem to lie at a particularly nonresonant point in the timpani range, and will therefore be difficult to tune accurately.

The one general principle for tuning any timpani is: *the tension must be kept equal at all points around the perimeter of the head if a clear tone is to result.*

The student will require some reference device to obtain his pitch unless he happens to be blessed with absolute pitch. A circular pitch pipe is recommended for the beginner, although the one or two octave transpositions are somewhat of a problem to some students. For students who have well-developed relative pitch, an A 440 tuning fork is all that should be necessary. General musicianship studies such as melodic and harmonic dictation, solfeggio, and related studies are requisite for the high school and college timpanist who expects to develop himself fully. For young students, the most practical method of objectifying pitch relationships is the use of the sol-fa syllables. Unfortunately for many young percussionists, the elementary school music curriculum does not include the learning of syllables in many districts at present. The instructor in this case will probably find that time spent at the beginning of tuning study in learning the rudiments of syllable singing will be time well spent, for without some groundwork in pitch relationships most beginners will find timpani tuning completely impossible. The relation of *do* to *sol*, and *fa* to *do* must be established in the first stages of timpani tuning study. All of the intervals must eventually be mastered.

Before any timpano head can be played upon it must be put in tune with itself, i.e., it must be tensioned so that it produces the same frequency of vibration at each point around its perimeter. All types of kettledrums have handles or keys by which tension can be applied to the counterhoop, and it is by means of these handles or keys that the head can be put into tune with itself. Hand-tuned drums have no additional means of regulating the tension. When making this preliminary tuning, adjust the handles to bring their areas of the head to the pitch of the portion selected as the playing spot.

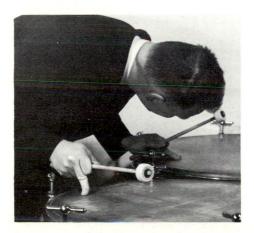

Figure 6.31. Timpanist in position to testing tuning.

The best way to test the tuning at each handle is to flick the middle fingertip sharply on the timpani head to set up a vibration which can be heard at close range, but is unaudible a distance away. There is a knack to listening for the fundamental tone of the timpani. At the moment of impact many overtones will be heard. The true fundamental isolates itself from the aggregate sound as a "ringing" tone *slightly after* the moment of impact. The player must crouch over to bring his ear close to the edge of the timpani head to hear the ring that is made by the finger-flick. See Figure 6.31. For beginners, it is recommended that they first hum the pitch to themselves before matching it on the drum.

If hand-tuned timpani are available it is recommended that tuning study begin on them. To prepare the hand-tuned timpani for playing tune the low drum to *A* and the high drum to *d* 𝄢 The usual procedure is to grasp a pair of handles at once, one with each hand in the following order:

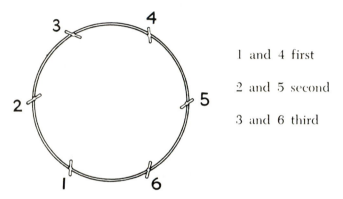

Figure 6.32. Diagram of numbered tuning handles.

1 and 4 first

2 and 5 second

3 and 6 third

Practice will show the approximate amount of turn needed at each handle to tune the various intervals. It is a good plan to try to tune rapidly enough so that the ring which results from the finger-flick can be heard rising or falling in pitch.

To settle the head after tuning, make a quick circular motion around the drumhead with the hand, using a downward pressure. This will tend to lower the pitch a little but will prevent the head from going flat while it is being played upon. To compensate for this flatting, tune slightly sharp before settling the head.

The essential feature of all pedal tuning devices is that a downward pressure of the toe on the foot pedal *raises* the pitch, and an upward movement (toe up—heel down) of the pedal causes the head to slacken and thus *lowers* the pitch. To prepare the pedal timpani for playing, the heads of both kettles should be set at their extreme low notes. For the 28″ kettle, release the pedal pressure by putting the heel to its lowest position. Now tune the head to the low *F* (low E on the 29″) by means of the tuning

handles. This creates the proper amount of tension on the head, enabling it to sound its best throughout its range. The tone of the timpani will not be full and resonant unless great care is taken to tune the extreme low notes accurately preparatory to the rehearsal or performance. The 25″ kettle is set at its low note, B♭, A on the 26″, by the method just described.

The pedal-tuning operation is somewhat simpler than hand-tuning in that the three tuning steps are accomplished with one movement of the foot pedal. Otherwise, however, the techniques are the same. The player must set the head ringing by the finger-flick, listen at a point near the head, and arrest the foot motion at the instant the pitch of the timpani's ring has reached the new pitch. It is usually easier to approach the new note from below when tuning with the pedal, in the manner of the string player's tuning procedure. Approaching a note from below also seems to set the head better, resulting in a truer pitch because the head has less tendency to pound flat.

Rotary timpani are tuned by turning the bowls clockwise to raise the pitch and counterclockwise to lower it. Grasp one or two of the tuning handles to turn the kettle. Notes at the upper end of the register require quite a lot of torsion to be exerted because of the resistance of the taut head, so the kettle sometimes must be steadied while turning. Familiarity with a particular set of rotary timpani enables the player to learn the approximate amount of turn needed to tune the various intervals. One model, recommended for school use, has a pointer and preset tabs around the edge of the counterhoop to indicate where to stop the rotation for each note. This model is shown in Figure 6.5.

As a guide to instruction in beginning the study of timpani tuning, there follows a set of stepwise procedures for making each tuning change.

1. Set starting note.
2. Play until tuning change indicated. Damp last note.
3. To change note, flick head with finger, ear close to timpani.
4. Hum, or think, next note.
5. Turn handles, adjust pedal, or rotate bowl until new note is reached. Tune slightly sharp.
6. Settle head.
7. Play new note.
8. Check accuracy of tuning; adjust if necessary. (A good way for beginners to check pitch accuracy is to have them softly sing or hum the pitch into the head. If the head is in tune, it will resonate sympathetically.)

Take time to tune each interval accurately at first. Students should practice with the aim of reducing the time needed to accomplish the foregoing steps. Most good method books for the timpani devote a number of exercises to the problem of making tuning changes. In these studies, as well as in most actual music, the direction to change note will occur during a long rest. See example below:

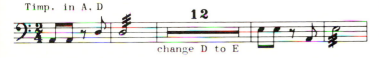

Timp. in A, D

change D to E

In such an actual musical context the player must maintain the count while at the same time accomplishing the steps of his tuning change. Needless to say, this demands a real power of concentration.

A mechanical aid to timpani tuning has been on the market for a number of years. The so-called *tuning gauges* attach to the inner sides of the timpani bowls, and consist of rods which move up and down with the action of the pedals and pivoted indicators activated by the pedal motions which point to preset note tabs. A pair are shown in Figure 6.3. Although somewhat expensive (approximately $60 each for the conventional type and up to $175 each for the newer deluxe type), these gauges are not recommended for use with calfskin timpani heads because they are too inaccurate. Once set to the pedal tuning of low *F* for the large drum, for example, then any variation in atmospheric conditions would throw off all the readings on the gauge. Any experienced timpanist will vouch for the fact that these changes do occur, and often suddenly, as in an auditorium where ventilation is accomplished by opening of stage doors, side doors, etc. Air conditioned halls, theaters, and auditoriums are likewise subject to minute-by-minute fluctuations in the relative humidity. Tuning gauges could be an aid in tuning timpani equipped with weatherproof plastic heads. They could be very useful for training young players as well as for saving time for the instructor, but it should always be borne in mind that the final arbiter is the *ear*. Students using timpani with tuning gauges should be taught not to depend completely upon the readings of the gauges, but to *listen* at all times. The speed at which the pedal is raised or lowered, or the bowl rotated, can affect the accuracy with which the gauge measures the tension on the head. Gauges can be of some use to the timpanist in coping with the problem of making many rapid tuning changes in a limited amount of time where approximate accuracy would be superior to guesswork. It is chiefly in such emergency situations that the tuning gauges are used by professional timpanists. Although some tuning gauges appear to be more accurate than others, one is reminded that no tuning gauge actually measures pitch; rather, the tuning gauge only measures a distance of movement of some portion of the tuning mechanism, depending upon the type of tuning gauge.

NOTATION

Timpani music is written in the F clef, sounding as written. The one exception occurs in some editions of certain Baroque and early Classic works, where the early custom of writing all timpani parts for the tonic and dominant notes as *C* and *G* is still followed. In each such case the actual pitches are clearly specified at the beginning of the first line of music. Most timpani parts specify the

written:

Timp. in D, A

sounding:

Timp. in D, A

starting notes for each kettledrum at the top of the page and/or the beginning of the first line. There is no standard order, however, and this can be confusing. A helpful aid is the staff with the actual pitches clearly shown. If such

Timp. in B♭, E♭, F   Timp. in F♯, B, E, F♯

an indication is not printed on the page, it is a simple matter to draw one in in pencil at the top of the page. If succeeding movements of a composition require different settings, these should be pencilled in at the start of each movement.

Unfortunately, there is not yet a standard method of indicating retunings, especially within a movement of a composition, and there is a difference of opinion as to how they should be written. One method entails the assignment of Roman numerals to each timpano. The drums would be numbered from left to right, the lowest being (I). This method appears the most logical, as we are accustomed to thinking from the left to the right, and associating low to high. However, some composers using this type of system have been known to number the drums from right to left, which can be quite confusing.

Occasionally, when a retuning involves a wide interval, there can be some doubt as to whether this is upwards or downwards. This can be clarified as follows:

An alternative method of indicating retuning, which combines the elements of clarity and simplicity, involves writing the pitch letter names, i.e., A-C-E-G. Then, when one or more of the pitches requires change, it can be indicated by simply circling it. Thus, the tuning above could become A-C-(F)-G. The circle can greatly enhance and facilitate retuning because it serves to draw attention to the new pitch.

Abbreviations for timpani are timp. or tp. The word timpani is derived from the Greek "tympanon" and the Latin "tympanum" meaning a small hand drum. In the Middle Ages the name meant kettledrum. The Italian form, "timpani" (singular "timpano"), and the term "kettledrum" are in most common usage today. The words "tympani", "timpany", and "tympany" are incorrect as Italian terms, there being no letter Y in the Italian alphabet. For the foreign equivalents, see the table of foregin language percussion terms in Chapter 2.

Rolls for the timpani are indicated by three slanted dashes through the note stem:  . The final note of a tied-over roll is the concluding sound of that roll:  . One slanted dash through a note stem means to divide that note into eighth notes; two slanted dashes—sixteenth notes. In some classic scores three dashes must be interpreted as thirty-second notes, *not* a roll. The famous passage from Beethoven's *Ninth Symphony* quoted is an example at the bottom of the page.

In older music rolls are often indicated by means of the trill sign:

However, the use of the trill is rather inaccurate as a symbol for a timpano roll inasmuch as a trill is actually a musical ornament consisting of the rapid alternation of a given tone with the diatonic second above it.

Grace notes are not uncommon in timpani writing. When they are encountered they should be played with single sticking:

Tremolos between two tones are indicated thus:

In this case the roll is simply split between the two kettles. Notation of glissandi should be properly understood.

In example one above, the F is struck and the pedal depressed until the B♭ is reached and then the head is damped. If the glissando is notated as in the second example above, the F is struck and the pedal is depressed. When the B♭ is reached, it is also struck and then the head is damped. In other words, if the note on which the glissando concludes is a grace note, only the first note is struck; however, if both the first and last notes are written as full value notes, then both get a separate attack.

TRICKS OF THE TIMPANIST'S TRADE

When it is necessary to change the tuning of one or more timpani during the course of a composition, it is a great help if the new note or notes can be picked out from the general sound to serve as cues. These cues can then

Symphony No. 9   Beethoven

be pencilled into the part at the points during rests and tacet portions of the piece.

In tonal music it is usually possible to get adequate cues to ensure that the drums can be kept in good tune. In compositions where the tonality shifts rapidly or in atonal compositions, the timpanist will be on his own, so to speak, and must use any and every aid available as pitch reference.

An "ear" for timpani tuning can be trained, but the novice can be easily discouraged by the slow rate of progress. Listening intently to the progressions of harmony and melody at all times is the best way to develop the ear. As has been mentioned, the formal study of solfeggio, with copious amounts of dictation, is a great help in training the timpanist to tune accurately. Even such relatively simple devices as memorizing the sound of intervals by identifying them in familiar tunes is a real help. Use of the sol-fa syllables has also been mentioned as a useful device. For the beginner, the first step in ear training is to match tones with the singing voice or hum tone. A piano or other bass register instrument can be utilized to sound the tones, which can first be matched by the voice, later by the timpani following the procedure of tuning. The ideal timpani student may be one who has had previous training in piano, marimba or xylophone.

It is very helpful to the timpanist to be able to think, hum, or sing a reliable *A* at any time. Practice with an *A* fork or pitch pipe should be started early and continued until the student can remember the sound and reproduce it at any time. Some students will experience great difficulty in learning to do this, others will find it quite easy. One aid for the orchestra timpanist is to associate the memory of *A* with the sound of the open *A* as it predominates when string instruments tune up. For *A*, the next most useful note is probably small *d*, a fourth above.

It will often be found useful to preset the outer kettle, or kettles, when more than a pair are used, to the extremes of the range required in a given composition. Thus, if the lowest note needed is *E* and the highest *g,* the timpanist should tune the lowest kettle (extreme L) to sound *E* when its pedal is in heel-down position, and the highest kettle (extreme R) to sound *g* when the pedal is in toe-down position. He will then be reasonably close to these notes when the pedals are moved back to these positions, should they have to be changed during intervening parts of the composition.

The placement of the timpani in the symphony orchestra has not been the subject of serious acoustical study. Expediency is usually the criterion for placement. The author would tend to agree with White, who advocates that the timpani be placed near the trumpets and French horns. In music of the Baroque, Classical, and to some extent the Romantic periods, the kettledrums formed a sort of bass register to brass parts. The timpani, even in more modern works, often enter with the brasses, and many of their rhythmic figures are identical. For this reason alone the idea of placing the kettledrums alongside, or directly behind, the brasses merits consideration. The timpani should *not* be placed next to the bass drum, as the large heads of each tend to pick up much unwanted sound through sympathetic vibration.

Round fibre or padded thin wooden head protectors should be kept over the heads of the timpani when they are not in use. If a four-kettle set-up is employed and the composition being played requires that only the two inner kettles be used, leave the fibre head covers *on* the outer drums to keep their heads from ringing sympathetically.

When the school music instructor identifies a student as showing aptitude and probable talent for timpani playing, he should lose no time in placing the student under the guidance of the best private timpani instructor in the area. The mastery of these demanding instruments is a lifetime of study and entails in nearly every case serious private study with an expert teacher. This is very important, even if it involves travel to a distant city for lessons. Perhaps extra long lessons only once or twice per month are still far better than no lessons whatsoever. In addition to private study with a capable professional timpanist, it will also prove very helpful for the student to study recordings and scores to really discover how the timpani parts actually fit into various compositions.

Finally, readers of this fourth edition *Guide* are encouraged to read the doctoral dissertation of the author of the edition at hand. The dissertation is really a treatise on timpani, though the actual title may be somewhat deceptive. Full information is provided in the bibliography located at the end of the *Guide*.

Notes

1. J. Fred Seitz, *Modern School of Timpani Playing* (Elkhart, IN: Leedy Mfg. Co., 1943).
2. Charles L. White, *Drums Through the Ages* (Los Angeles: Sterling Press, 1960).

CHAPTER 7

Other Percussion Instruments

THE TRIANGLE

The triangle is the most frequently used of the small percussion instruments often referred to as "traps." It is an ancient instrument, often depicted in early Renaissance paintings being played by angels and members of heavenly choirs. These paintings usually show the triangle as having three or more circular jingles attached to the lower leg of the triangle. This early form of the triangle was known as a *cymbale,* and represented an intermediate step in the development of the triangle from its ancestor, the *sistrum,* an instrument developed in ancient Egypt consisting of a frame with handle and thin metal rods which would rattle when the instrument was shaken. The triangle in its present form came into use in the orchestra in the early years of the eighteenth century. Both Haydn and Mozart scored for the triangle, and both employed the instrument to lend a Near-Eastern coloration to certain passages. The bass drum, cymbals and triangle were adopted into the orchestra originally to obtain the effects of the Turkish music which was having considerable influence on European composers of the eighteenth century.

Much tonal variation is possible from the triangle, and is dependent upon the weight of the beater used, the spot struck, and the kind of stroke. Each triangle has its own distinctive set of frequencies, which consist of clashing upper partials of the unheard fundamental. The best triangle tone does not exhibit any definite pitch, but only a shimmering metallic quality which has considerable brilliance. The tone of a triangle has the ability to cut through the total orchestral texture, even when played very softly.

Triangles are made in a variety of sizes, from tiny 3" models to the 12" to 14" large sizes. Their diameters may vary from about 1/4" to 1/2", the 7/16th" diameter being the most popular for smaller triangles. Plated steel is used for both the triangle and the beater. In public school situations, the most common error noted in relation to triangle and beater selection is the using of too large a size.

In school bands and orchestras where one triangle must do general duty the recommended size is the 8" model. This triangle is large enough to produce the heavier tones when needed, yet light tones are possible by the

Figure 7.1. Triangle.

use of light beaters and light strokes. The symphony orchestra percussion equipment should include a 6" and a 10" triangle in addition to one or more around 8" in size. When selecting triangles the purchaser should be governed more by the sounds obtainable than mere dimensions. Although professional quality triangles and beaters (such as Alan Abel, Danmar, Grover, Latin Percussion, Perdell, Andrew Feldman, Stoessel) represent a somewhat larger initial expenditure, the investment will result in increased durability and superior tone quality.

The usual triangle beater is a steel rod about nine inches long. The weights vary, and it is recommended that at least three to five different weights be available to the player. Perdell makes a set of five pair of matched beaters in a handy denim case for carrying and storage protection. Experimentation will show which sizes work best for a particular triangle. The triangle will not sound good if it is struck with wood, such as a snare drumstick. However, this is called for sometimes, as a special effect.

An extremely important item is a good device for holding the triangle. The commercial holder consists of a metal clamp which attaches to the music stand and has a loop of gut from which to suspend the triangle so that it will be at the correct angle for easy playing. Unless a very thin gut string is used, there will be considerable deadening of the tone. A discarded violin gut *D* or *G* string is right for the purpose. A very satisfactory triangle holder can be made from a wooden clothes pin, or the clamp section of the clip used to keep music from blowing off music stands. See Figure 7.1. Drill two small holes about an inch apart in the underside of the clothes pin or clip to accommodate the loop of gut. Secure a piece of gut string to form a loop which will suspend the triangle about one inch below the clamp. The advantage of such a holder is that it can be removed from its place on the music rack and replaced after playing easily and quickly.

Another useful type of triangle holder can be made from the base section of the common collapsible music stand. A metal rod of the same diameter as the upper section of the music stand, three to four feet long and bent to a right angle at the top, forms the upper section for this handy type of holder. Two holes must be drilled near the end of the angled rod through which the gut loop can pass. The great advantage of the floor stand triangle holder is that it permits the player to use two beaters, yet still maintains the triangle in a position which is both convenient and high enough so that the tone will carry.

When the triangle is played it should be held up in front of the player about chest high. Only in emergency, when there is not time to take the triangle off the music stand, should the triangle be left clamped to the stand. The tone of the triangle will project well if it is unimpeded by music stands and the backs of seated musicians. Figure 7.2 shows the best method of holding the triangle in playing position.

Notation for the triangle varies considerably. In composite scoring, where snare drum, bass drum, cymbals, triangle, etc., are all printed on one or two staves, the triangle notes are usually placed on the upper line or in the upper space of the top staff. In most cases notes to be played on the triangle will be clearly marked *triangle, tri.,* or *trgl.* Sometimes the noteheads will be x-shaped to set them off from snare drum notes on the same staff. If a tie or slur mark extends after a triangle note, allow the tone to ring. Staccato dots are often used to indicate that the tone of the triangle should be damped quickly. Rolls are indicated by three slanted dashes through the note stem or under or over whole notes, or by the trill sign.

The usual playing spot is the outside of the right leg of the triangle, but triangles vary in this respect, and the player must determine by experimentation the optimum playing spot for the particular triangle. There is no rule or custom to prohibit the use of any spot on the triangle if it produces a good tone. Assuming that the triangle is held in the left hand and played with the right, then the most convenient playing surfaces would be the inside of the lower leg and the outside of the right leg.

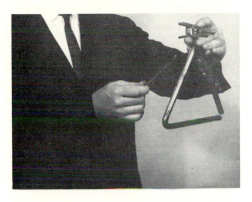

Figure 7.2. Triangle playing position.

A light wrist motion should be used in striking the triangle. The tone should be drawn out of the instrument. The sound to avoid is a clang which sounds like a dinner bell, or a roll which sounds like a fire gong. Such poor tones from triangles are all too common, and are due to using too heavy a beater, too heavy a stroke, or both.

Damping is possible by the R finger tips or can be done with the fingers of the L hand while holding the clamp. A light contact of the fingertips is sufficient to stop the tone.

The triangle roll is produced either by a series of quick wrist motions with the beater held close to a corner of the triangle or by the use of two beaters on the outside legs of the instrument. The upper corner is easier, as the beater is not working against gravity as it would be in one of the lower corners. The wrist shake must be well controlled so that the force of the alternating contacts of the beater with the legs of the triangle will be equal. The single strokes will produce a good sounding roll if they are rapidly executed. See Figure 7.3. In the two-beater method, a certain disadvantage lies in the fact that the triangle will have to remain clamped to the music stand and cannot be brought up to its best playing position. See Figure 7.4. In such a situation the floor stand triangle holder would solve the problem.

Figure 7.3. Triangle roll.

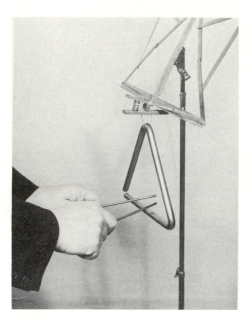

Figure 7.4. Triangle roll, two beaters.

TIPS FOR GOOD TRIANGLE PLAYING

1. Avoid too large a triangle or beater.
2. Hold triangle at proper height (between chest and eye level) so sound will project.
3. Do not grasp beater with all fingers. Use thumb and index finger.
4. Use a thin gut or nylon string to suspend triangle.
5. For small, *piano* sounds use tip of beater.
6. A tapered beater is most useful for executing a crescendo roll. Start at tip for *piano* and progress to thicker diameter of beater as roll crescends.
7. For very rapid rhythmic passages use suspended triangle with two beaters which are matched.
8. Always have concept of drawing tone out.

There are two generally accepted striking spots which will result in the following sounds:

for "ping" sound

for "shimmer" sound

Rolls can also be executed by rapidly alternating the beater between the base and the side.

THE TAMBOURINE

The tambourine is probably the most ubiquitous percussion instrument in the history of civilization. Prior to its introduction into the symphony orchestra it was used in most nations in all corners of the globe. Evidence of early use can be found in Egypt, China, Peru, Greenland, Britain, Babylon, Greece, Arabia and many other countries, back to antiquity. Its popularity was perhaps due to the fact that it could be easily carried while playing, making it a popular instrument of the dance. Tambourines had been known from the early second millennium B.C. in Mesopotamia, where they may well have been associated with the cult of the Mother Goddess; the tambourine was almost always associated with women, even in later Greek and Roman times. It consisted in its early forms of a skin stretched over a wooden ring, and was played with the fingers striking the skin. Subsequently, jingles of small bells or metal discs were attached to it. It probably came to Europe late in the twelfth or early thirteenth century. Biblical mention of the timbrel, the old name for the tambourine, can be found in the King James version of the Bible: "Miriam, the prophetess, the sister of Aaron, took a timbrel in her hand; and all the women went out after her with timbrels and with dances." (Exodus 15:20).

The tambourine is a hybrid instrument, being a membrane covered frame drum with metal jingles. Like the triangle, it is an ancient instrument and is thought to have

Figure 7.5. Tambourine.

evolved from the sistrum. Modern tambourines consist of a circular maple shell with apertures cut at equidistant points through which pins are mounted to hold the tiny pairs of plated cymbals, called jingles. One side is covered with a calfskin head, tacked down tautly, and shellacked to make it somewhat impervious to weather conditions. Some tambourines have a double set of jingles mounted on each pin. Diameters vary from 6″ to 10″. Tambourines with plastic heads and head tensioning mechanisms are the most predominantly used instruments. This type of tambourine is pictured in Figures 7.6, 7.7, and 7.9.

A good quality 10″ tambourine with either single or double jingles is recommended for school use when one tambourine is to do general duty. Most of the cheap imported tambourines have flimsy shells which warp or crack easily and heads of inferior quality.

There is no particularly standard way of notating tambourine music. When the percussion parts are printed on one or two staves, the tambourine notes are usually placed on a line or space above the snare drum part. In any case, the notes to be played by the tambourine are clearly indicated by the word *tambourine, tamb., tam.,* at the beginning of the line of music, or at such places as the tambourine enters. Some of the common foreign equivalents for *tambourine* are: *tambour de basque,* (Fr.); *tamburino, tamburo basco,* (It.); *beckentrommel,* (Ger.); and *tamburin,* (Ger.).

To hold the tambourine, grasp the open side of the shell just over the small hole drilled in the shell with the fingers of the left hand. Place the L thumb on the outside of the shell and parallel with the head. Do not put the thumb or a finger in the hole on the side of the shell. For a playing position which will best project the sound to the audience, hold the instrument at almost face level (not above eye level). So many tambourine players, as well as players of the other miscellaneous hand held percussion instruments, insist on playing these instruments at a low, almost subterranean level. Visually and audibly this is poor positioning. Projection to the audience is most important. See Figure 7.6.

There are at least four types of strokes used for executing single strokes on the tambourine.

1. The usual stroke for medium to loud notes is made by forming the fingers and thumb of the R hand into a small tight "ball" of flesh and bringing this sharply into contact with the tambourine head, using a sharp wrist action. See Figure 7.6. It is best to hold the tambourine practically stationary and move the R hand, because to do the reverse will produce many extra jingle sounds as the tambourine is moved. There must be resiliency to the stroke. *Exception:* when the tone must be damped suddenly, the hand should remain in contact with the tambourine and held firmly there for a second or two until the jingles have stopped vibrating.

2. For notes of soft volume, hold the tambourine as in (1), but instead of striking the tambourine with the "ball" of flesh formed by the fingers and thumb, tap the head near the edge with the tips of the first three fingers. See Figure 7.7. A variation of the foregoing stroke, used when very soft notes are needed, is to contact the tambourine head with the heel of the playing hand and tap lightly with the finger tips. This muffles the resonance of the tambourine and aids in controlling the volume. The tambourine solo in the *Danse Arabe* of Tschaikowsky's *Nutcracker Suite* traditionally is played in this manner.

3. When the tambourine part contains soft rhythm figures which are too rapid to execute with a single hand, the tambourine may be placed head side down on the knee, which has been raised by placing the foot on a chair or stool. In this position it is possible to use both hands to play the rhythm pattern.

Figure 7.6. Usual playing position and stroke.

Figure 7.7. Finger-tip stroke.

Figure 7.8. Knee position.

Figure 7.10. Tambourine roll.

Rap the frame of the tambourine with the extended fingers of each hand, in the manner of the bongo player. The instrument is held secure by the weight of the forearms as they rest on its near edge.

A variant of the foregoing method is to place the tambourine head down on the trap table. The tone in this case will be somewhat muffled, but for soft passages it is quite satisfactory.

4. For parts which call for loud volume and rapid strokes, use the raised knee position, grasp the tambourine firmly, and strike the tambourine down on the knee and up against the R hand on alternate notes. Figure 7.9 shows the correct position.

There are two standard roll techniques. For long and/or loud rolls, hold the tambourine in the standard manner, but with the arm straight up, and rotate the wrist as rapidly as possible. If this rotary motion is rapid and well controlled a very satisfactory roll will result. It is the only way to sustain a long trilled note. End the shake with a light tap of the R.

The second method produces a true roll by opposing the extended R thumb tip in a counterclockwise rotary motion around the perimeter of the head near the shell. The thumb works "against the grain," and thus causes a series of fine vibrations which are useful in playing a short and/or soft note which calls for a trill or roll. Moisten the thumb tip with saliva in order to cause enough friction to set up the vibration. Start rotating from the bottom near the L handhold and work up and around as far as it is possible to go, keeping the thumb always at the same angle to the head. The L handhold must be quite firm. As an aid in securing enough friction, some percussionists apply powdered rosin to the outer surface of the tambourine head. It must be applied often, usually before each playing period. Others glue double-O sandpaper around the outer edges of the tambourine head. Probably the best insurance for the thumb roll is to rub the thumb on a cake of the sticking agent used by bank tellers and secretaries. It can be procured at a stationery shop for a few cents a cake.

One of the hazards of tambourine playing is the tendency of the instrument to sound unwanted jingle noises when it is picked up preparatory to its entrance, or when

Figure 7.9. Knee and hand position.

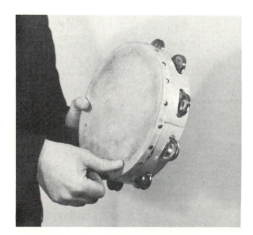

Figure 7.11. Tambourine thumb roll.

replacing it on the trap table after use. Always keep the instrument flat when moving it to minimize extraneous jingle sounds.

THE TAM-TAM (GONG)

The tam-tam, or gong, is of ancient Oriental origin, and until rather recent times was reserved for musical passages with exotic flavor, as in "Orientales" and other descriptive forms. Modern composers use the tam-tam more for the sake of its inherent power to cap a climax or give an electric quality to the orchestral timbre than for any Oriental connotations.

The terms *gong* and *tam-tam* mean the same thing, at least in modern usage. Originally the word tam-tam was derived from an African word meaning simply *drum* (no doubt the same word from which we have derived *tom-tom*). Technically, a gong is a metal plate which emits a definite pitch, but such instruments are rarely used in Western music. The term gong has now become attached to the instrument of indefinite pitch which is also called the tam-tam. It should be pointed out that some scores call for "tuned gongs" and will list the desired notes. Very few organizations have such instruments and, normally, these have to be rented. The term "tuned gong" is proper when referring to these type instruments. The term "tuned tam-tam" is never proper. Conductors and percussionists must be careful to distinguish between *tam-tam* and *tom-tom*, two very unlike instruments with similar names.

The tam-tam is one of the slowest speaking of the instruments. Its sound, when struck a sharp blow, does not appear to reach maximum intensity until a second or two after the blow.

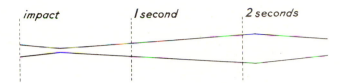

Figure 7.13. Diagram of tam-tam sound showing relationship of time and volume.

Its after-ring, in the case of the large gong of good quality, is extremely long in duration. The amplitude of vibration at the center of the instrument is wide, particularly when it is struck a heavy blow.

Small gongs do not have the crashy tone and long sustentation characteristic of the larger sizes. Some of the best gongs, such as Wuhan authentic Chinese gongs are imported from various areas throughout Asia and are now distributed by leading percussion instrument manufacturers. The Paiste Company is producing beautiful, quality tam-tams and/or gongs. The most popular diameters are 24″, 26″, 28″, 30″, 32″, 34″, and 36″. For young school bands and orchestras the smaller of these sizes is adequate, but for high school, college and professional use a gong at least 28″ in diameter is recommended. Like cymbals, gongs are very expensive, with list prices ranging from $300 to $1500 for the sizes just mentioned. A heavy gong stand of pipe or tubular steel is required to hold the instrument steady. One type consists of a wide multi-legged base with a single supporting upright on which is mounted a circular frame within which the gong hangs. The best type of stand for suspending a heavy gong is the full circular ring stand supported by two feet which are mounted at right angles to the instrument itself.

The tone of a tam-tam is very dependent upon the beater used to strike it. A common type of commercial tam-tam beater has a rather heavy metal handle and a beater ball covered with lamb's wool. The center core of the tam-tam beater is usually weighted with lead in order to give it sufficient weight to bring out the full tone of the instrument. The larger the gong the heavier the beater must be. In addition to the lamb's wool previously mentioned, several kinds of material are used to cover gong beaters. Soft chamois, layers of wool cloth, and felt are often used. For rolls on the tam-tam two beaters somewhat smaller than the beater used for single notes are needed. A pair of bass drum beaters will usually suffice for the purpose, especially if they are wrapped beforehand with a layer of thick felt.

Notation for the tam-tam is not standardized. Because the instrument is used sparingly in most compositions which call for it, the composer or arranger usually labels each note *gong*, *tam-tam*, or *T.T.* The notes usually appear on the lower lines or spaces of the F clef. Occasionally a special kind of notehead, such as a diamond-shape or an *x*, is used to indicate gong notes. A slur or tie

Figure 7.12. Tam-tam.

after a note for the gong means to let the instrument ring beyond its written value at the discretion of the player. The direction "let ring" (in French— "laissez vibré") means to allow the tone to sustain without any damping whatsoever.

The point at which a tam-tam is struck influences the high and low partials that are included in the overall sound-range. A tam-tam struck dead center will produce a deep, sustained sound with the lower partials more predominant. Struck near the edge, a tam-tam sounds more high toned, bright, and "rustling." The higher partials sound out. The optimum playing spot to produce a deep, rich sound, rising gradually, and incorporating the full range of highs and lows is an area found slightly above, below,

Figure 7.14. Impact of the tam-tam stroke.

or to the side of the center. The percussionist must experiment under a variety of playing conditions and with a variety of beaters to determine the best playing spot on a particular tam-tam.

The stroke on the tam-tam is much like that used for the bass drum. The beater is grasped in the same manner as the bass drum's, with the thumb on top of the handle. For very light strokes only the wrist is needed, but for most gong tones the forearm is also brought into play. The concept of drawing the tone out of the instrument is particularly applicable in the case of the tam-tam. The player must be thoroughly familiar with his instrument in order to know how much force to use to obtain the various volume levels. A small variation in the force of the blow may result in a big difference in volume.

If there is opportunity to do so, the gong should be "warmed up" just before its entrance by brushing it lightly with the beater to start the vibration in advance of the actual note. This warming-up makes volume control a bit easier and also tends to cause the gong to speak more quickly after the impact.

The tam-tam roll is made with two beaters held in the manner of the two beaters used in the bass drum roll. Single strokes are alternated, more slowly than in the bass drum roll.

The tam-tam can be damped gradually or suddenly, depending upon the musical context. To damp the gong gradually, run the hand opposite to the beater hand slowly across the back surface of the gong. If the note to be damped in this manner is very loud, both hands will be required, one brushing against the back and one against the front. To damp the gong suddenly, press both hands against the front and back of the instrument at its center. To damp very loud crashes suddenly, one or both knees can be utilized to contact the vibrating gong. Figure 7.15 shows the gong being damped in the ordinary manner. Figure 7.16 illustrates the manner of damping with the knees.

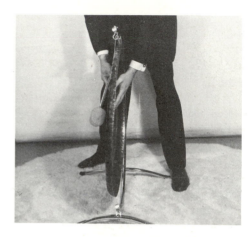

Figure 7.15. Damping the tam-tam with the hands.

Figure 7.16. Damping the tam-tam with the knees.

THE WOODBLOCK

The woodblock is another of the small percussion instruments to be adopted into Western music from its orig-

Figure 7.17. Woodblock played with xylophone stick.

inal oriental usage in ritual and ceremonial music. During the early part of the jazz era in America the woodblock became associated with ragtime and Dixieland drumming. It is sometimes used to create a synthetic ragtime, soft-shoe, or Dixieland effect. In concert music it is used in a variety of ways, sometimes simply to provide a hollow wood sound as a contrast to the drums and the metal sounds of cymbals, triangle, or bells.

A good woodblock for general purposes would be one about 8″ × 2½″ × 3″. This block will have one high pitched side and one lower in pitch, the difference in pitch resulting from a difference in width and location of the slotting. A block of this size can produce a heavy "bonk" and is also capable of making the lighter tap sounds.

The woodblock may be held in the L hand and struck with the R, using a xylophone mallet or snare drumstick. If rapid figures are called for the block can be placed on the trap table and played upon with two sticks.

Two kinds of tone are obtainable and the choice of tone is a point of musical judgment. The heavy "bonk" sound is good for single notes where medium or loud volume is indicated. It is produced by striking the block on its top surface with the shoulder or butt end of a snare

drumstick in such a manner that the maximum wood-against-wood contact is made. For a very heavy sound use hard rubber xylophone mallets. To produce light tapping "ticky" tones, play on the top of the block with the tips of the drumsticks. The sticks may be held with snare drum handholds, or both may be held as the R snare stick is held. The latter is usually more convenient when the block is placed on a rather low table.

A roll is possible on the woodblock, although it is seldom called for in band or orchestra music. The double-stroke snare drum roll is used, with the stick tips playing on the top surface of the block. See Figure 7.19.

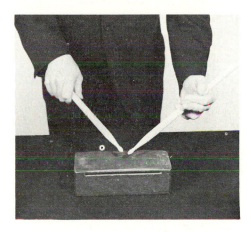

Figure 7.19. Woodblock roll.

Figure 7.20. Castanets.

THE CASTANETS

The castanets are of Spanish origin and are used in band and orchestra music when the composer wishes to impart a Spanish flavor to a piece such as a tango or other dance. The authentic castanets played by the Spanish dancers are pairs of shell-like wooden clappers, held by means of cords which are passed over the thumbs and dangled rather loosely in the palms of the hands. The rhythms are tapped with the four fingers on the outer shells which then contact the inner shells with a resonant "clack." To play castanets in this manner is an art. By way of making it easier for percussionists to play castanet rhythms, the castanet shells are mounted opposite one an-

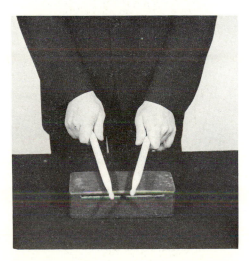

Figure 7.18. Woodblock played with snare drumsticks.

other, separated by a broad wooden handle. When the handle is shaken the castanets clap against the upper portion of the wood handle. One or two pairs of castanets can be mounted on a single handle.

The castanets are held in front of the player about chest high, with the handle at right angles to the floor. To sound the castanets, shake the handle back and forth so that the shells will alternate to sound the desired rhythm pattern. The L hand is held behind the castanets to assist in control and in readiness to damp at the end of the pattern, or on the cut-off. See Figure 7.21.

Another style of castanet playing is sometimes used, especially in loud passages, wherein the castanets are struck against the raised knee on the downstroke and

Figure 7.21. Ordinary playing position for castanets.

Figure 7.22. Knee and hand method for rapid castanet playing.

against the cupped L hand on the upstroke. Precise rhythms are difficult to execute in this manner.

The chief difficulty in castanet playing lies in shaking the handle in exactly the right way to sound the desired rhythm. This is not at all easy to do because the loosely mounted shells are very prone to sound extra clacks before, during, and after the playing of the notated rhythm pattern. An excellent device, for making clean and precise castanet playing possible is in wide usage nowadays. It

consists of a single castanet shell, or pair of shells, mounted on a resonant block of wood and held at an angle to this block by means of a spring. The player has merely to tap out the desired rhythm with a pair of snare drumsticks, xylophone mallets, or his fingers on the top of the castanet. A spring causes the castanet to snap up instantly to position for the next note. The sound compares very favorably with the authentic paired castanet arrangement. See Figure 7.23.

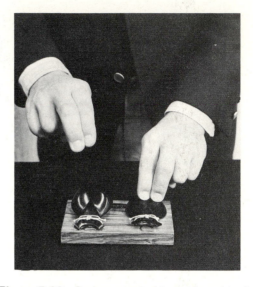

Figure 7.23. Spring-mounted type of castanets.

Castanet music is usually notated on one of the upper lines or spaces of the F clef, or on a single line running above or below the staff. In any case the part will be clearly marked *castanets, cast.* or *casts.*

When a roll is indicated for the castanets the handle is shaken back and forth as rapidly as possible, as shown in Figure 7.24. If the spring-mounted type of castanets are used, the correct roll for them is made by rapid single strokes of the drumsticks, mallets, or fingers.

Figure 7.24. Castanet roll.

TEMPLE BLOCKS

The temple blocks come from the Orient, where they are still used in Chinese temple ceremonies. The usual set consists of five blocks, each with a different pitch. The pitches are indefinite, but unmistakably "higher" or "lower." See the table of percussion instruments, Chapter 2, for a picture of the temple blocks. The set of blocks is mounted on a frame with the lower pitched blocks to the left. They may be struck with xylophone mallets, felt timpani sticks, yarn or cord wound marimba or vibraphone mallets. Until very recently composers and arrangers wrote for the temple blocks only to suggest an Oriental atmosphere or as horsehoof imitations. At present the temple blocks are being employed to a greater degree for their own inherent sound, which is more mellow and mysterious than the ordinary woodblock, by many eminent composers.

RATCHET

This curious sound effect has been used by many composers in a variety of idioms. Richard Strauss, Offenbach, and Honneger *(Jeanne d' Arc)* have scored for the ratchet. See the table of percussion instruments, Chapter 2, for a picture of the ratchet. The instrument consists of two tongues of wood which are made to vibrate when a notched cylinder is cranked. The chattering sound made by the ratchet has no clear associative or imitative qualities. The ordinary manner of playing the ratchet is to attach it by means of a clamp to the hoop of a bass drum or edge of a trap table. To sound the ratchet, the handle is turned clockwise. It is necessary to turn the handle at a constant rate of speed in order to maintain a steady volume of sound. See Figure 7.25.

Figure 7.25. Ratchet.

SLAPSTICK

The slapstick and the whip-crack are essentially alike. Figure 7.26 illustrates the type which is activated by a

Figure 7.26. Whip-crack.

Figure 7.27. Slapstick.

whip-cracking motion. Another type is shown in Figure 7.27, which consists of two flat boards which are slapped shut by means of handles. It is probable that the slapstick reached its hey-day during the vaudeville era when the pit drummer was called upon to accompany the stage comic's pantomime with sound effects.

Figure 7.28. Sleigh bells.

SLEIGH BELLS

Sleigh bells used as musical instruments are highly suggestive of Christmas, Santa Claus, sleigh rides, etc. Waldteufel, Leroy Anderson, and even Mahler *(Fourth Symphony)* have scored for sleigh bells. The most convenient way to play rhythm figures cleanly on sleigh bells is to mount them on a flat board, which can then be shaken up and down. See Figure 7.28. To play softly, damp several of the bells with the hand and allow only two or three to vibrate. Commercial sleigh bells consisting of 25 bells with a handle are available.

CHAPTER 8

Latin-American Instruments

In this chapter descriptions, photos of correct playing positions, techniques, and idiomatic rhythm figures of the percussion instruments generally classified as Latin-American rhythm instruments are given. In dance bands the rhythm patterns as given can be used. Concert band and orchestra arrangements usually have parts for these instruments written out, although often it is desirable to substitute authentic beats for those notated. The Latin instruments are easily obtainable and are relatively inexpensive. All school bands and orchestras should have claves, maracas, guiro, bongos, and cowbell at the disposal of their percussion sections.

CLAVES

The claves are rosewood sticks about 6″ or 7″ long and about an inch in diameter. In a good matched pair one clave will be of a higher pitch that its mate. The claves are very important in the dance rhythms of Afro-Cuban origin, namely the rhumba, bolero, beguine, mambo, cha-cha-cha, and guaracha.

In these dances they play a two measure pattern:

which is repeated over and over from start to finish of the piece. The pattern measures may be reversed if the rhythmic structure of the melody conforms more closely to that order:

In either case the pattern, once set, is never changed.

One clave rests lightly between the ends of the fingers and thumb of the left hand with the palm up and cupped to add resonance. This stationary clave is struck by the right clave held lightly by the tips of the thumb and index finger. The less contact of flesh with the claves, the more resonant the tone. See Figure 8.1.

Two round pieces of hardwood approximately 6″ long and 1″ in diameter can be procured very easily from any school woodshop, and can serve as an inexpensive substitute for the authentic claves.

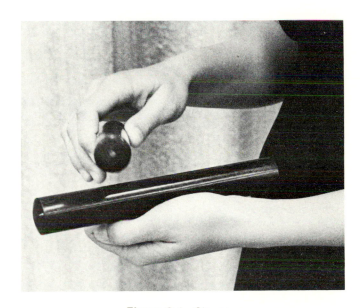

Figure 8.1. Claves.

MARACAS

The maracas are hollow gourds, or plastic substitutes, filled with shot or seeds and fitted with handles. They are used in all Latin dances except the tango.

The most important basic function of the maracas is to provide a steady flow to the music by sounding a continuous eighth note pattern:

It is usually best to stick strictly to this eighth note rhythm, although authentic Latin players often add to or modify this beat.

Figure 8.2. Maracas.

Shake the maracas up and down in short arcs, using a sharp wrist motion in order to cause the seeds to strike the inside of the shells simultaneously. This will help to make the sound crisp and rhythmic. To produce a good sound for soft passages and to avoid the grace note effect, hold the maracas as shown and tap on the top of them with the forefinger of each hand.

The samba is an exception to the foregoing in that both maracas are held in the right hand, one up and one down. The rocking motion of the right forearm, back and

Figure 8.3. Method of holding maracas for the samba.

then forward, is done either in a quarter note rhythm with the second and fourth quarter accented:

or in eighths, with every second eighth accented:

COWBELL

The cowbell is a necessary ingredient of the modern Cuban rhythm section in playing the mambo, cha-cha-cha, and also in the Brazilian samba. The cowbell is held in the left hand with the large end to the right. It is usually

Figure 8.4. Cowbell.

struck with a snare drumstick, but it can also be struck with a clave which has been well wrapped with tape. A variety of tones can be obtained from the cowbell, depending upon which part of the bell is struck. Cowbells less than 6″ long do not produce a full enough tone for an authentic sound. The cowbell as it comes from the music store is not ready for use until it has been wrapped near its large end with several winds of tape. An unwrapped cowbell usually emits too harsh a clang, and the tape serves to deaden it somewhat.

A simple basic beat for the mambo is:

where the first and third beats of the measure are loud (open end of the bell) and the second and fourth beats are softer because they are played near the closed end. See diagram page 149. Typical variants for the mambo and cha-cha-cha are:

Cha-cha-cha

The pattern for the samba is:

The dome of a cymbal struck with the shoulder of a snare drumstick may serve as a substitute for the cowbell.

BONGOS

The bongo player is the "free agent" of the Latin percussion section, since he is not expected to stick rigidly to a steady rhythm pattern but is free to improvise "fill-ins" and "licks" as the spirit moves. The bongos themselves are small bucket-like single-headed drums which are held between the seated player's knees, with the deeper toned bongo to the right. The bongos should be tuned so that their interval corresponds to a third or fourth. Bongos may also be mounted on a floor stand.

Figure 8.5. Bongos.

Bongos are struck with the extended index and middle fingers of both the right and left hands. In symphonic scores it may be necessary to use small snare drumsticks or timbale dowels to obtain sufficient volume. The piercing "pop" of the bongo is achieved by the simultaneous striking of the edge (rim) and the head proper, as in the snare drum rimshot. Since this is done with the fingers, however, it is rather painful until the player has toughened up his fingers through much bongo playing. The novice or school player will probably find that one or more of

the beats given following will suffice for the bulk of his playing. He should not, at the beginning, try for fancy "licks."

Basic beats for

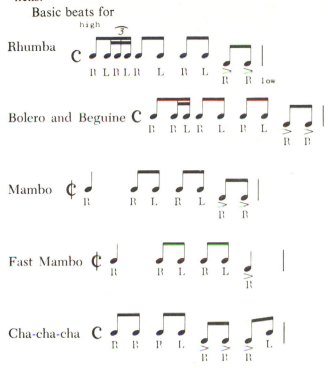

CONGA DRUM

The conga drum is the large single-headed drum which is slung over the shoulder, held between the knees,

Figure 8.6. Conga drum.

fitted with adjustable legs or mounted (sometimes in pairs) on a sturdy and versatile floor stand. See Figure 8.7. Other names for this instrument are *tumbadora,* or simply *tumba.* In appearance it resembles an elongated nail keg, and its main function is to provide a steady bass-register beat.

The basic pattern following may be played in the rhumba, mambo, bolero, beguine, cha-cha-cha. It is not generally used in the samba or tango. The basic beat for the conga is:

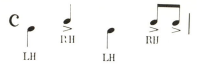

The extended fingers of the left hand strike the drumhead lightly on the first and third counts of the measure, while the right hand plays the second beat at the edge with fingers extended and the "four-and" with the flat of the hand in the center of the drumhead. The edge tone is rather high in pitch, while the tone at the center is very deep. Pitch gradations can be obtained by placing the elbow of the left arm on the head and exerting different pressure while playing with the R hand.

A tom-tom or snare drum with snares off may substitute for the conga drum. Because the rims of the tom-tom or snare drum make the hand and finger technique painful for the player's right hand, a drumstick or mallet can be used to sound the second and fourth beats.

Courtesy Latin Percussion, Inc.

Figure 8.7. Mounted congas.

GUIRO

The guiro is made from the shell of a dried gourd, or may be made of wood in the shape of a fat cigar. Its top

Figure 8.8. Guiro.

surface is notched, and holes are cut in the under side for the thumb and fingers of the left hand, used to hold the instrument. When a stick, back of a comb, triangle beater, or two-pronged wire scraper is rubbed across the notched surface, a resonant scratching sound is emitted. Other names for the guiro are gourd, scratcher, scraper, reco-reco.

Various rhythms are used in the several Latin dance forms. Some of the typical patterns are:

1. Slow rhumba, bolero

down up down up etc.

2. Fast rhumba, mambo

down up down up down up

down up down up down up

3. Cha-cha-cha

down up down up down

4. Samba

down up down up down up

TIMBALES

The pair of timbales are used in authentic Latin bands as the basic drum sound. The distinctive feature of the timbales is their metal shell, usually of copper or spun brass. Timbales have only top heads, which are tucked directly on the counterhoops—there are no flesh hoops. The pair of drums are mounted on a stand with the higher pitched drum to the right. The usual dimensions for timbales are 7″ × 13″ and 7″ × 14″. Very often a cowbell is mounted between the timbales. See Figure 8.9 for an illustration of the timbales mounted with cowbells.

Timbales are played with either very small drumsticks or dowels about 3/8″ in diameter, held in the overhand manner of the timpani stick. Rolls are single stroked. Rim shots are frequently utilized for the fill-in beats which lend color and excitement to the mambo, cha-cha-cha, etc. In the slow Latin dances such as the bolero and beguine, the "paila" style is employed. "Paila" means literally *pail*, and to play in this style the right stick strikes against the outer shell of the high timbale in a steady eighth note pattern, while the left stick alternates the afterbeats on the heads of the two drums. Some of the typical timbale beats are:

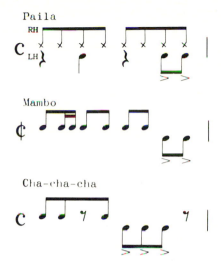

The beats for the several Latin rhythm instruments contained in the preceding section may be substituted for written-out parts as scored in band and orchestra arrangements of Latin music. In most cases the arrangers of these selections have been content to notate parts for the rhythm instruments without a working knowledge of the authentic beats used by the Latin players themselves.

The bass drum is not considered to be a Latin rhythm instrument, but it is often helpful to use it to help maintain good rhythm in the band or orchestra. When the bass drum is used it should *always* play one of the following patterns:

1. For Bolero, Beguine, Mambo, Cha-cha-cha

2. For Samba

3. For Tango

The bass drum should *never* anticipate the third beat of the measure thus: . This is an obsolete rhumba beat once used by American drummers. It has never been used by authentic Latin players, although many arrangements still appear with this incorrect bass beat.

The snare drum with snares turned off may be substituted for the timbales, and American drummers have developed a cross-stick technique for Latin playing. A good

Courtesy Latin Percussion, Inc.

Figure 8.9. Timbales.

basic beat for the mambo and cha-cha-cha in which the left stick is held across the snare drum so that its butt end

is on the head, and the shoulder of the stick makes contact with the rim, indicated in the foregoing by the x's. Figure 8.10 shows the snare drum being played in this manner.

Figure 8.10. Stick positions for Latin-American beats on the snare drum.

The pattern for the snare drum in the slower dances, such as the bolero, is:

As an aid in adapting the Latin-American rhythm instruments for use by the full percussion section of the band or orchestra, the following composite pattern measures are given following.

Bolero, beguine

Mambo

Cha-cha-cha

*not regular claves beat

Samba

Tango

CHAPTER 9

Set Drumming

Dance band, stage band, and jazz drumming are highly specialized skills, and it is difficult to present adequate concepts via the printed page. The eager and interested student may be guided using the information and suggestions contained in this chapter, but for that student who shows real aptitude for this phase of percussion playing, it is strongly recommended that private study, listening, watching, and trying out for himself the techniques of the modern jazz drummer follow up the introductory stages. Every well-rounded percussionist must have a basic knowledge of the fundamental dance rhythms and should have an opportunity to practice with a pedal bass drum set-up. The author would strongly recommend that every student percussionist, at some point early in his school career, be given some training and guidance in the technique and style of dance band drumming. Music instructors from elementary school through college would reap many benefits from encouraging, rather than discouraging, their drum students to play jazz. Not only are dance band and jazz drumming fun and hence interest-building devices, but the rhythmic discipline and precision required in these styles of music contribute to the total musical development of the student. For those students who develop their talents sufficiently, there is the additional prospect of earning money to help defray college tuition expenses and a later vocational or avocational source of income.

The usual dance band set consists of a bass drum with pedal, snare drum, one or two top cymbals, sock (variously called hi-hat, foot, off-beat, after-beat, etc.) cymbals with foot pedal stand, one small mounted tom-tom and one large floor tom-tom, plus a cowbell. As a basic minimum for any kind of dance band, the drummer must have a bass drum with pedal and a snare drum with floor stand. The best size bass drum is a 22″ diameter model, and for the snare drum the 5″ × 14″ or 6½″ × 14″ models are the most popular. Starting with these absolutely essential items, next would be added a ride cymbal on shell-mounted holder or floor stand, preferably an 18″ or 20″ diameter. A crash cymbal is also needed.

Courtesy Ludwig Drum Co.

Figure 9.1. Dance band drum set.

Next in importance is the sock cymbal set-up, using 13″, 14″, or 15″ cymbals. For additional information on the make, type, and diameters of cymbals for dance band use, refer back to the Chapter 4 section on Cymbals. One small 9″ × 13″ tom-tom, shell mounted, is the next logical addition. For Latin music, a large cowbell is indispensible (it should be wound with tape to eliminate the excess ring). A large 16″ × 16″ tom-tom with legs attached would round out the set to that normally carried by the professional drummer.

There are three basic functions of the dance band drummer. The one which is most often overlooked completely by the novice is in fact the most important, namely the providing of a steady beat upon which the group can lean. In addition to keeping a steady beat, he must contribute interesting and musical fill-ins and "licks." His third function would be to take an occasional break of 2, 4, or 8 measures, and very occasionally he might solo for a whole chorus or more. The instructor and students should discuss fully the implications of the foregoing statements. Many young students are completely unaware of the qualifications necessary for good dance and jazz drumming and of the real contribution of the drummer to the total ensemble.

BASIC 4/4 PATTERNS FOR FOXTROT AND JAZZ

One important rhythm pattern that is necessary for dance or jazz playing must be learned so thoroughly that it becomes an automatic response. The beat is usually written:

but is often played with a more relaxed, or jazz, feel, approximating the notation

The beat should be practiced using the R stick only (it is nearly always played with one brush or one stick) on the pad. Various tempos should be set and maintained over a number of repetitions of the one measure figure. When this can be done fairly automatically, add the R foot, tapping on all 4 beats of the measure:

This is called "4-beat."

Next, try beating the R foot only on 1 and 3, keeping the same R stick pattern.

This is called "2-beat."

The L stick's job is to furnish the strong after-beat characteristic of much dance (foxtrot) and jazz music.

We now have:

and in "2-beat":

Note that the R and L sticks coincide exactly on beats 2 and 4.

The final coordination to be added is the L foot, which operates the sock cymbal pedal. Like the L stick, its function is to emphasize the after-beat. The sock cymbal

maintains its afterbeat pattern with rigid monotony, regardless of any L stick variations and in total disregard of the bass drum's pattern.

In "4-beat":

In "2-beat":

Use: RH on top cymbal or sock cymbals
LH on S.D.
R foot on B.D.
L foot on sock cymbal pedal

This completes the basic foxtrot (jazz) drum pattern. The student should practice the pattern as given at the drum set until it is quite automatic, a task requiring considerable perseverance. *Only* when this elemental pattern has been made secure can the player's thought be extended to the embellishing figures which serve to create interest through variation. Again, the author would strongly urge *analytical listening* to experienced and talented modern drummers on record, TV, radio, and especially in live performance. The student should have no qualms about copying the styles and tricks of his favorite players. The materials of the modern dance drummer are a composite

Figure 9.2. R stick on ride cymbal, L on snare drum. Over-shoulder view.

heritage of styles and tricks passed along from drummer to drummer over the past sixty-odd years, and are in truth "public domain."

Figure 9.3. Same as Figure 9.2. Side view.

Figure 9.4. Playing rhythm with brushes. Over-shoulder view.

Figure 9.5. Same as Figure 9.4. Side view.

FILL-INS AND SOLOS

The modern drummer has an opportunity to assert his creativity in improvising fill-ins, two and four measure breaks, and extended solos. Since the advent of so-called progressive jazz in the late 1940's, the style of drumming has undergone a radical change from the older conception which emphasized a steady, swinging beat underlined principally by a rigid and heavy bass drum. Today's drummer keeps the "time" mainly by the ride cymbal rhythm and thus frees the bass drum foot from its former monotonous duty. This new freedom makes possible left hand and right foot combinations which serve both to punctuate the flow of the music and to fill in gaps in the melodic structure behind ensemble riffs and during improvised solos by the other instruments. Such fill-ins vary in length from a single well-placed note to a measure or more. No rule can be laid down regarding the placement of tasteful fills, except to state that they can often be inserted at the ends of phrases. The fill-in should have the quality of *leading in* to the next musical idea or providing a rhythmic springboard from which the ensemble or soloist can surge forward. For this reason most fills should arrive at their climax with a heavy accent on the first beat of the new phrase. Three rather simple examples of fill-ins are notated following.

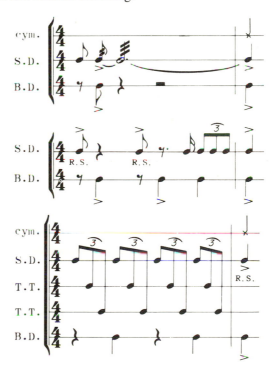

Short solos of two, four, or eight bars duration are sometimes called breaks. The novice is well advised to work out and memorize some two-measure patterns before attempting longer solo breaks. He must keep in mind that whatever he plays must be interesting and, more importantly, maintain the pulse of the beat. It therefore is best

EXAMPLES OF SIMPLE TWO MEASURE BREAKS

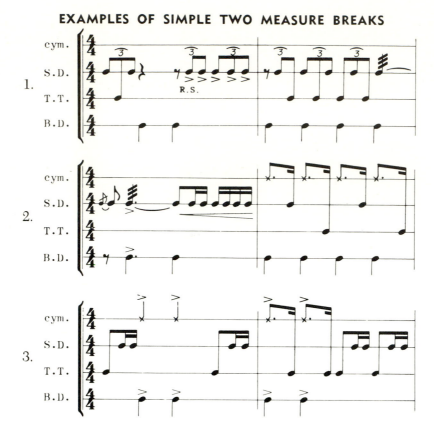

to keep the pattern simple enough so that the rhythm will be perfectly clear to himself, the other musicians, and the listeners. When working out such two-bar breaks in practice sessions it is a good policy to count each beat aloud or mentally. Three examples of simple two measure breaks are above.

When the student has perfected several two-bar break patterns, various combinations of these can be strung together to form four measure phrases. It is important to keep the count, either orally or mentally, during practice. By this means a feeling for the phrase can be acquired. Eventually the drummer will wish to improvise four bar breaks without dependence upon previously worked-out patterns, and should in time develop a sense of phrasing which will permit him to fill in the four bars without counting each beat. The same remarks would apply generally to the eight measure solo break. Longer solos, however, require more musical planning, that is, the drummer should structure his solo so that it will show not only his technique but also his musical feeling. This is not easy for everyone to accomplish, and requires long hours of practice at the drum set. Several suggestions may help to guide the novice:

1. Try to have an idea for a rhythmic motif *before* launching into the solo.
2. Begin with a fairly simple exposition of the motif.
3. Stay with either a double or triple division of the beats and build toward a climax, then introduce a new idea.
4. Save the heavy cymbal crashes for the final climax.
5. Don't try to fill up every beat with 32nd notes! A few well-placed rests during the solo can be very effective.
6. Try to get contrasts in volume, motion, and timbre.
7. Spend a lot of time listening analytically to live or recorded drum solos.
8. Practice working out ideas at the drum set.

READING STOCK AND SPECIAL ARRANGEMENTS

Arrangers of popular, commercial, and jazz music do not attempt to write their drum parts literally. Instead, they notate the skeletal outline and trust that the player will have the requisite skill and experience in the various styles to interpret and embellish the part. This is a good system, for it minimizes reading difficulties (which would be great indeed if arrangers wrote out everything exactly as they wished it to be played), and it allows an outlet for the creativeness of the individual drummer. An example often cited by writers on jazz notation to illustrate the comparative freedom of interpretation in this idiom is the standard cymbal ride rhythm:

May be played as follows:

(very slow tempo)

(very fast tempo)

It is assumed by the arranger that the drummer will choose from among these various possible interpretations the one which "feels right" for the tempo and style of the arrangement. In other words, the ride rhythm figure

is a notational convenience or conventionalized way of indicating any or all of the foregoing examples. And so it is with many of the conventionalized notational usages in drum parts, or "charts," to borrow from the jazzman's jargon. For example, the chart may indicate only the rhythm figures that are to be played *with the ensemble,* leaving long sections marked simply "16 bars straight rhythm," "light rhythm next 8," "32 bars shuffle," etc. It is expected that the drummer will know what is meant by these conventionalized signals and govern his interpretation accordingly. Stock arrangements usually have every measure written out, but the drummer does not take them literally. In both stock drum parts and special arrangement charts the drummer should observe carefully the introductions, first and second endings, indicated fill-ins and solo spots, and endings in order to play the tutti licks in unison with the ensemble. The remainder of the phrases will usually be played with an appropriate steady rhythm figure, and whether or not the measures are written out or simply indicated, they should be counted in order to keep the place. In most situations the drum part should be considered as a guide, rather than played literally, in the sense that the percussion part of a symphonic composition would be played "as written."

SOCK CYMBAL TECHNIQUE

Many drummers use a rocking motion of the left toe and heel in playing after beats on the sock (hi-hat) cymbals. The heel is lifted off the pedal as the toe is depressed on the second and fourth beats of the 4/4 measure. This style of playing the sock cymbals is less fatiguing to the ankle and leg muscles than the constant straight downward press of the toe section of the foot. Another advantage is that the rocking motion helps to maintain a steady beat.

In playing the ride rhythm figure

with the stick on the sock cymbals, the foot continues its strict afterbeat pattern. This will produce an open sound on the first and third beats, closed sounds on the second and fourth. Most drummers prefer to cross the R over the left to reach the sock cymbals, as illustrated in Figure 9.6. For loud playing the cymbals are opened an inch or more. The amount of opening is controlled by the left foot; for wide opening use large rocking motions, for less opening use smaller motions. A good effect can be obtained by allowing the cymbals to separate only slightly when playing the ride rhythm. In this way the cymbals continue to "zizz" against each other during the first and third beats. This style is particularly effective behind legato ensemble writing, and can be used as a contrast to the more choppy open-and-closed style.

The R stick may either strike the cymbals at an angle (shoulder of stick) or, for a softer effect, the tip of the stick may be used on the top of the upper cymbal.

Remember that whether or not the sticks are playing rhythm on the sock cymbals, the basic afterbeat produced by the rocking motion of the left foot is continued.

Figure 9.6. R stick on sock cymbal.

SPECIAL STUDY FOR SPEED

THREE HAND AND FOOT COORDINATION STUDIES

BASIC DRUM PATTERNS FOR VARIOUS DANCES

The dance band drummer must be conversant with other common dance rhythms in addition to the foxtrot pattern. There follow typical basic drum patterns of some of the more common dances. Many of these dances are dated and are seldom played by today's bands; however, they are still called for, occasionally, and a passing knowledge of them will assist the drummer. Like the foxtrot pattern, these are skeletal and would need embellishment and variation to sound authentic.

Basic Waltz Beat

The waltz is the easiest of the common dance beats. It should be played rather "straight" and be fairly free from "fill-ins."

Use: Brushes, usually. Loud last choruses will require sticks in a large band. If desired, the drummer may swish the L brush during the 2nd and 3rd beats and the two written ♩'s with the R brush. This is for "American" or rather slow waltzes. The faster Viennese waltz requires sticks, and is played with the characteristic anticipation of the 2nd beat:

played:

Tango

The tango is also a fairly regular beat. It should be played with a good drive and heavy accents on the final eighth of each measure. Do not turn off the snares.

Bolero

The rhumba as such has been ousted from its place as the foremost Latin American dance by the bolero, mambo, and cha-cha-cha. The dance which corresponds most closely to the slow rhumba is called the bolero, and its basic beat is:

Snares off. Use of sock cym. is optional. There are a number of variations possible in the bolero, especially in the timbres used. The Latin drummer plays a steady eighth note pattern on the metal shell of his R timbale, playing a pattern of

with his L hand on the pair of timbales. Most American drummers use the L stick held across the snare drum so that its butt end is on the head, and the shoulder of the stick makes contact with the rim. This might be notated thus:

x above the note means L stick on rim. The bass drum pattern should be observed carefully. Figure 9.7 shows the drummer playing a bolero.

Mambo

The second rhumba derivative is the mambo, which means literally "Cuban Jazz." Like American jazz it has a monotonous driving beat upon which various ensemble

Figure 9.7. Drummer playing a bolero.

riffs and solos are grounded. There is a definite tendency for our American jazz to incorporate some of the elements of the Latin style, and conversely, their music is constantly under the influence of our modern jazz. The basic mambo ingredients are a heavy cowbell on the first and third beats, and a continuous pattern played on timbales, conga drums, or on snare drum and tom-tom. The bass drum has several options, but it is not under any obligation to play a unison rhythm pattern with the string bass. One basic mambo pattern might be notated thus:

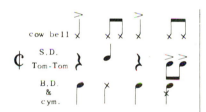

The authenticity of this basic pattern will be enhanced if the player uses the tip of the R stick near the clamp end of the cowbell on the ♪'s, and plays the heavily accented ♩'s with the shoulder of the stick at the open end of the bell. This is diagrammed following.

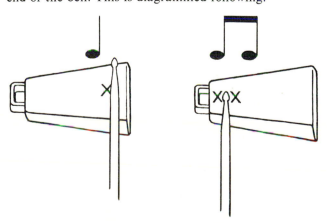

The L hand notes should be split between two pitches, a high (snare drum with snares off) on the 2nd beat and a lower sound (small tom-tom) on the 4th beat. As a variation useful in final loud ensemble choruses or behind trumpet or piano montunas (long, free solos based on one or two chords), the cowbell beat may be transferred to the

top cymbal. A good effect is to strike the cymbal on the dome section, alternating the tips and shoulders of the R stick. An example of the kind of variation often used by Latin drummers for the R hand on the cymbal dome:

Cha-cha-cha

Figure 9.8. Drummer playing a cha-cha-cha.

The cha-cha-cha drum pattern is basically very similar to the mambo. The tempo for most cha-cha-chas is fairly slow, however, which allows time for the quick cowbell grace notes shown in the example below. Figure 9.8 illustrates the position of the drummer as he plays the fourth beat in the cha-cha-cha measure.

Samba

This dance was imported from Brazil, and is basically in "2 beat" rhythm. The bass drum plays strictly on 1 and 3 of a ¢ measure, as in a march or polka. The L is played with a brush, and provides the afterbeats.

The ♩ on the 2nd beat should be pushed down into the head, while the ♫'s on the 4th beat should be "open". The R has a tricky pattern, played with a stick on cowbell or snare drumhead:

The combined pattern is:

If two cowbells are available, a good effect is gained by alternating the high bell on the first pair of ♪♩'s and the low bell on the next ♪♩. As an acceptable alternative, the domes of two cymbals can also be used. The sock cymbal can be used on the 2 and 4.

Bossa Nova

The bossa nova is based on the foregoing samba and is also in a "2 beat" rhythm. The bass drum plays the following pattern:

The left foot plays the sock cymbal on the 2 and 4 beats—

The right hand plays a pattern of straight eight notes on the cymbal with a snare stick or brush

The left hand plays with a snare stick which has been placed on the snare drum so that its butt end is on the head and the shoulder of the stick makes contact with the rim. The left hand then lifts only the end of the stick touching the rim for accented beats

The combined pattern is:

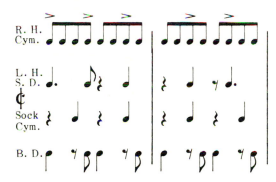

Rock Beat

Starting in the early 1960's, the "rock and roll" music took its place in the forefront of the pop music field. A definite "rock" style developed culminating in its use in musicals and even a "rock opera." As is the case with any beat style, there are many possible and acceptable variations; however, the rock beat has as its basic ingredients the following:

The right hand can easily be converted to triplets to give a ternary feeling:

As a general rule, it is important to understand that Latin and rock rhythms are interpreted literally as opposed to converting them to the 12/8 feeling of the swing patterns.

TUNING THE DRUM SET

There is a tendency to muffle drums more than necessary when playing live in a concert hall or club. After adjusting and tuning the set, have someone strike each drum while you listen at a distance. Acoustics will often vary from room to room and from concert hall to concert hall. The drums may sound great on stage and "dead" in the audience. Or, they may seem "dead" on stage and "loud" in the audience. Some of this can be corrected at a rehearsal by simply moving instruments around and by adjusting microphones and amplifiers. The following procedures may be followed to adjust for room acoustics: (1) If the room is too live and the sound bounces around, use a little more muffling. (2) If the room is dead, use less muffling to obtain more sound.

One common error is to tune and muffle drums at rehearsal in an empty night club or concert hall. When the place is full of people, the drums may be too dead or overly muffled. A good general rule is to have each drum "ring" just a little more than one would like to hear. In the audience, the drums will sound just right in most clubs and halls. Occasionally one will encounter a bad performance site in which no amount of tuning and/or muffling appears to help.

One should think of the drum set, even the basic four-piece outfit, as a "choir"; that is, snare drum as soprano, ride tom-tom as alto, floor tom-tom as tenor and bass drum as bass "voice."

The two tunings which are quite popular today are a "live" resonant sound, used by most jazz and commercial drummers, and a "wet" loose sound used by most rock drummers. The "live" resonant quality is a clear, ringing tone while the "wet" loose quality is muffled and heavier. The "wet" sound evolved as a result of advanced recording techniques where each drum is individually miked. A flat defined sound is necessary so that the sound of each drum will not leak into other microphones. Most rock drummers now tune for this same sound in live performance. Each sound has its place and both maintain the same pitch relationships between drums.

A mistake made by many drum set players is that of tuning relative pitches too closely. Whether the player selects an outfit utilizing only two tom-toms or a complete set of melodic toms with double bass drums, the primary goal of a multiple tom set is to have a definite melodic pitch difference between the drums. If a group of toms is used, tune them a third or fourth apart to obtain greater clarity of relative pitch. Never allow two drums to sound identical in pitch. Appropriate and consistent selection of heads can also assure a more uniform sound.

Regardless of the type of tuning dictated by personal preference and/or situational requirements, efforts spent in making adjustments will be in vain if one does not tune each tension rod around the entire circumference of the head. A few turns of the drum key can alter considerably the sound of any drum. However, if time is taken, and care is given to tensioning, the reward is evident in improved tone quality.

As was stated in the opening paragraph of this chapter, only a cursory look at set drumming would be attempted. Many fine books and studies are available for the serious set drummer and these should be pursued by such individuals. What has been attempted in this short discussion of set drumming is to cover the basics. These serve as a departure for the more complicated aspects of jazz drumming.

The old concept of once a drummer had mastered playing the basic four-quarter time, got in those four beats per bar, and kept an even tempo he was a set drummer, is a thing of the past. The contemporary jazz percussionist has a most demanding job. He is expected to play in any meter, superimpose one time over another, at times be independent of the rest of the rhythm section by executing a polyrhythmic pulse over the established time, and be proficient on all other percussion instruments.

Although set drumming is an art in itself, the time has come when being a set drummer only will not suffice. Stage bands, show bands, and recording groups demand total percussionists. This should be impressed upon all young drummers.

CHAPTER 10

The Marching Band Percussion Section

INSTRUMENTATION

The day when a collection of snare drums, tenor drums, cymbals, bass drums, and bell-lyras would suffice for a marching band percussion section is no longer. The contemporary marching percussion section has expanded to include a large percentage of all the percussion instruments.

Today's marching bands are rapidly expanding their percussion sections to include at a minimum bass drums, cymbals, snare drums, tenor drums, bongo-timbale clusters, timp-toms, and portable marching timpani. Depend-

ing on the size of the band, and personnel permitting, the percussion section is further augmented to include such instruments as pitched bass drums, claves, maracas, guiros, tambourines, triangles, cowbells, and castanets.

Band directors, composers, and arrangers have begun to realize the many color possibilities inherent within the percussion section. This first became apparent with contemporary music being written and arranged for symphonic bands and orchestras. Augmentation of percussion sections became necessary with many compositions demanding as many as six to ten percussionists. These cre-

Figure 10.1. California State University, Sacramento Marching Band Percussion Section.

ative new sounds this augmentation provided to the concert ensembles now have been incorporated (to a lesser degree) within the marching band with pleasing results to performer and listener alike. Marching percussion no longer is relegated to the singular, rather boring task of keeping the beat.

The following listing of marching percussion instrumentation for the various school levels is approximate. Specific situations may dictate more or fewer instruments depending on player competency, type of music used on the march, and size of organization.

RECOMMENDED MARCHING PERCUSSION EQUIPMENT AND GENERAL SPECIFICATIONS FOR VARIOUS SCHOOL LEVELS

Equipment	Specifications

Elementary and Junior High School Level

1. Snare Drum	double tension 10″ × 14″ (9″ × 13″ available for smaller players)
2. Tenor Drum	double tension 12″ × 15″
3. Bass Drum	double tension 10″ × 26″
4. Cymbal	15″ to 18″ medium
5. Miscellaneous small equipment such as tambourines, claves, and maracas when and if desired.	

High School Level

1. Snare Drum	double tension 12″ × 15″
2. Tenor Drum	double tension 12″ × 17″
3. Bass drum	double tension 10″ × 26″ to 14″ × 28″
4. Cymbal	18″ to 20″
5. Timp-tom Trio	tenor or baritone set (three drums per set)
6. Mounted Bongo-Timbale Cluster	tunable bongos
7. Miscellaneous small equipment such as tambourines, claves, maracas, cowbells, etc., when and if desired.	

College, University Level

1. Snare Drum	double tension 12″ × 15″
2. Tenor Drum	double tension 12″ × 17″
3. Regular Bass Drum	double tension 14″ × 28″
4. Pitched Bass Drum	double tension 14″ × 20″ to 16″ × 32″
5. Cymbal	18″ to 22″
6. Timp-tom Trio	tenor, baritone, and bass sets. (three drums per set)
7. Mounted Bongo-Timbale Cluster	tunable bongos
8. Marching Timpani	20″ to 29″
9. Miscellaneous small equipment such as tambourines, claves, maracas, cowbells, etc., when and if desired.	
10. Mallet instruments—Bells, marimba, xylophone, vibes	portable, with special horizontal carriers

Remember, the above listing is only an approximate recommendation. Situations may and very probably do exist where it would be desirable for high school groups to utilize pitched bass drums, all three timp-tom trios, marching timpani, and mallet percussion.

PROPORTION AND BALANCE

A critical point to consider when formulating a marching percussion section is the proportion of percussionists to the total band membership. Although *extremely* important to marching bands, percussion all too often dominates the total band sound. This is unmusical and must be guarded against.

A marching band of forty can sound just as good (not as powerful, but just as musical) as a two hundred and fifty piece band. This requires careful attention to instrumentation, placement of various instruments, and musical arrangements utilized to mention only a few variables. Here, since we are concerned only with percussion, we shall proceed with a discussion of the proper proportion of percussion instruments to the total marching band membership.

In a band of forty-eight members, there should be no more than six to eight percussionists. Bands of from forty-eight to eighty-eight should maintain a percussion section of eight to twelve players. Bands of over one hundred may have from ten to sixteen percussionists. Good marching bands never permit their percussion sections to overpower the rest of the band. On the other hand, they maintain a section which will provide power when needed and a full, exciting sound when performing as a solo section.

It is equally important to maintain a satisfactory balance between instruments within the percussion section. Generally two or three snare drums balance with one tenor drum. One or two regular bass drums will suffice for an entire percussion section. Likewise, one or two cymbals will be satisfactory. When using timp-toms, bongo-timbale clusters, pitched bass drums, and marching timpani, it is assumed that only one of a kind or set will be utilized; otherwise, the total sound becomes "muddy" and those individualized instruments begin to lose their effectiveness. More than one of a kind of the mallet instruments usually creates precision problems due to the sharp and penetrating sound of each note played on a bell-lyra and xylophone.

MARCHING PERCUSSION TECHNIQUES AND SPECIAL CONSIDERATIONS

Snare Drum

For purposes of projection and power, snare drummers generally should play with open rudiments and make considerable use of full arm strokes. For appearance, they should use identical stickwork and equal stick arcs. Large sticks such as 2B or 2S should be used to aid in projection of sound. Nylon tips are recommended.

Ease of carriage and precision in marching can be facilitated by the use of a device known as a "hi-stepper" mentioned in Chapter 3. This device positions the drum up, out, and away from the body and legs. This gives more freedom of movement to the drummer and maximum control of the drum. Its use almost necessitates playing with the matched grip.

Web slings for carrying field snare drums and tenor drums are included in the purchase price of new instruments, as is one pair of sticks or beaters. The sling passes over the right shoulder, from right to left across the front and back of the chest, and suspends the drum on the player's left side about belt height. To put on the sling preparatory to attaching the drum:

1. grasp the latch (heavier) end with the right hand, eyelet at the top;
2. grasp hook (lighter) end with the left hand;
3. stretch left arm out away from body;
4. bring right hand over head and then down across front of chest so that sling rests on right shoulder and finally—
5. put hook through eyelet.

When ready to play, bring the drum up to playing level with the left hand, and latch through carrying hook on the rim of the drum. See Chapter 3, page 43, Figures 3.27 to 3.30.

Another device which is an aid when using the sling is called a *leg rest*. It attaches to the lower portion of the drum and has a crescent-shaped metal strip which fits around the player's leg above the knee. The leg rest is adjustable and assists in holding the drum in its playing position at all times, thus helping to eliminate bruised legs and missed beats caused by the drum's twisting due to the body's natural movements and/or windy weather.

For flashy appearance and durability the so-called pearl, or sparkling pearl, finishes are recommended. A new plastic material called "vistalite" is also available in transparent tints of blue, red, green, amber, and yellow. Plastic heads should be used on all drums to be played outside.

Tenor Drum

The tenor drum can be played slung over the shoulder in the manner of the snare drum, or it can be carried by means of the vertical holder in front of the player's chest and played with the Scotch bass drum technique. The latter method offers more possibilities for flash and is easier on the player than the traditional sling. Manufacturers' catalogs contain photos and information about the vertical tenor drum holder. Tenor drumsticks are equipped with hard felt beater balls and thongs which interlace through the player's fingers to make twirling of the sticks possible. See Figures 10.2 to 10.4. Many tenor drum parts consist mainly of single notes. Should a roll be called for, the single stroke timpani-style roll is used. By using regular snare sticks, much more complicated parts can be written for and assigned to the tenor drums. The tone of the tenor drum usually is midway in general pitch range between that of the snare drum and the regular bass drum. Its heads will not ordinarily need to be tensioned as much as those of the snare drum. A very suitable substitute for the tenor drum is a field drum with its snares removed or simply turned off.

Bass Drums—Regular and Pitched

The Scotch style of bass drumming is usually employed on the regular bass drum. This technique makes use of two beaters with looped thongs which lace around the player's fingers and wrist so as to allow for twirling. Both heads of the drum are played upon; therefore, both heads must be tuned or tensioned exactly the same. This should be a rather high, crisp tone. The regular bass drum part is primarily responsible for maintaining the beat or pulsation of the music. It usually does not become too involved; however, in antiphonal or multi-voiced cadences, it can assume an individual line.

A rather new concept in marching bass drums is the use of pitched bass drums. Some bands and drum corps

Figure 10.2. Tenor drumstick handhold, step 1.

Figure 10.4. Twirling the tenor drumstick.

Figure 10.3. Tenor drumstick handhold, step 2.

are using two to six pitched bass drums (each drum tuned to a different pitch). This provides a new and interesting line both rhythmically and melodically to the percussion section. Wooden ball mallets are used in playing the bass drumhead—the larger the diameter of the bass drum head, the larger the ball end of the mallet should be. The use of pitched bass drums probably should be utilized only by larger bands at the high school and college levels.

Cymbals

Marching cymbals should be used with some discretion. Too often, as with bass drummers, cymbal players in a marching band are permitted to play continuously; hence, they relinquish their effectiveness to monotony.

Due to the physical stamina required to play marching cymbals, there exists the temptation to utilize too small cymbals and they neither project nor give the beautiful brilliance required outside. As suggested in the above equipment listing, no smaller than 18″ cymbals should be used by high school and college bands. Many bands use two different sets such as an 18″ pair and a 20″ pair. This gives added depth of sound and range of color. Obviously, more than one cymbal player creates a problem of precision and both players must be rhythmically very secure.

Cymbal players should use plenty of motion in the ordinary up-and-down strokes, and extend the cymbals well over the head in the flare stroke used for climaxes and solo crashes.

As mentioned in Chapter 4, marching cymbals should be held by putting the hands through the straps for purposes of security and twirling the cymbals for showmanship. Use of light-weight gloves is a great aid in protecting the hands of players during rehearsals.

Timp-tom Trios

One of the newest additions to the list of marching band percussion is the timp-tom trios. See Figure 10.5. These are groupings of three one-headed drums varying in sizes from 10″ × 14″ to 16″ × 28″ and are played with a pair of wooden ball end mallets. Each group of three drums is provided with a carrying holder and balanced slings and is completely portable. Each trio is carried by one person and is individually tunable by means of a key in the same manner as a snare drum is properly tensioned. Tune each head as recommended by the manufacturer.

Figure 10.5. Tim-tom trio.

There are three different trios—tenor, baritone, and bass. They bridge the tonal gap between the tenor drums and bass drums. Since these are basically solo instruments, it is not necessary to have more than one of each combination within any organization. Many bands use only one set in which case the baritone set is recommended.

Timbale-Bongo Cluster

A specially designed holder and sling for carrying a set of timbales and bongos has been manufactured. It is similar to the holder used by the timp-tom trios. See Figure 10.6.

This "cluster" of four instruments gives added tonal color and projection at the higher pitch end of the percussion section and can be utilized in cadences or as a feature solo instrument in Latin American and similar musical selections. Hard rubber mallets or a pair of small, in diameter, snare drum sticks played with the matched grip are recommended. Experience in playing timpani is beneficial in playing the timbale-bongo cluster as well as the timp-tom trios.

Tune the bongo heads a fifth apart, keeping the pitches as high as practical. The timbale heads then should be tuned a fourth apart at lower pitches than the bongos. (It is recommended that the smallest timbale head be tuned a perfect fifth below that of the largest bongo head.)

Figure 10.6. Timbale-bongo cluster.

Marching Timpani

Completely portable, machine model, marching timpani made of fiberglass are available. These are designed with a special sling and retracting leg supports. These lightweight instruments are equipped with a tuning handle and gauge. They come in sizes of 20″, 23″, 26″, and 29″. Mallets of hard piano felt or hard solid felt should be used.

These instruments are effective in giving more depth of sound to a band performing a concert selection and in enabling the percussion section to contribute more melodic and even harmonic support to the organization.

Normal timpani technique should be utilized. Only personnel familiar with timpani performance should play these instruments. See Figure 10.7.

Courtesy Ludwig Drum Co.

Figure 10.7. Marching timpano, legs retracted.

Marching Bells, Xylophone, Vibes and Marimba

Special portable marching versions of these instruments are among the most recent additions to cadences, interludes and spectacular solo percussion features found within the newest, most innovative marching band and drum corps arrangements. These instruments add the full melodic dimension to the contemporary marching percussion section. All four of the instruments have the versatile capability to function in soloistic as well as in tutti passages for additional tone color and texture. This new role for melodic percussion avoids the intonation problems usually associated with the old practice of doubling a bell lyra in unison with the piccolo.

The xylophone and marimba are equipped with synthetic bars and the bells and vibes with various metallic alloys, all of which are virtually impervious to climatic variances. The marimba and vibes have resonators while the vibes are further equipped with a battery operated motor.

The marching xylophone is especially useful because it sounds one octave higher than written, just like the larger concert model. The xylophone has a particularly penetrating quality and is ideal for melodies as well as countermelodies. Ranges of the four marching melodic percussion instruments are as follows:

Bells	G–32 to C–61
Xylophone	G–32 to C–61
Marimba	C–13 to D–39
Vibes	F–6 to G–32

TUNING THE PERCUSSION SECTION

Much neglected is the "tuning" of the percussion section of a marching band. It is a time consuming task and one which must be supervised (at least in the public schools) by the director. In the more mature organizations, the section leader usually can handle this. The results are well worth the efforts.

First of all, it should be pointed out that the extent to which this "tuning" is carried is entirely contingent upon the desires of the individual director and the instrumentation of the section. As an absolute minimum, all like instruments should be "tuned" or tensioned to the same response, i.e., all snare drums should sound alike, etc.

As the next logical step, there should be a low, medium, and high response range from the section as a whole utilizing the bass, tenors, and snares respectively. Otherwise, much of the effectiveness of modern day "antiphonal" percussion cadences is lost.

To carry this tuning process to its ultimate using the basic instruments of a marching percussion section, a triad can be created using the bass as the tonic, the tenors as the third, and the snares as the fifth of the triad. This gives depth of sound not only to the percussion section, but also to the entire band. It assists in projection and "cleanness" of sound of the percussion section and gives a true meaning to the term "antiphonal cadence." As other of the instruments are added to the section, they should add depth and extend the tonal spectrum of the percussion sound.

Each drum lug should be tuned with equal tension to ensure a balanced head. This is especially important when mounting a new head. Each drum *must* be in tune with itself before any attempt is made to tune all snares alike, for instance. In multiple sets, i.e., timp-tom trios, bongo-timbale clusters, etc., it is essential that each drum in the set be in tune with itself in order to realize the greatest degree of pitch clarity and differential between different size drums in each multiple set. Figures 10.8 and 10.9 are self-explanatory for tuning ten and twelve lug drums respectively.

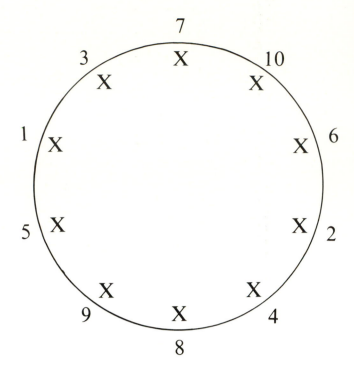

Figure 10.8. Criss-cross tuning procedure for a ten-lug drum.

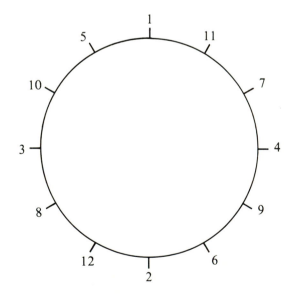

Figure 10.9. Criss-cross tuning procedure for a twelve-lug drum.

SMALL LETTERS INDICATE OPTIONAL PITCHES
LARGE LETTERS INDICATE PREFERRED PITCHES

MIDDLE

Instrument	C²	D	E	F	G	A	B	C³	D	E	F	G	A	B	C⁴	D	E	F	G	A	B	C⁵	D	E	F	G	A
SNARE DRUM 12"X15"																											
TENOR DRUM 12"X15"																						b	c	D		f	G a
TENOR DUO 10"X14" & 9"X13"																							C	E			
TENOR DUO 12"X15" & 10"X14"																					B	B	D		F		
TENOR TRIO 10"X18"-16"-14" DIA.																					B	B	D		F		
TENOR TRIO 12"X18"-16"-14" DIA.																				A		C		E			
BARITONE TRIO 14"X22"-20"-18" DIA.															D			F		A		C		E			
BARITONE TRIO 14"X24"-22"-20" DIA.														B	D			F		A							
TIMPANO 20"														B	D			F									
TIMPANO 23"											D			B													
TIMPANO 26"								B				G			D												
TIMPANO 29"											F#				D				G								
BASS DUO 14" DEPTH X 26"-22" DIA.															D				G								
BASS DRUM 14"X22"															D												
BASS DRUM 14"X26"														B													
BASS DRUM 14"X28"																											
BASS DRUM 16"X30"					G																						
BASS DRUM 16"X32"			F																								

Figure 10.10. Pitch chart for marching drums.

GENERAL INFORMATION

The percussion section of a marching band must perform musically to be effective. This means the section must play dynamics, *not just loudly*. It must read music, although it should have well-rehearsed fake patterns for all common meters which it can utilize from time to time. The section should not be used continually. Besides the fact that percussionists need to rest periodically, the relief offered by the complete absence of the percussion sound is often extremely effective.

Nowadays percussion feature numbers are included in the repertoire of most marching bands. These usually present good challenges to members of the section and are thoroughly enjoyed by audiences.

CADENCES

Drum beats used on the march are called cadences, street beats, or tap steps. They are utilized as signals and to move the band while at the same time giving the brass and woodwind players an opportunity to rest their embouchures. The following cadences are examples of various styles progressing from the old style traditional marching beats and cadences (#1–#8), through the more recent style utilizing interplay between the snare and tenor drums (#9–#13), to the contemporary sound of multi-percussion marching instruments (#14–15). Cadence #16 is an excerpt from a contemporary score of a percussion feature which highlights multiple cymbals, bass drums, and timpani plus xylophone and bell parts.

OLD STYLE TRADITIONAL MARCHING BEATS AND CADENCES

1. Funeral March Beat —— muffle S.D.

2. Old French Street Beat

3. The Roll-off

The Roll-off ¢

4. The Halt Cadence

The Halt Cadence

5.

6.

TWO TYPICAL STREET BEATS

7.

8. Add flams on accented beats in #7 and #8 for a more martial sound.

Cadences With Tenor Drum Added

Cadences 9 through 13 utilize the more recent concept of interplay between the various percussion "voices" particularly between the snare drum and tenor drum parts. The cadences get progressively more difficult.

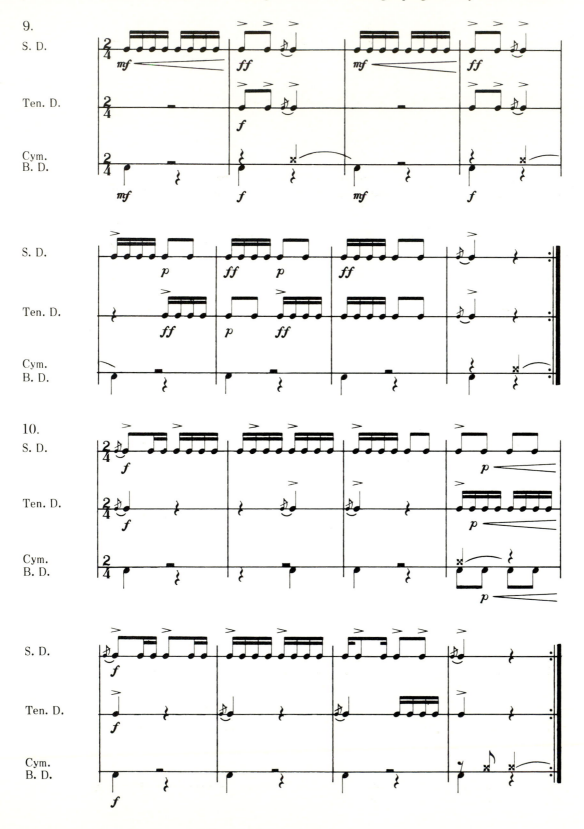

CONTEMPORARY CADENCES WITH MULTIPLE-PERCUSSION

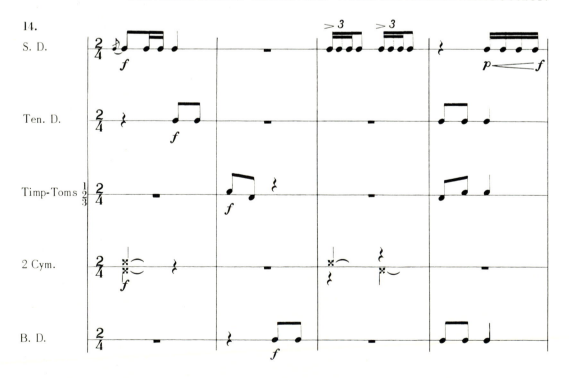

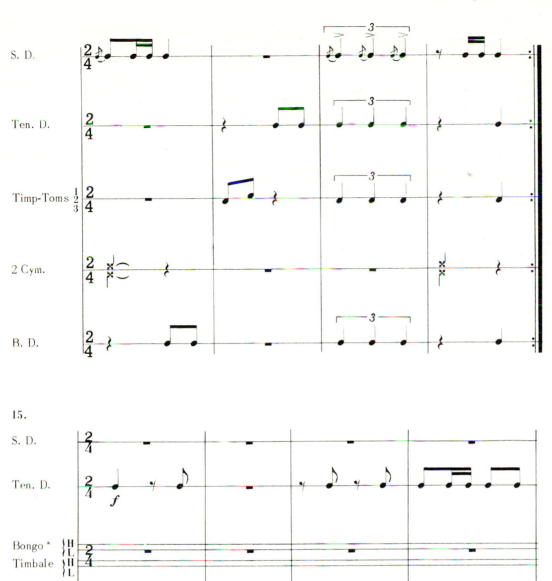

15.

*H – High; L – Low

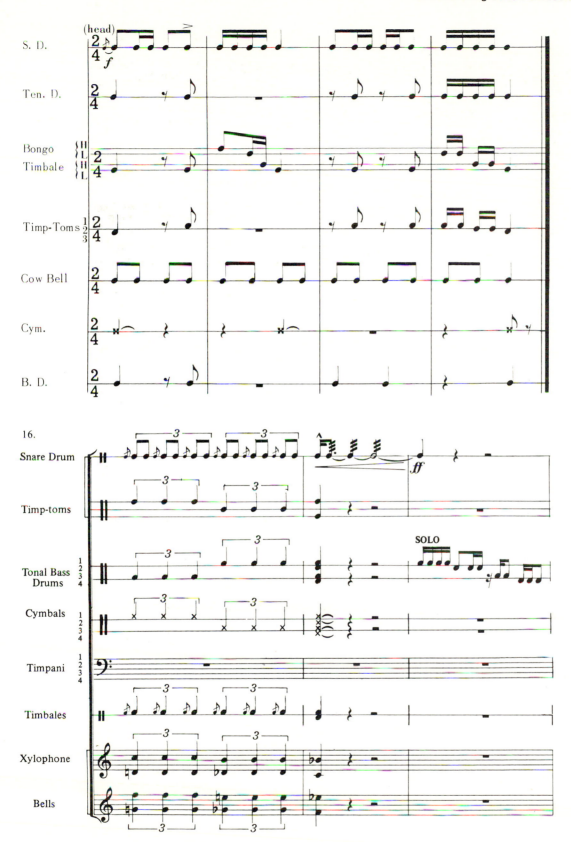

SELECTION, CARE AND STORAGE OF PERCUSSION EQUIPMENT

Determining basic needs. Persons charged with the responsibility of purchasing and maintaining percussion instruments must be aware of the minimum essential needs of their particular musical organization. In many school districts it is customary for all instruments to be issued from a central office, while in others the instrumental music teacher makes purchases direct from local retail houses from either district or school funds. Under either plan, it behooves the persons responsible to make the best possible use of the monies available. The *Guide* has included recommended specifications for all of the instruments in several of the chapters by means of tables classified by school grade level. The seemingly endless array of brands, types, sizes and price ranges in the complex percussion palette can be especially frustrating to the nonpercussionist music director. Consulting the manufacturers latest catalogs and visiting instrumental displays at music conventions can be of assistance in selecting the exact instrument for your particular situation. It can also be very helpful to contact the percussion specialist at a nearby college or university for advice and opinions on various percussion gear *before* expending large sums of money.

As a further aid in determining the percussion instruments which should make up the basic inventory for the various schools groups, the following are suggested lists.

Elementary School
(orchestra and/or band)

bass drum

pair of cymbals

concert snare drum (one or more)

triangle

tambourine

woodblock

set of bells

castanets

sticks, stands, beaters, holders as needed for foregoing items as well as cases and covers

Junior High School
(orchestra and/or band)

pair of timpani

bass drum

concert snare drum (one or more)

pair of cymbals

suspended cymbal

set of bells

triangle

tambourine

woodblock

castanets

Latin rhythm instruments

sticks, stands, beaters, holders as needed for foregoing items as well as cases and covers; if band marches, add Scotch bass drum, one or more field drums

High School
(orchestra and/or band)

4 timpani

bass drum

concert snare drum (one or more)

field drum (one or more)

pair of cymbals

suspended cymbal

set of bells

xylophone, marimba, vibraphone

chimes

tam-tam (gong)

triangle (small and large)

tambourine

woodblock

temple blocks

castanets

Latin rhythm instruments

sticks, beaters, stands and holders as needed for foregoing items as well as cases and covers; for marching band, add

Scotch bass drum, smaller pair of cymbals, one or two tenor drums, timp-tom trio, bongo-timbale cluster, one or more horizontally carried mallet instruments; for dance band set-up, see Chapter 9, page 143.

College, University or Professional Orchestra or Concert band

set of four timpani, five preferred

bass drum

concert snare drum (one or more)

field drum (one or more)

set of concert tom-toms (4), preferably set of (8)

pairs of cymbals (two sizes)

two suspended cymbals (two sizes)

set of bells

xylophone

vibraphone

marimba

chimes

tam-tam (gong)

triangles (3)

woodblocks (2)

tambourines (2)

temple blocks

castanets

sleigh bells

ratchet

Latin rhythm instruments

sticks, beaters, stands and holders as needed for foregoing items as well as cases and covers; for marching band, add Scotch bass drum(s), additional pair of cymbals, one or two tenor drums, one or more horizontally carried mallet instruments for dance band set-up, see Chapter 9, page 143.

Care of percussion equipment. Much unnecessary wear and tear on percussion equipment results from ignorance of proper procedures for routine care or from failure to heed common sense rules of instrument care.

Drumheads, especially calfskin, are easily damaged and broken and account for a large part of the percussion repair bills, yet it is quite possible to make heads wear and retain their life if they are given good care. Snare drum batter (top) heads should be set at an even and tight playing tension (with equal tension on each tuning rod) on a dry day when the head is contracted to its maximum. The

snare (bottom) head should be set at this time also, but higher than the batter head. A tight batter head depresses *only slightly* when at proper playing tension; the snare head depresses a little less. One very important point: *do not* change the tension once it has been satisfactorily set. Constant loosening and tightening soon causes the head to slip on the flesh hoop, and eventually it is impossible to keep it taut. The only time one would need to use the tuning key would be when required to play the drum on a very rainy, humid day, when the head would be too slack to play on. If it is tightened up under such circumstances be sure to loosen it the same amount after playing, as if there is a quick drop in the humidity a split head can result. There is one additional reason for tightening the heads, and that is the natural settling and stretching of the calfskin. A newly mounted head, for instance, will require several tensionings before it is settled. For long periods of storage, loosen calfskin drumheads about ½ turn. Plastic heads need not be loosened for storage. Additional information about drumhead care, with particular reference to plastic heads, is contained in Chapter 3, pages 31–32.

The wire brushes, if used a good deal in dance band playing, will tend to blacken and roughen up a calfskin batter head. One good way to prevent this roughing up (the wires eventually poke tiny holes in the head) is to bend the last ⅜" of the wires upward with a pair of pliers. This will prevent them from digging into the head, as they then strike or rotate at an angle. This procedure is not necessary if a plastic batter head is used, or if the newer types of brushes with nylon strands are used.

Instructors, conductors and percussionists will find it most convenient, practical and economical in the long run to purchase drumheads ready mounted on the flesh hoops. Be sure, when ordering by mail or by phone, to give the exact diameter of the shell as measured from *outside to outside* edges. When mounting plastic heads, make sure that the portion of the drum's shell over which the head passes is absolutely smooth. See Chapter 3, pages 31–32 for the step-by-step procedure used to mount drumheads.

Bass drumheads should be cared for in quite a different manner from the snare drumheads. Most bass drumhead trouble stems from a failure to tune with an equal number of half-turns at each tuning handle. On all drumheads, equal tension at all points around the circumference is absolutely requisite to good tone production. The collar should be measured with a ruler when setting the tension on a newly mounted bass drumhead. The hoop (rim) should protrude an equal amount from the head at each tuning handle.

Another important matter which is often overlooked is the proper tuning of calfskin bass drumheads. Unlike the snare drum, they should be checked before and after each use. For detailed instructions concerning the tuning of the bass drum for playing and storage, see Chapter 4, page 75. Plastic bass drumheads do not require these routine adjustments.

Calfskin timpani heads should be cared for in much the same manner as the calfskin bass drumheads. Equality of tension around the circumference is of the utmost importance. After the playing period on a day when the humidity is average, set the 25″ kettle to *d* and the 28″ kettle to *A*. This will put about the right degree of tension on the heads for storage. Timpani heads should *not* be loosened to their lowest notes for storage. It is much better for the life of the head to keep it under tension. On very humid days leave the heads a tone or so lower than the usual *d* and *A* to allow for a possible sudden weather change.

See the section on *Timpani Heads,* Chapter 6, page 108, for additional information, particularly regarding plastic heads. On Timpani equipped with plastic heads, pedals must be left in the "heel down" position.

To eliminate the annoying squeaks and creaks often emitted by the timpani when the heads are being stretched in tuning, rub lanolin, paraffin or powdered graphite around the entire perimeter of the bowl on its top edge where it comes in direct contact with the head. (The head must be removed from the bowl for this operation.)

To prevent the spread of a small tear in a timpani head (calfskin type) cauterize by heating the point of a needle red hot and pierce the head to form a tiny circular hole at each end of the tear. Breaks in the head up to a couple of inches in length can be rendered harmless by this method. The head should not then be played upon at the point of the tear. Adhesive or Scotch tape should not be used in an attempt to repair a kettledrum head, as even a small piece of tape deadens the tone considerably. Tears, holes, or breaks too large to cauterize will necessitate replacement of the head. Save the discarded timpani head—portions of it can be cut out to re-head tambourines, bongos, and even snare drums, though timpani heads are generally much thicker than snare drum heads, an important consideration.

Drums and timpani should be kept free from dust and dirt, and their chrome-plated and copper parts cleaned with the appropriate metal polish. Cymbals can be cleaned with Copper-Clean or Bon-Ami, following the directions on each can carefully. It is dangerous to buff cymbals with a power buffer, as enough heat may be generated to affect the delicate temper of the alloy.

Whatever metal cleaner or polish is used, be sure that it is of high quality and of the non-abrasive type. Finally, be extra careful to remove all metal cleaner or polish substance from cymbal grooves, as any remaining residue will impair the vibrations of the instrument.

A canvas or vinyl cover *and* a hard fibre case should be provided for each drum in order to afford maximum protection during moving and storage of instruments.

Once drum tension is set, it is best to just leave it alone. However, for long periods of storage it may be advisable to loosen each tension rod one full turn, as all heads, even plastic, can and will stretch a slight amount. In the process of storing heads in a slightly loosened position, the life of the head can be prolonged considerably, thus allowing the higher sounds to be more easily obtained.

Timpani should be stored in cabinets or in fibre carrying trunks if they are not to be used for a considerable period of time or if it is necessary to leave them any place where there is danger of damage to the heads or bowls. The copper kettledrum bowls are extremely susceptible to dents. A good protective device is the hood type of padded mackintosh cover which hangs down to envelop the bowl. These can be purchased from the manufacturer or made up locally from heavy fabric, mackintosh or canvas. Moving parts of the machine timpani should be lubricated once or twice a year. Be careful not to get any oil or grease on the ratchet portion of the pedal tuning mechanism of Dresden or the old style Leedy timpani. The newer types of silicone lubricants work very well and appear to be less messy than conventional lubricating substances.

The moving of percussion equipment should always be supervised by the instructor of young school groups. High school and college bands and orchestras should appoint a responsible member of the percussion section to be in charge of all moving of these delicate instruments. If drayage company employees do the moving they should be well briefed on the proper handling of percussion instruments. Items which require special attention are:

1. All drum and timpani heads should be covered with fibre disk-type covers.
2. Xylophone, marimba, bell or vibraphone resonators should be wrapped or cased, as they are easily dented.
3. Timpani should be moved in their trunks. If no trunks are available, use the hoods just described. If neither trunks nor hoods are available, wrap each timpano with a large and thickly padded movers quilt. Always be sure that the wheels are locked after the instruments are placed in the vehicle of conveyance.
4. Removable sets of xylophone, marimba or vibraphone bars should be wrapped, even when moved in their cases.
5. Fibre carrying cases should be used for snare drums and for all small items such as the "traps," sticks, beaters, holders, etc.
6. Cymbals should be laid flat where nothing will rest on them. Do not toss cymbals into a box of miscellany where their edges are exposed to bending stress. A cymbal carrying bag with zipper opener is on the market, and is highly recommended.
7. A large trap case on wheels, of the type used by drum set players, is especially helpful for moving stands for snare drums and cymbals as well as other related equipment.

Two types of percussion instrument storage cabinets are illustrated in Figures A1–A3. The cabinet shown in Figure A1 is designed for use in the band or orchestra rehearsal room. The model shown in Figures A2 and A3 double as storage units and trap tables. Both come equipped with rubber casters which are not shown in the photographs.

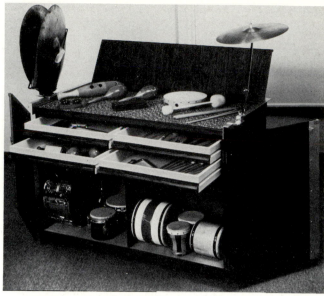

Courtesy Wenger Corp

Figure A3. Unit doubles as a trap table.

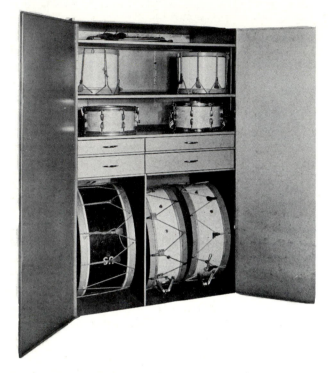

Courtesy Norren Co.

Figure A1. Percussion storage cabinet.

Courtesy Norren Co.

Figure A2. Percussion storage unit.

ASSIGNMENT OF INSTRUMENTS WITHIN THE PERCUSSION SECTION

The assignment of instruments within the percussion section of the orchestra or band may follow one or the other of two basic plans, namely, *rotation* or *specialization*. Under the policy of rotation the several percussionists would change to a different instrument for each selection or to a different instrument at each rehearsal. A policy of specialization would mean that a particular instrument would be covered at all times by a particular player. The usual specialized assignments are timpani, snare drum, cymbals, bass drum, and mallet instruments. In the large concert band the snare drum part is sometimes doubled. The small instruments such as triangle, tambourine, woodblock, and the like are usually covered by whichever percussionists are not engaged on their special instruments at the time.

In a percussion instrument class the rotation system is recommended, as every student should be given the opportunity to gain a basic playing knowledge of each of the percussion instruments. In elementary and junior high school bands and orchestras, rotation of players is also recommended, since at this stage trying out firsthand the techniques of all the instruments satisfies the tendency of young people to explore and provides a basis for later specialization. Many school instructors use a system of rotation at the beginning of each school year and continue its use until spring concert time approaches, at which time specific instrument assignments are made. These assignments are based on the particular aptitudes of the percussion section members as demonstrated throughout the earlier parts of the school year. High school situations vary, because some students enter the orchestra or band with several years of experience and/or private study on one or another of the percussion specializations, while others have only a basic generalized sort of background. Still others will likely be pianists or other instrumentalists, with little or no technical skill on any of the percussion instruments. In situations which present such diversity, the practical solution is specialization according to the training, experience, and talents of the members of the section. In high school organizations where more uniform backgrounds are to be found, rotation is probably the most satisfactory method for all concerned. The talented, ambitious, and serious student in any band or orchestra should be encouraged to develop his talents on all of the instruments. For example, a highly musical person with several years of private study on the marimba should not only be used as the mallet specialist in the band or orchestra but also should be trained to cover some or all of the other parts. College instrumental majors who are preparing to teach music should gain as much experience as possible on all of the percussion instruments. This is often achieved by playing percussion instruments with the training orchestras or bands in addition to the major performing groups. Percussion majors should concentrate on obtaining a well-rounded skill in each of the special areas during college years. Later professional work may require their specialization in snare drum or timpani for example, but the college years are the best time to perfect techniques along the broad front in order to achieve the status of a true professional percussionist. The present-day symphony orchestra, recording, and studio professional is expected to be able to perform creditably on each and every one of the percussion instruments regardless of the particular specialized duty he may have in the organization.

Some policy or system should be used to ensure that all the parts will be covered with a minimum of delay and discussion at rehearsals. A useful device is the penciling in of the player's first name above each entrance, instrument by instrument. In orchestrations with a separate part for each instrument the names can be written at the top of the sheet of music. In high school, college, and professional groups this method of instrument assignment works well. Assignments are usually made by the section head. In younger bands and orchestras, the instructor should make the assignments to ensure equitable rotation among the students and to eliminate squabbling within the section. Parts should be marked before the music is passed out. In compositions calling for many rapid changes in instrumentation, care must be taken to consider the time factor involved in changing from one instrument to another. When one player is required to change from one instrument to another during a composition, it is helpful if a penciled notation "change to" or simply "to" is made in the music immediately after the last note played on the original instrument.

Given the complex nature of many modern compositions, organizing the percussion section can become a major source of frustration for the ensemble director. Figures A4 through A6 offer three different types of charts to assist with organizing the percussion section. After all the performance parts are assigned, a filled in copy of the chart should be placed in each folder of percussion music as well as in the conductor's folder also. Considerable amounts of rehearsal time will be conserved as a result of using one or more of the organizational charts which follow. A well-organized percussion section is especially enhanced if the director will announce the rehearsal schedule in advance. This will allow the percussion section to be properly prepared with the correct instruments, mallets, etc. without wasting any time.

Another advantage to using the organizational charts is that the director and/or section leader can determine at a glance whether or not all players receive the opportunity to play all the instruments. Furthermore, a contingency plan can be developed listing substitute players in the event one or more players are injured or become ill before a major performance, be it a concert or contest. The organizational chart will also expedite productive rehearsals in the event that an assistant or substitute director assumes the responsibility for rehearsals.

Figure A4. PERCUSSION ASSIGNMENT CHART

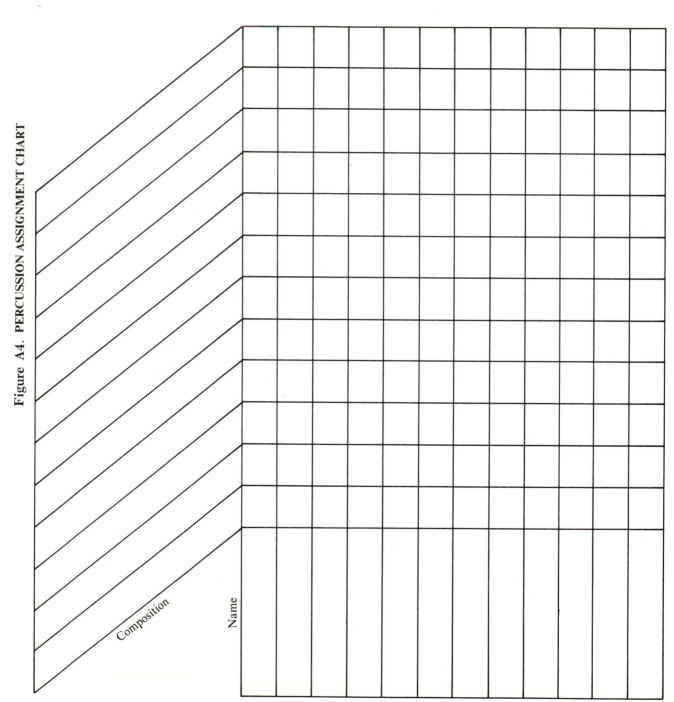

SECTION LEADER

Write in composition title on slanted lines. After name write in instrument(s) played.

Fill out for each concert and give a copy to your director.

Abbreviations and/or symbols:

SD = Snare Drum

FD = Field Drum

BD = Bass Drum

Timp = Timpani

Xyl = Xylophone

Vibe = Vibraharp

Mar = Marimba

Bells = Orchestra Bells

WB = Woodblock

TB = Temple Blocks

Tamb = Tambourine

△ = Triangle

= Crash Cymbals

= Suspended Cymbal

= Chimes

Composition

Name

Figure A4. Percussion assignment chart.

Figure A5. PERCUSSION ORGANIZATIONAL CHART

SECTION LEADER—Use this organizational chart to list equipment needed for band, orchestra or percussion ensemble. Write in title of composition and check appropriate equipment box.

(MAKE A COPY FOR YOUR DIRECTOR)

[ACCESSORIES]

Composition	SD	BD	CYM	TIMP	BELLS	XYL	MAR	VIBE								

Figure A5. Percussion organizational chart.

Figure A6. ORGANIZATION CHART

NAME	Snare Drum	Bass Drum	Cym.	Timp.	Mar.	Xyl.	Bells							

Figure A6. Organization chart.

The following commentary pertains to the percussion parts for *Variations on a Korean Folk Song* by John Barnes Chance. The complete timpani and percussion parts appear on the next eight pages. The composition requires five percussionists and one timpanist.

The notes followed by ties must be allowed to ring, even when the tie is succeeded by rests. It is helpful to indicate the initial timpani tunings directly on the timpani part in the upper left-hand corner: F, B♭, D♭, G♭ or, use a small section of staff:

Measure(s)	Performance Suggestions
9	strike triangle with large beater; allow triangle to ring
39	use hard yarn, cord-wound or felt mallet on gong; temple block sticking pattern depends on blocks mounted in-line or staggered and on player covering the part; use medium hard xylophone mallets on blocks; hard rubber on xylophone
49	pair of cymbals used here
51–76 53	general purpose mallets on timpani; triangle beater on cymbal dome; be sure gong, suspended cymbal and triangle are steady and precise
63	medium to hard yarn or cord mallets on vibraphone; clear execution of octaves, lest false grace note sound results
68	pair of cymbals indicated again

Measure(s)	Performance Suggestions
71	use appropriate gong mallet, not bass drum stick which is too light
116 (allegro con brio)	play 4-stroke ruffs on snare drum just *before* the beat and main note *directly on* the beat
	regular staccato mallets on timpani, short mallet height and use staccato technique (squeeze mallets with thumb and first two fingers; not possible to observe rests in timpani part here due to speed
147	snare drum to be played with closed rolls only
150	brass mallets on orchestra bells; five-stroke rolls on snare drum in first seven measures; bass drum and cymbals *must* be precise
178	timpani solo here with staccato mallets on muted heads; use actual timpani mutes or small piece of cloth on each drum; triplet figure at *sostenuto* must be steady
184	the triplet figure remains constant
190	large (20″ or 22″) suspended cymbal struck with large yarn marimba mallets such as Musser M-12
199	snare drum grace notes played closed; new timpani tuning is: F, G♭, A♭, B♭; unfortunately, all four of these pitches sound best on two largest drums (32″ and 29″); play F and G♭ on 32″ and A♭ and B♭ on 29″

Q.M.B. 348

Printed in U.S.A.

Figure A7. Variations on a Korean Folk Song, John Barnes Chance. © Copyright 1967 by Boosey & Hawkes, Inc. Reprinted by permission.

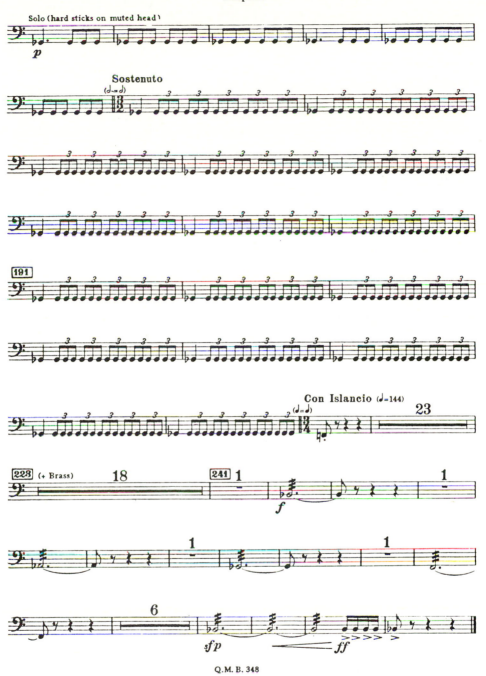

Figure A7. *Continued*

VARIATIONS
ON A KOREAN FOLK SONG

JOHN BARNES CHANCE

Q.M.B. 348

Printed in U.S.A.

Figure A7. *Continued*

2   Percussion

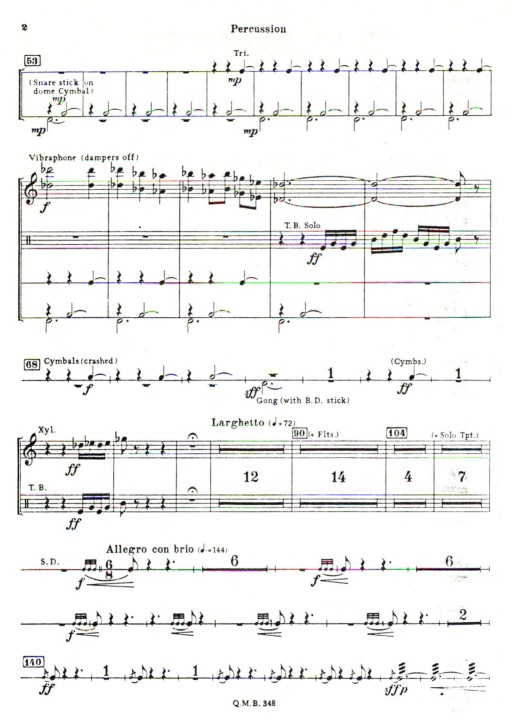

Q.M.B. 348

Figure A7. *Continued*

Q.M.B. 348

Figure A7. *Continued*

Q.M.B. 348

Figure A7. *Continued*

Q. M. B. 348

Figure A7. *Continued*

6 Percussion

Q.M.B. 348

Figure A7. *Continued*

On the next two pages are the percussion parts for two standard marches from the band repertory, with suggestions for performance.

Figure A8. "The Black Horse Troop" (march) by John Philip Sousa using the following material: the march size part for drums, one page only. Reprinted by permission. Sam Fox Publishing Company, Inc.

The bass drum notes can be doubled with cymbals to good effect if the cymbals are not too large and heavy. In measure 5, the pattern should be reversed so that flams are played *on* the beats. The flam accent number 2 can also be used. In 6/8 marches, that certain lilting quality is greatly enhanced with the sticking pattern of RRLLRR or LLRRLL. The consecutive flams in line 5 are played on one side; do not alternate. The short rolls should be tied in a consistent manner. Be sure to observe the correct bass drum rhythm, especially in line 7, measures 6 through 9, and do not anticipate the second beat of the bar in 6/8.

All ruffs must be interpreted with the main note on the beat. The ties must be carefully observed as they are of the essence in this particular march. All eighth notes must be played very evenly, especially in the trio, to reinforce the tutti rhythm in the winds. As in other marches, all dynamics must be strictly followed so that the percussion contribute musically to the piece. Percussion parts must always be checked against the conductor's score to be sure that all articulations are present. Percussion parts are often notoriously lacking many of the signs necessary for correct performance.

SIDE DRUM

COLONEL BOGEY
March

KENNETH J. ALFORD

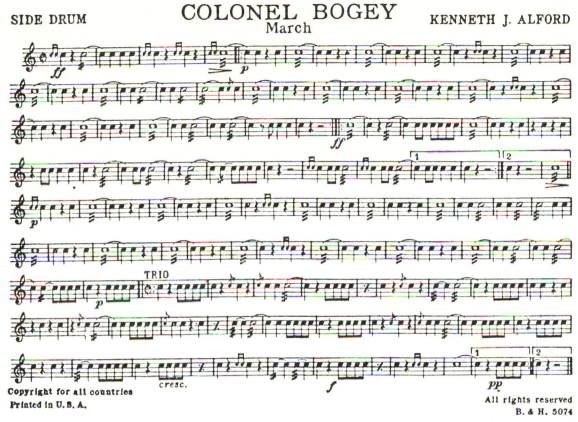

Figure A9. "Colonel Bogey," Alford. © Copyright 1914, 1916 by Hawkes & Son (London) Ltd.; renewed 1941, 1943. Reprinted by permission of Boosey & Hawkes, Inc.

HOW TO MARK PERCUSSION PARTS

In addition to the marking of instrument assignment, experience has taught percussionists the value of certain other aids to good performance which can be penciled into parts. School music instructors should encourage their students to use pencil marks freely, following the lead of the professionals who make very liberal use of markings and rarely trust to luck or memory. There follows a list of some of the more common pencil markings used as performance aids by professional percussion players:

1. Rests, when they occur as a series of individual measures, should be numbered thus:

2. Repeat or ditto measures are very frequently encountered in drum parts. They should be numbered, either with a number for each measure, on alternate measures, or at each fourth bar, thus:

Note that the numbering corresponds with the measure *according to its place in the phrase.*

3. Cues of other instrumental parts penciled into the drum or timpani parts are often helpful as insurance against losing the count during long rests. For example:

4. Eyeglasses are conventionally used to alert the player to a trouble spot such as a quick tempo change or unexpected fermata:

5. Cuts are marked with double slash marks which include the portion of the music to be left out. These slash marks are then connected by a continuous line which may traverse bars, lines, or even pages of music. See example A below:

6. Accents and dynamic markings may be written in where they are not indicated in the score, but are desired by the conductor. Those accent and dynamic marks which require special attention may be overmarked with heavy pencil lines.

7. When abrupt changes in tempo and/or meter occur, or if there is likely to be some doubt about the conductor's choice of beat pattern, musicians usually mark the parts with slash marks above the initial measure of the piece or at the measure where a change occurs. See example B:

8. Indicate all changes of instrument or beater by "change to."

9. Timpani players should note in pencil tuning cues from other instruments during the course of a composition where frequent tunings are necessary.

10. Timpani tuning changes should be noted in pencil if they are not printed in the part, i.e., "E to F♯."

11. Timpani note settings should be penciled in at the beginning of each piece or movement if they are not already printed in the part.

12. Make note of passages in mallet instrument, timpani or snare drum parts which require unusual sticking by the use of *R* and *L*.

13. Choice of most appropriate sticks, mallets or beaters should be penciled in where necessary, such as "soft mallets," "wood sticks," "two beaters."

14. V.S. (volti subito—It. "turn quickly") should be marked in large letters at the end of a page which requires a quick turn.

15. Brackets should be drawn to enclose rhythmic figures which cross bar lines or are otherwise not readily apparent, as in A and B below.

SUBSTITUTION OF PERCUSSION INSTRUMENTS

Occasions will arise in all but the most completely equipped bands and orchestras when it will be necessary to substitute an available instrument for one called for in the score but not procurable. It usually is better to improvise a substitution rather than leave the part out entirely. The following list of possible substitutions does not

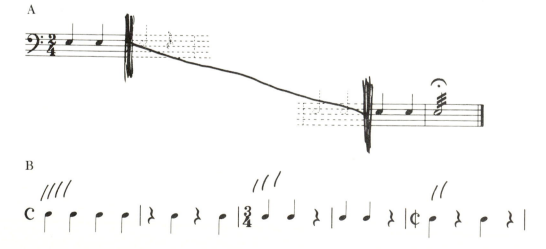

exhaust the potentialities, but may prove useful to the director as a guide in making necessary percussion instrument substitutions. It should be noted that, as a general rule, instruments of a similar pitch range and timbre are used as substitutes for the indicated instruments.

1. The bass drum can be used to play certain important timpani parts if these are of vital rhythmic or timbre importance. The bass drum cannot contribute the harmonic effects of the timpani, however. It is possible to use the large (16″ × 16″) tunable tom-tom from the dance drummer's set-up to substitute for the timpani in certain cases. With careful tuning these can be made to sound a fairly clear fundamental tone.

2. A triangle beater, spike, or snare drumstick striking the dome section of a suspended cymbal can be used to serve as a triangle, and has been used to substitute for even a bell note.

3. The best substitute for the tambourine is the snare drum played near the rim.

4. Castanet parts can be played by striking the top of a woodblock with the tips of snare drumsticks.

5. Woodblock notes can be obtained by using a snare drum rim shot of the cross stick variety (see Chapter 3, page 63). Very light woodblock notes can be imitated by playing on the rim of the snare drum.

6. Xylophone and marimba are interchangeable, provided the appropriate kinds of mallets are used. In making the xylophone serve as a marimba, use soft rubber or yarn-covered mallets. To play a xylophone part on the marimba, use medium or hard rubber mallets. As a general rule, play xylophone parts in the upper octaves of the marimba. Play marimba parts on the lower octaves of the xylophone.

7. Bells and vibraphone parts can be substituted for each other. Do not use the "vibra" mechanism when playing bell parts on the vibraphone. Transpose written bell notes up two octaves if played on the vibraphone. Make the opposite transposition if playing vibraphone notes on the bells.

8. Chime parts can be played on the bells or the vibraphone, doubling at the octave in the lowest possible range.

9. Here is an ingenious substitute for the tuned antique cymbals (crotales) called for in Debussy scores and other works. Remove the bell bars corresponding to the pitches of the antique cymbals called for (e″ and b‴ in DeBussy's *L'Apès Midi d'un Fune*). Place these bars on a pair of heavy rubber bands stretched around a cigar box with its top removed. Use metal bell mallets on the bars, striking very lightly.

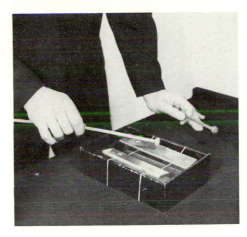

Figure A10. Bell bars can substitute for antique cymbals.

10. The triangle can be used to substitute for the bells, although this is not a satisfactory substitute if the passage is melodic in nature.

11. The snare drum, especially the field type with snares turned off, makes an excellent substitute for the tom-tom. The field drum with no snares may serve very satisfactorily as a tenor drum.

12. A large and heavy suspended suspended cymbal, 22″ or larger, struck with a large marimba mallet such as a Musser M–12 can be used to substitute for a tamtam (gong).

13. The woodblock can be substituted for temple blocks. To obtain two tones from a single block, strike with the tip of the snare drumstick on top of the block for a light, high pitched tone, and with the shoulder of the stick on the edge for a deeper, more resonant tone.

14. Different size snare (with snares off), field, or tenor drums or any combination of these played with medium or hard timpani sticks can be substituted for a set of concert tom-toms. Modern scores, particularly band scores, call for these instruments frequently.

When all of the written parts cannot be covered by the number of percussionists available, it becomes necessary to ensure that the most important instruments will be heard and only the least essential will be left out. Every case demands the attention of the director, and no two cases will be exactly alike. The two general rules that may guide the director or percussionist are: 1) leave out those notes or passages which contribute least to the total musical effect, and 2) leave out those passages which are played by another percussion instrument in the same general pitch-timbre range. As an illustration of the latter rule, if timpani and bass drum play a similar rhythm pattern the bass drummer can be spared to play a triangle part not covered by another player. Another illustration: when gong and cymbal notes coincide, and the player cannot reach both instruments at once, leaving out the cymbal notes would probably be best, since the gong is more powerful and would tend to dominate the sound anyhow.

STAGE DEPORTMENT FOR THE PERCUSSION SECTION

The watchwords for the percussion section in concert are: 1) no unnecessary movement and 2) no unnecessary sound.

The first step to unobtrusive and efficient concert performance is to arrange the instruments, stands, music, trap tables, sticks, beaters, etc., in their most convenient location before the first downbeat. Each player should be responsible for the items of equipment he is to use during the concert, and the section head should oversee the group's preparations. Due to the complicated percussion set-up required by many contemporary compositions, ample time between pieces must be allowed. It is always wise for the conductor to make a visual check with the percussion section leader prior to giving his downbeat to make sure the section is prepared.

It is presumed that the parts have been definitely assigned and marked for the individual players during rehearsals. There is no excuse for confusion over who is to play what at concert time. During rehearsal periods one further matter should be worked out, and that is the timing of standing for entrances after rests. Incidentally, rests should be counted silently, and with a minimum of lip movement. Cross-checking of the count among the players may be done by a prearranged signal, such as a nod of the head or a small movement of the hand at each rehearsal letter. Lip-reading, provided that it is done discreetly, is an additional check. Each percussionist should have a chair and should sit during long rests and tacet portions of the program. In moderate or slow tempos a rest of over 16 or so measures will allow the player ample time to be seated and rise again for the next entry. One simple rule for rising for an entrance would be to rise four measures in advance in slow or moderate tempos, eight measures in advance in allegro and presto passages.

Particular care should be taken to eliminate the distracting extra sounds from the percussion section which mar so many performances. Dropped snare drumsticks can be prevented by a concert rest position which uses *both* hands, one at either end of the pair of sticks. See Figure A11. Some band directors prefer a more military rest position in which the pair of sticks is tucked under the right arm with the ends held from underneath by the right hand. See Figure A12.

Figure A11. Concert rest position.

Figure A12. Military concert rest position.

Do not allow the triangle beater to touch the triangle while getting into playing position, or let the triangle dangle where it will strike a stand, drum or timpani handle.

The tambourine is a treacherous instrument to prepare for playing and to put down after playing. The tambourine must be moved very slowly and carefully in order to keep the jingles from sounding.

A great aid to quiet functioning in the percussion section is a felt or baize-covered trap table. The type of folding tray stand used by bus boys is an excellent and portable base for a trap table. Cymbals, as well as the small traps, sticks and beaters should be placed on this table when not actually in use. Commercial trap tables are available, also.

Snares should always be turned off at the conclusion of a snare drum passage preceding a long rest. This practice must be rigidly adhered to, as the buzzing of the snares during quiet passages is very annoying to the other musicians and to the audience. The snare drummer must also develop the habit of turning the snares back on just prior to entry—it is embarrassing to start a snare drum passage with a tom-tom tone.

Figure A13. Trap table.

Percussion students should be trained to arrive early in order to arrange their instruments and to tune them properly before the rehearsal or concert hour. The snare drumheads should be set, snare tension adjusted, bass drumhead loosened to its proper playing tension, and the timpani set for the tunings required in the first piece on the program. All the instruments should be tested prior to the playing period, and a thorough check made to see that all music, instruments, sticks, beaters, etc. are in order, and that music stands are placed so as to allow good sightlines to the conductor.

Snare drummers should try to avoid testing drumhead and snare tension during a performance. If it becomes necessary to make adjustments, test during a tutti passage where the sound will not be noticed.

The timpanist has a special problem in timing his tuning changes so that they will not be audible to the audience. He should use the finger flick and not the sticks to test intonation. If possible, he should locate the harmony or single tone to which he is tuning in a preceding passage. For instance, he may get his cue from a tuba note F♯ four measures ahead of his own entrance on an F♯, and test his tuning quietly as the tuba sounds his note.

TWENTY MOST COMMON FAULTS OF SCHOOL PERCUSSION SECTIONS

1. Poor handholds, poor wrist action.
2. Snare drums set too low.
3. Snare drums not set on stands correctly.
4. Music stands too low for drums, timpani—too high for mallet-played instruments.
5. Not watching conductor closely enough, with resultant rushing or dragging.
6. Snare drumheads too loose.
7. Bass drumheads too tight.
8. Excessive noise, talking, fooling.
9. "Scurrying," which is distracting to audience.
10. Uneven tension on timpani, bass drum and snare drumheads.
11. Poor choice of sticks, beaters or mallets for the purpose at hand, i.e., snare drumsticks too light, timpani sticks too fluffy, triangle beaters too heavy, bell mallets too soft, etc.
12. Double stroke roll on timpani.
13. Hands through loops of cymbal straps. (except for marching band)
14. Triangle left on stand while being played.
15. Snare drum snares vibrating sympathetically.
16. Failure to damp properly and at the right time (timpani, bass drum, cymbals, triangle, bells, chimes).
17. Failure to make the most of dynamic constrasts.
18. Careless counting.
19. Failure to listen to total ensemble sound.
20. "Faking."

Annotated Bibliography

PERCUSSION INSTRUMENT TEACHING AND REFERENCE MATERIALS

I. Snare Drum

CIRONE, ANTHONY J. *The Orchestral Snare Drummer*. Belwin Mills, Melville, New York.

A non-rudimental approach to the teaching of snare drum. This is an excellent and very sensible book which introduces the beginner to simple ensemble playing, flexibility and basically sound musicianship.

————. *Portraits in Rhythm*. Belwin Mills, Melville, New York.

Fifty studies for snare drum with heavy emphasis on dynamics and musical form. For the advanced snare drummer.

FENNELL, FREDERICK. *The Drummer's Heritage*, Carl Fischer Inc., New York.

A collection of old popular airs and official U.S. Army music for fifes and drums combined with similar pieces for field trumpets, cymbals and drums. An excellent source for the student of rudimental snare drumming. All of the music in this volume is recorded on Mercury MG 50111 *The Spirit of '76* and MG 50112 *Ruffles and Flourishes*.

GOLDENBERG, MORRIS. *Modern School for the Snare Drum with a Guide Book for the Artist Percussionist*. Chappell and Co., New York.

Probably the outstanding book in its field, this book treats snare drumming from a practical performance standpoint rather than a rudimental one. Graded study material, including numerous duets, runs from easy to very difficult. In addition to the snare drum, excerpts and studies cover the bass drum, cymbals, numerous small percussion instruments and the Latin-American rhythm instruments. Percussion scores for 16 pieces from the standard orchestra literature are included, with notes on practical performance practices for each. Other features are the complete score of Varèse's *Ionisation* and a glossary of percussion terms in three languages.

HARR, HASKELL W. *Drum Method for Band and Orchestra*, Books One and Two. M. M. Cole Publishing Co., Chicago.

Though somewhat dated and traditional, Book One is very helpful for beginners in developing a solid background upon which to build fine musicianship.

————. *Supplementary Reading Material*, Books 1 and 2.

These two books provide extensive extra reading material to augment the two volumes mentioned above. There are exercises in various meters and styles with helpful explanations at the beginning of each exercise.

McMILLAN, THOMAS. *20th Century Orchestral Snare Drum Studies*. Creative Music, Glenville, Ill.

An excellent collection of representative snare drum rhythm patterns from contemporary orchestral literature. Examples of the rhythms of such composers as Bartok, Chavez, Copland, and Stravinsky, only to mention a few, are presented. A great opportunity for the advanced drummer to study such devices as asymmetrical meters, asymmetrical divisions, shifted accents, changing meters, superimposed rhythms, etc.

PAYSON, AL. *The Snare Drum in the Concert Hall*. Payson Percussion Products, Park Ridge, Illinois.

This book is directed to the drummer who is interested in any or all facets of concert percussion playing, be it symphony orchestra, concert band, opera, ballet or chamber music. The user of this book must be at least at the intermediate level in technical proficiency and reading skills.

PODEMSKI, BENJAMIN. *Standard Snare Drum Method*. Belwin Mills, New York.

Although a somewhat dated method book, its chief value lies in the many and varied exercises and etudes for the snare drum which provide excellent reading material.

PRICE, PAUL. *Beginning Snare Drum Method*. Morris, New York.

A musical approach to the snare drum. Includes some 250 studies derived from the rudiments, many of which are in 8 measure tap step form. The treatment of the roll, and the fine photographic illustrations of playing positions, handholds, etc., make this a good book for either individual or class instruction. Developed by a college percussion instructor, and particularly adapted for use with mature students.

STONE, GEORGE L. *Stick Control for the Snare Drummer*. Geo. B. Stone and Son, Inc., Boston.

A very thorough book for developing technique using progressively arranged permutations of stickwork patterns of certain rhythmic figures. Very useful for attaining fine technique as well as for maintaining it. Excellent supplemental material for the serious and diligent snare drum student.

WHALEY, GARWOOD. *Fundamental Studies for Snare Drum*. JR Publications, New York.

A perfect book for teachers interested in a method book for beginning snare drum. It contains many things a new student must learn including basic time signatures, dynamic marks and even simple duets.

————. *Intermediate Duets for Snare Drum*.

This book fills a void for there are few studies that present snare drum duets suitable for intermediate students. Each part is extremely musical, helping to develop techniques important for playing with an ensemble or for solo playing.

————. *Musical Studies for the Intermediate Snare Drummer*. JR Publications, New York.

This collection of musical pieces will increase technical facility and develop musicianship. It includes the extensive use of dynamic marks, changing meters, drags, flams and rolls.

————. *Primary Handbook for Snare Drum*. Meredith Music Publications, Fort Lauderdale, Florida.

A comprehensive and musical beginning method that includes rudiments, reading, duets, repetition exercises, multiple drum studies and composition assignments.

————. *Recital Solos for Snare Drum*. Meredith Music Publications, Fort Lauderdale, Florida.

Thirty musically challenging solos for concert or contest, intended for the intermediate to advanced student.

————. *Solos and Duets for Snare Drum*. Meredith Music Publications, Fort Lauderdale, Florida.

A collection of educational and musically challenging solos and duets for contest or recital. Solos include idiomatic techniques that explore a variety of unique sound possibilities on snare drum and multiple drums. A superior collection for the intermediate to advanced performer.

II. Mallets

BARNETT, WALLACE. *The Mallet Percussions and How To Use Them*. J. C. Deagan, Inc., Chicago.

This guide contains brief but pertinent resumes of each of the mallet instruments. This pamphlet could be an aid when purchasing keyboard percussion. The publication also contains a compilation of performance material, from all publishers, in which the mallet instruments are used.

BURTON, GARY. *Four Mallet Studies*. Creative Music, Glenview, Ill.

A study of the problems involved in playing with four mallets. Although much of the technique discussed is applicable to all mallet instruments, the book concerns itself with the "vibes." It deals with holding the mallets (with good pictures), hand and mallet independence, and voicing techniques. All areas contain a considerable number of exercises and examples. This is a good book for the aspiring jazz vibe player.

————. *Solo*. Creative Music, Glenview, Ill.

A collection of six unaccompanied solos for the vibraphone. Sticking, use of the damper, and chordal structures are well marked. These solos range from medium difficult to very difficult.

CIRONE, ANTHONY J. *Portraits in Melody*. Belwin Mills Publishing Corp., Melville, New York.

This is an advanced book consisting of fifty studies for marimba and xylophone, mostly for two mallets. Tempos and suggested stickings are included throughout, although the author makes it clear in his preface that other stickings are possible. Cirone is a percussionist with the San Francisco Symphony Orchestra and a faculty member at San Jose State University.

DEVENS, GEORGE. *Lesson Plan for Mallet Instruments*, a Musical Approach to Technique for Vibes, Marimba, Xylophone. Henry Alder, Inc., New York.

Guide to ideas on technique studies, to be extended and transposed to all keys. Intended as a foundation book for the mallet player preparing for jazz or studio field. Stress is on technique building, not reading.

FIRTH, VIC. *Mallet Technique*. Carl Fischer, Inc., New York.

This book contains 38 studies for xylophone, marimba and vibraphone by the solo timpanist and principal percussionist for the Boston Symphony Orchestra. Three tempo markings are indicated (beginner, intermediate, advanced) for each study.

GOLDENBERG, MORRIS. *Modern School for the Xylophone, Marimba, Vibraphone*. Chappell and Co., New York.

A complete method for the mallet-played instruments. Scale and chordal studies in all keys, with related melodic materials comprise the first half of the book. These are graded from easy to very difficult. The latter half of the book contains excerpts from standard orchestral literature. A must for all serious students of the mallet instruments.

GORNSTON, DAVID. *Foundation Studies for Vibes, Xylophone or Marimba.* David Gornston, New York.

Contains graded original major and minor scale and chord studies, plus 15 pages of studies adapted from Klosé and other sources. These studies run a full page each and are excellent for the building of a fine mallet technqiue.

GREEN, GEORGE HAMILTON. *New Elementary Studies for Xylophone and Marimba.* Leedy and Ludwig, Elkhart, Indiana.

Mallet studies for the beginner, including all of the major and minor scales. Exercises are adequate from a technical standpoint. No excerpts or pieces.

KRAUS, PHIL, ed. ALLEN, DOUG. *Modern Mallet Method,* Vol. I Elem., Vol. II Inter., Vol. III Advan., Belwin Mills, Melville, New York.

Progressively arranged technique exercises, mostly in sequence form. Little melodic material. Theory, especially harmony, well treated. Good supplementary material for the ambitious student preparing for jazz and studio work.

PETERSON, HOWARD M. *Rubank Elementary Method—Marimba or Xylophone,* Rubank, Inc., Chicago.

A foundation course for individual or like-instrument class instruction. Contains basic technical studies, mostly easy, and many familiar tunes. Some of the melodies are arranged as duets and trios. Good beginning book for young students.

SCHAEFER, FLORENCE. *Xylophone and Marimba Method,* Vol. I. Henry Alder, Inc., New York.

Basic mallet instrument instruction for the very young beginner. Uses folk song materials, quizzes, tests, blank pages for notes, and similar teaching aids. Contains 174 short exercises. Adapted for private or class instruction.

STEVENS, LEIGH HOWARD. *Method of Movement for Marimba,* Marimba Productions, New York.

Based upon the author's innovative rotary-stroke method of playing the marimba, there are 590 exercises designed to achieve mastery of this unique technique which has revolutionized mallet playing. This volume is intended for the serious mallet student who is dedicated to complete and independent control of four mallets.

STONE, GEORGE L. *Mallet Control for the Xylophone, Marimba, Vibe.* Geo. B. Stone and Son, Inc., Boston.

Supplemental sequential studies for the mallet-played instruments, to be memorized and transposed to other keys. Designed to build a sound and facile technique. Studies are made up of diatonic scale patterns, arpeggiated chords, and double stops.

WHALEY, GARWOOD. *Fundamental Studies for Mallets.* JR Publications, New York.

This is a valuable beginning book which integrates reading, technique and memorization of familiar tunes. Many of the transcriptions emanate from the symphonic and keyboard literature.

————. *Musical Studies for the Intermediate Mallet Player.* Meredith Music Publications, Fort Lauderdale, Florida.

A complete intermediate method book that is well organized and very musical. Includes studies in technique, reading, duets and four-mallet playing.

————. *Primary Handbook for Mallets.* Meredith Music Publications, Fort Lauderdale, Florida.

A complete method that includes studies in reading, techniques and creativity. A graduated book for beginning students.

III. Timpani

ABEL, ALAN. *20th Century Orchestra Studies for Timpani.* G. Schirmer, Inc., New York.

The author has compiled and annotated 69 pages of timpani excerpts from the works of 22 different contemporary composers. The book is helpful for the serious and aspiring orchestral timpanist as well as to anyone in need of modern excerpts.

ATKINS, THOMAS N. *The Musical Timpanist.* Kendor Music, Inc., Delevan, New York.

Written by the timpanist of the Indianapolis Symphony Orchestra, the book contains twenty lessons, each with specific goals intended. There are many tuning exercises throughout as well as photographs with explanations of the various makes and models of timpani mechanisms.

BEGUN, FRED. *Twenty-One Etudes for Timpani.* Meredith Music Publications, Fort Lauderdale, Florida.

The technically and musically challenging solos provide advanced solo literature for three, four and five drums, all of which must be pedal timpani. There is a diagram at the beginning of each etude explaining which drums to use, as well as helpful stickings and other performance suggestions.

DOWD, CHARLES. *The Well-Tempered Timpanist.* Belwin Mills Publishing Corp., Melville, New York.

This book contains 770 technical studies for the practicing timpanist. There is material for two, three, four and five drums.

FIRTH, VIC. *The Solo Timpanist.* Carl Fischer, Inc., New York.

Designed for the advanced player, this is a fine collection of 26 etudes for solo timpani. Each of the etudes deals with problems related to some of the most difficult works in the classical and modern repertoire, problems such as complicated meter changes, technique on six timpani, piano-staccato playing in the low register, cross sticking, tuning, and melodic passages.

FRIESE, ALFRED, and LEPAK, ALEXANDER. *Timpani Method.* Henry Adler, Inc., New York.

A truly complete timpani method, including extensive modern repertoire. Recognizes *intonation* as the central problem in timpani playing and devotes many pages to tuning study. Presumes the use of pedal timpani. Some studies for 3 and 4 kettles. In four parts: Basic Theory, Technique and Facts, Intonation, and Repertoire. A must for all serious timpani students.

GOODMAN, SAUL. *Modern Method for Timpani.* Mills Music, Inc., New York.

A complete timpani method in four sections: 1) Fundamentals, 2) Exercises for the Development of Technique on 2 Drums, 3) 3 and 4 Drum Technique, including Pedal Timpani, 4) Repertoire. Careful and copious explanations accompany the musical studies. An excellently selected repertoire of 22 selections, plus 2 original solos. Author was timpanist of New York Philharmonic. A must for serious timpani students.

HARR, HASKELL W. *Method for Timpani.* M. M. Cole Pub. Co., Chicago.

An inexpensive beginning timpani method, satisfactory for young elementary students. Contains some of the author's rudimental snare drum solos adapted for the timpani.

LUDWIG, WM. F. *Ludwig Timpani Instructor.* Ludwig Drum Co., Chicago.

A beginning method book included with all new WFL timpani. Diagrams and illustrations show proper playing positions, handholds, etc. In addition to the tuning and technique studies, information is given on the care of the timpani heads, storage, etc.

SEITZ, J. FRED. *Sietz, Modern School of Timpani Playing.* Leedy Mfg. Co., Elkhart, Ind., (out of print).

A complete timpani method, containing historical information and many illustrations. Theory of music and lists of musical terms and foreign language percussion terms are included. Tuning and technical studies

for two to five kettledrums comprise the first section of the book. Orchestral excerpts make up the bulk of the book (130 pages), including all of the Beethoven symphonies and excerpts from the principal Wagnerian operas.

WHALEY, GARWOOD. *Fundamental Studies for Timpani: Musical Studies for the Intermediate Timpanist.* JR Publications, New York.

These two volumes contain numerous exercises ranging from elementary techniques to frequent dynamic changes, tuning changes, musical expressions, glissandi and changes of meter.

————. *Primary Handbook for Timpani.* Meredith Music Publications, Fort Lauderdale, Florida.

This comprehensive course of study for the beginning timpanist contains many fundamental elements of timpani playing. There are many two-drum exercises and diagrams are used throughout to help the student to understand each fundamental technique. A number of tuning studies are also included.

IV. Comprehensive Percussion Methods

BARTLETT, HARRY R. *Percussion Ensemble Method for Teacher Education.* Wm. C. Brown Co., Dubuque, Iowa.

Designed as a semester course text for the college-level instrumental class. Aims to develop the basic skills of playing all the percussion instruments through ensemble studies and pieces. The snare drum is considered as the basic instrument. Includes studies and pieces for various combinations of snare drum, bass drum, cymbals, timpani, mallet-played instruments, the small percussion instruments, Latin-American instruments and the dance band drum set. Emphasis is on musical and practical performance techniques.

FIRTH, VIC. *Percussion Symposium.* Carl Fischer, Inc., New York.

A very fine manual defining and illustrating the complete percussion section. It covers the areas of tone production, sound projection, instrument range, selection of correct sticks, proper care of instruments, and interpreting percussion notation. Although not a method book in the general sense, this publication is a source of practical reference for all those interested in the art of percussion playing.

GARDNER, CARL E. *Gardner Modern Method for the Instruments of Percussion.* Carl Fischer, New York.

In three parts. Complete in one volume or separate. Part One: Drums, Cymbals, Accessories (120 pp.), Part Two: Bells, Xylophone, Vibraphone, Marimba, Chimes (105 pp.), Part Three: Timpani (95 pp.). A standard method book presenting a unified approach to all the standard instruments of the percussion family. Thorough and correct expository text, clear instructions in technical matters. Copious studies, with many drawn from the standard literature. Many of the excerpts, however, are from works seldom played today. Originally copyrighted in 1919, the newly revised and enlarged edition dates from 1938.

SPOHN, CHARLES and TATGENHORST, JOHN. *The Percussion.* Allyn and Bacon, Inc., Boston.

A basic manual covering all the percussion instruments with an appendix containing exercises dealing with basic problems encountered on these instruments. Much supplemental material would be needed if this manual were being used as an instructional text; however, it is a good book for use by school music teachers as a reference source.

V. Set Drumming

BURNS, ROY, and MALIN, LEWIS. *Practical Method of Developing Finger Control.* Henry Adler, Inc., New York.

Photos illustrate snare drumstick handholds used in modern jazz drumming. Stress is on the fulcrum (grip), finger control and bounce technique. Designed for pre-jazz training. Some reading material is included written for four-way hand and foot coordination at the drum set. Studies are in the form of short patterns.

CHAPIN, JIM. *Advanced Techniques for the Modern Drummer.* Jim Chapin, New York.

The exercises in this book are designed to aid the jazz and dance drummer in perfecting the independent hand and foot coordinations characteristic of modern drumming. Most of the studies consist of one or two lines of counterrhythms against the basic cymbal jazz beat and steady bass drum beat in "two" or "four." Snare drum technique and some experience at the drum set are prerequisites.

DAWSON, ALAN, and DeMICHEAL. *A Manual For the Modern Drummer.* Berklee Press Publications, Boston.

A three part book dealing with the fundamentals of set playing, dance-band drumming, and jazz drumming. Presents the basic beat patterns of all major dances and follows each with suggested variations and embellishments. Offers background material on various styles and name players.

LUDWIG, WM. F. JR. *Modern Jazz Drumming.* Ludwig Drum Co., Chicago.

Supersedes Bill Ludwig Jr.'s original book on dance drumming, called "Swing Drumming." Attempts the difficult task of conveying the skills of dance band and jazz drumming via the printed page. Its value is much enhanced by the 130 photos and diagrams which clarify the concepts presented. A good book for the drum student beginning work at the drum set.

MORELLO, JOE. *New Directions in Rhythm.* Jomor Publications, Chicago.

This book was written in answer to many requests from students and professionals and illustrates exactly how Joe uses the cymbals, bass drum, hi-hat and left hand in playing the 3/4 rhythm of the jazz waltz and the 5/4 rhythm.

————. *Off the Record.* Jomor Publications, Chicago.

The drum solos in this book are transcribed from recordings of the Dave Brubeck Quartet on Columbia Records and Joe Morello's own recordings on RCA Victor. All solos are note for note transcriptions as played by Joe Morello and have been edited by the artist himself. Each solo is preceded by two or four measure exercises which were suggested by the ideas expressed in the solo.

————. *Rudimental Jazz.* Jomor Publications, Chicago.

This is a modern application of the "old" rudiments to the drum set. Many of NARD's 26 rudiments are discussed with extensive examples and exercises given utilizing these rudiments in jazz drumming. This is a good book for those brought up on the "rudimental system" and are now learning dance and jazz band drumming.

RALE, PHIL. *Latin-American Rhythms for the Drummer.* Remick Music Corp., New York.

Adaptations of rhythms of the Latin dance forms for the drummer working at the drum set. Some illustrations and adequate exercise material. Mambo and cha-cha-cha not included, as this book was published prior to their introduction into this country.

REED, TED. *Progressive Steps to Syncopation for the Modern Drummer.* Ted Reed, New York.

Study material for "double drums." Exercises vary in length, many full page solos. Syncopation, ties and accents are main problems stressed. No rolls or rudiments. A practical reading book for the ambitious student learning to work at the drum set.

RICH, BUDDY. *Modern Interpretation of Snare Drum Rudiments.* Henry Adler Inc., New York.

Ghost written by Henry Adler, this book attempts to adapt the standard rudiments to usable form for dance band and jazz playing. The entire first half of the book consists of the 26 rudiments in varied notations. Although the rhythms derived from the rudiments do not seem "modern" today, the book does contain a lot of good reading material for snare drum sight-reading.

ROGERS, DENNIS G. *Solo Studies for Drum Set*. (3 vols.). Southern Music Company, San Antonio.

Each of the three volumes contains 9 etudes based upon one or more of the drum rudiments. Stickings and dynamics are clearly indicated throughout. The books provide a smooth transition from the snare drum to the drum set with the elements of technique and musical concepts.

ROTHMAN, JOEL. *The Complete Jazz Drummer*. JR Publications, New York.

This companion book to the *Complete Rock Drummer* deals exclusively with jazz drumming. Geared to intermediate and advanced students, as well as to professional players, this single volume contains hundreds of pages of exercises on the topic of jazz.

————. *The Complete Rock Drummer*. JR Publications, New York.

With over 500 pages, this is a virtual encyclopedia of rock drumming. Almost 200 pages demonstrate an array of coordination exercises for the cymbal, bass and snare drum, as well as for the hi-hat. Rock beats are presented in many different meters including odd time signatures and an entire section is devoted to playing with two bass drums.

————. *The Complete Show Drummer*. JR Publications, New York.

This volume is intended to help the player learn how to handle show charts with smoothness and ease. The book contains hand-written arrangements of typical show drumming charts. The material progresses developmentally from easy to fairly difficult arrangements. Two special sections at the end contain helpful information as to how show charts should be interpreted.

STERNBERG, SIMON. *Modern Drum Studies*. Alfred Music Co., Inc., New York.

A practical study book for double drums. The first section of the book consists of 312 30–40 bar studies, mostly 4/4, progressing very gradually from easy to very difficult. All are scored for snare drum and bass drum. The idioms are not rudimental, but neither are they jazz. Mastery of these studies provides ample foundation for the reading at sight of typical show drum parts. Contains a section on Latin-American rhythm instruments, and concludes with a short section on timpani.

WILCOXON, CHARLEY. *Drum Method*. Chas. Wilcoxon, Cleveland.

An attempt to integrate the original 26 rudiments and "swing" rhythms with most studies and solos written for snare drum, cymbals, etc., and bass drum. Designed for the drum student beginning study at the drum set.

VI. Marching Band Percussion

CASAVANT, A. R. *The Antiphonal Drum Section*. Southern Music Company, San Antonio.

A collection of exercises which may be used in whole or part as drum cadences or as drum music to be played in conjunction with standard marching music. These exercises or cadences serve as an introduction to the various types of contrasting rhythms that may be used with the snare, tenor, bass drum, and cymbals.

FOSTER, ROBERT E., WANAMAKER, JAY A., DUFFER, BOB and COWLES, KRAIG. *Championship Auxiliary Units*, Alfred Publishing Co., Inc., Sherman Oaks, California.

Part two of this book is entitled "Contemporary Marching Percussion Ensemble" and spans some 74 pages. There are many very detailed explanations which address the modern marching percussion section and its related problems as well as solutions.

PETERS, MITCHELL. *Drum Music To March By*. KSM Publishing Company, Dallas.

A collection of drum cadences with the first half of the book devoted to a wide selection of binary and ternary meter cadences with traditional style and instrumentation. The second part of the book presents cadences which are based on various styles of popular music such as "rock and roll."

RAPP, WILLIS. *Multi-Percussion Cadences*, Sets 1–5. Charter Publications, Inc., Valley Forge, Pennsylvania.

Each of the sets contains several lengthy cadences for the greatly expanded marching percussion section. The cadences include parts for timpani, marching mallet percussion instruments, etc.

SCHINSTINE, WM. and HOEY, FRED. *Drum Cadences for All Occasions*. Southern Music Co., San Antonio.

A booklet of march beats in a variety of styles, scored for snare drum, cymbals and bass drum. Based on 6 rudiments. A good source of beats for school marching groups.

Note: The major percussion manufacturers such as Ludwig/Musser and Slingerland/Deagan maintain educational departments which include specialists in all phases of marching percussion. Both of the above-mentioned companies also produce a number of educational aids, often distributed without charge, to assist directors with cadences, drum features, care and repair of all marching instruments and equipment, etc. Simply call or write the company of your choice and they will be most helpful.

VII. History of Percussion

BLADES, JAMES. *Percussion Instruments and Their History*. Praeger, New York.

Beginning with their primitive origins, the history of virtually all percussion instruments is traced in various parts of the world. With its hundreds of musical examples and rare illustrations, the book has become a benchmark work.

FARMER, HENRY GEORGE. *Handel's Kettledrums and Other Papers On Military Music*. Hinrichsen Edison Ltd., London.

A historical survey of English military music with considerable emphasis on the percussion involved. Purely of historical interest.

HOWARD, JOSEPH. *Drums In The Americas*. Oak Publications, New York.

Dr. Howard, one of the country's leading authorities on drums, discusses in this book the heritage of the drum in the Americas from its communal use as an instrument of warning through its final evolution as a musical instrument. Very nicely illustrated.

TITCOMB, CALDWELL. *The Kettledrums in Western Europe: Their History Outside the Orchestra*. Harvard University, Cambridge, Massachusetts.

This is a brilliant doctoral dissertation which concentrates on early kettledrum development. There are eight chapters, over 200 illustrations and a total of 550 pages.

WHITE, CHARLES. *Drums Through The Ages*. The Sterling Press, Los Angeles.

A very readable volume on the history and evolvement of percussion instruments around the world. Interesting as background material on percussion.

VIII. Orchestration of Percussion

ADLER, SAMUEL. *The Study of Orchestration*. W. W. Norton & Company, New York.

This is the first new major work on orchestration to appear in a number of years. The percussion instruments are finally treated as a choir and there is a chapter on scoring for percussion and keyboard, alone or in combination. There are many very appropriate and current musical examples and diagrams.

KENNAN, KENT. *The Technique of Orchestration*, 2nd Ed. Prentice Hall, Inc., Englewood Cliffs, New Jersey.

Although only two chapters of this publication are devoted to percussion, it is worth consulting regarding any problems involved in writing for percussion. This edition was published in 1970 so is generally quite up to date.

LEACH, JOEL and REED, OWEN. *Scoring for Percussion*. Prentice-Hall, Inc., Englewood Cliffs, New Jersey.

This book provides rather detailed analyses and description of the various percussion instruments along with a modern approach to understanding how to notate for these instruments. Areas included in the book are availability of the various percussion instruments, ranges and sizes of the instruments, transposition of the mallet instruments, ways of setting the instruments into vibration, various types of beaters available, standardized notation, and percussion as an integral part of the compositional scheme.

PAPASTEFAN, JOHN J. *Timpani Scoring Techniques in the Twentieth-Century*. University Microfilms International, Ann Arbor, Michigan. (Ph.D. dissertation, Walden University).

There are six chapters, two appendices, a glossary and a very complete bibliography. (UMI order no. LD 00327, 1979).

IX. Miscellaneous Percussion

DENOV, SAM. *The Art of Playing Cymbals*. Adler/Belwin, New York.

This is indeed a rare book covering these often neglected instruments. Written by the cymbalist with the Chicago Symphony Orchestra, the book is an excellent reference and method with photographs and diagrams that illustrate all phases of playing the cymbals.

GOLDENBERG, MORRIS. *Studies in Solo Percussion*, edited by Ralph Satz. Chappel & Company, New York.

There is a wealth of information here to develop skills necessary to perform multiple percussion solo literature. The etudes begin with only two drums, progress to three and then to four or more instruments including non-membranic percussion. There is a supplement of compositions written by Robert Russell Bennett, Morton Gould, Gerald James, Milton Kaye, William Kraft and Norman Lloyd.

MORALES, HUMBERTO and ADLER, HENRY. *Latin-American Instruments and How to Play Them.* Adler/ Belwin, New York.

A wide variety of instruments and rhythms are covered in this volume with many helpful techniques and stickings explained in great detail. The book concludes with examples for the full Latin-American percussion ensemble.

ADDITIONAL REFERENCES

ALTENBURG, JOHANN ERNST (1795), English translation by Edward H. Tarr. *Trumpeters' and Kettledrummers' Art.* Nashville, Tennessee: The Brass Press, 1974.

BACKUS, JOHN. *The Acoustical Foundations of Music.* New York: W. W. Norton & Company, 1969.

BANEK, REINHOLD AND SCOVILLE, JON. *Sound Designs, A Handbook of Musical Instrument Building.* Berkley, California: Ten Speed Press, 1980.

BARTHOLOMEW, WILMER T. *Acoustics of Music.* Englewood Cliffs, New Jersey: Prentice-Hall, 1942.

BRINDLE, REGINALD SMITH. *Contemporary Percussion.* London: Oxford University Press, 1970.

CIRONE, ANTHONY J. AND SINAI, JOE. *The Logic of It All.* Melville, New York: Belwin Mills Publishing Corp., 1977.

COPE, DAVID. *New Music Notation.* Dubuque, Iowa: Kendall/Hunt, 1976.

CULVER, CHARLES A. *Musical Acoustics.* New York: McGraw-Hill, 1956.

Dictionary of Percussion Terms. Morris Lang and Larry Spivack. New York: Lang Percussion Company, 1977.

Harvard Dictionary of Music. 2nd ed. rev. and enl. Cambridge, Massachusetts: Harvard University Press, 1969.

HOLLAND, JAMES. *Percussion.* New York: Schirmer Books, 1978.

MARCUSE, SIBYL. *Musical Instruments: A Comprehensive Dictionary.* Garden City, New York: Doubleday, 1964.

————. *A Survey of Musical Instruments.* New York: Harper and Row, 1975.

MOORE, JAMES L. *Acoustics of Bar Percussion Instruments.* Columbus, Ohio: Permus Publications, 1978.

MUELLER, KENNETH. *Teaching Total Percussion.* West Nyack, New York: Parker Publishing, 1972.

PEINKOFER, KARL AND TANNIGEL, FRITZ. *Handbook of Percussion Instruments.* Translated by Kurt and Else Stone. Melville, New York: Belwin Mills Publishing Corp., 1976.

PETERS, GORDON B. *The Drummer: Man.* rev. ed. Wilmette, Illinois: Kemper-Peters Publications, 1975.

PRESS, ARTHUR. *Mallet Repair.* Melville, New York: Belwin Mills Publishing Corp., 1971.

READ, GARDNER. *Contemporary Instrumental Techniques.* New York: Schirmer Books, 1976.

————. *Music Notation.* 2nd. ed. Boston: Crescendo Publishers, 1969.

————. *Thesaurus of Orchestral Devices.* New York: Pitman Publishing, 1953; reprint ed., Westport, Connecticut: Greenwood Press Publishers, 1969.

RICHARDS, EMIL. *World of Percussion.* Sherman Oaks, California: Gwyn Publishing Company, 1972.

SACHS, KURT. *The History of Musical Instruments.* New York: W. W. Norton & Company, 1940.

————. *Our Musical Heritage.* Englewood Cliffs, New Jersey: Prentice-Hall, 1948.

STONE, KURT. *Music Notation in the Twentieth-Century.* New York: W. W. Norton & Company, 1980.

WOOD, ALEXANDER. *The Physics of Music.* 7th ed. rev. J. M Bowsher. New York: Halsted Press, 1975.

DISCOGRAPHY

Classification

All compositions were included that used percussion in a chamber ensemble or mentioned a percussion instrument(s) in the title. Where possible the percussionist who performed on the recording is listed. Abbreviations of record company are the same as used by the Schwann Long Playing Record Catalog.

Concert Music

ANON. *18th Century Intraden and Sonatas for Trumpets, Drums, Horns and Organs.* Caskel, Percussion. DGG Arc. 3249 Stereo 73249.

ALTENBURG, JOHANN. *Concerto for 7 Trumpets and Timpani.* Consortium Musicum Odeon S 91421.

AMY, GILBERT. *Inventions.* Drouet, pc. Boulez Ensemble, Amy, cond. Everest 3332.

ANTHEIL, GEORGE. *Ballet Mecanique (1924).* Los Angeles Percussion Ensemble; Kraft, cond. Urania 134 Stereo 5134. *Ballet Mecanique (1924).* New York Percussion Ensemble, Surinach. Col. CML 4956.

ARBEAU, THOINOT. *Orchesographie (1589).* T. & R. Schulze, Telemann Society Amphion CL-2143.

AUSTIN, LARRY. *Improvisations for Orchestra and Jazz Soloists (1963).* Cocuzzo, percussion. New York Philharmonic; Bernstein, cond. Col. ML6133 Stereo MS6733.

BACEWICZ, G. *Music for Strings, Trumpets and Percussion.* Warsaw National Philharmonic, Rowicki, cond. Phillips 900141.

BACH, JOHANN SEBASTIAN. *Chorale, "Herzliebster Jesu." Sonata in G Minor for Unaccompanied Violin.* Vida Chenoweth, Marimba Epic LC3818. *Toccata and Fugue in D minor. Toccata and Fugue in F major. Fugue in G minor. Fugue in C major.* New York Percussion Ensemble; Glick cond. Audio Fidelity 1812.

BACH, J. S., *Prelude XXII (arr.)* East Carolina University Percussion Ens., Harold Jones, cond. 12″ LP from East Carolina U. Greenville, N.C.

BADINGS, HENK. *Passacaglia for Tympani (sic) and Organ.* Piehler, organ. Lyrichord 7221.

BARTOK, BELA. *Concerto for 2 pianos, Percussion & Orch.* (1940). Goodman, Rosenberger, Bailey, Lang, Perc. New York Philharmonic; Bernstein, cond. Col. MS-6956.

BARTOK, BELA. *Music for Strings, Percussion and Celesta. (1935)* Orch. Suisse Romande; Ansermet, cond. London 6159. New York Philharmonic; Bernstein, cond. Col. ML 6356 Stereo MS 6956. BBC Symphony; Boulez, cond. Col. MS7206. Los Angeles Chamber Symphony; Byrns, cond. Cap. HBR21003. Berlin Philharmonica; von Kaajan, cond. Angel 35949. Budapest Orchestra; Lehel, cond. West 19004 Stereo 17004. Chicago Symphony; Reiner, cond. Vic. LM/LSC 2374. London Symphony; Solti, cond. Lon. 9399 Stereo 6399. Cologne Philharmonic; Wand, cond. Counterpoint 607 Stereo 5607.

BARTOK, BELA. *Sonata for Two Pianos and Percussion (1937).* Austin, Parry. Loveridge, Webster, Lees. Lon. Argo 89. J. & D. Schwartz. Percussion Westminister 17064. R. G. & J. Casadesus Drouet. Col. MS-6641. Farnadi, Antal, J. & O. Schwartz. Westminister 17064. Sandor, Reinhardt, Schad, Sohm Turnabout 34036. Tusa, Antal; Piano. Petz and Marton, perc. Qualiton 1280. Votapek, Vosgerchian, Faberman. Cambridge 803. Bartok, Pasztory Bartok, Baker, Rubsan Turnabout 4159. Brendel, Zelka, Schuster, Berger, Minarich, Zimmermann. Turnabout 34465. Eden & Tamir London 6583. Ponse, Frid, Dorati and Lon. Sym. members Mercury 90515.

BARTLETT, HARRY R. *Four Holidays for Three Percussionists.* American Percussion Society; Price, cond. Urania 106 Stereo 5106.

BATSTONE, PHILIP. *Mother Goose Primer.* UCLA Chamber Ensemble CRI S-243.

BEHREND, SIEGFRIED. *Xenographic.* Siegfried Find, percussion and Guitar DG L 3034.

BENSON, WARREN. *Three Pieces for Percussion Quartet; Variations.* Ithaca Percussion Ensemble; Benson, cond. Golden Crest 4106. *Trio for Percussion.* Percussion Ensemble; ice, cond. Period 743 Stereo S743.

BENSON, WARREN. *Symphony for Drums and Wind Orchestra.* Cornell Wind Ensemble, Stith, cond. Cornell U. 12.

BERIO, LUCIANO. *Circles.* Mainstream 5005. *Differences.* Mainstream 5004.

BERNSTEIN, LEONARD. *Serenade for Violin Solo, Strings and Percussion.* N.Y. Philharmonic, Bernstein, cond. Col. MS-7058.

BIRTWHISTLE, HARRISON. *Ring a Dumb Carillon;* Thomas, Hacker, Quinn. Mainstream 5001.

BLAKEY, ART. *Drum Suite.* Percussion Ensemble. Col. CL1002.

BOUCOURECHLIEV, ANDRE. *Archipel 1 for 2 Pianos and 54 Percussions.* J. C. Casadesus and Drouet, Percussion. Angel S36655.

BOULEZ, PIERRE. *Marteau sans maitre (1955).* Craft, Ensemble Odys. 32160154 Deroubaix, Boulez Ens. Turnabout 34081.

BOULEZ, PIERRE. *Pli selon pli (1960).* Boulez, cond. B.B.C. Sym. Col. M-30296. Thome, Philadelphia Composers' Forum Can. 31021.

BRANT, HENRY. *Hieroglyphics 3,* CRI S 260.

BRANT, HENRY. *Signs and Alarms and Galaxy.* Brant and Challiber Ens. Col. CML4956.

BREHM, ALVIN. *Dialogues for Bassoon and Percussion. (1936).* Paul Price, Percussion. Golden Crest 7019.

BROWN, EARLE. *Four Systems For 4 Amplified Cymbals.* Neuhaus. Col. MS7139.

BROWN, EARLE. *Hodograph I. (1959).* Time 58007 Stereo 8007. Kraus, Percussion Mainstream 5007.

BROWN, RAYNER. *Five pieces for Organ, Harp, Brass and Percussion.* L.A. Brass Ensemble. Avant 1001.

BROWN, THOMAS. *Tropicussion.* Sandy Feldstein, Percussion Golden Crest 1005.

BUSSOTTI, SYLVANO. *Coeur pour batteur—Positively Yes.* Neuhaus, Percussion. Col. MS7139.

CAGE, JOHN. *Amores For Prepared Piano and Percussion.* Manhattan Percussion Ensemble, Price, cond. Mainstream 5011. *She is Asleep. First Construction in Metal,* Price, Manhattan Percussion Ensemble Avakian 1.

CAGE, JOHN AND HARRISON, LOU, *Double Music for Percussion Quartet.* (1941) Manhattan Percussion Ensemble; Price, cond. Mainstream 5011.

CARTER, ELLIOT. *Double Concerto for Harpsichord, Piano and Orchestra.* English Chamber Orchestra. Col. MS-7191.

CHAVEZ, CARLOS. *Xochipilli Macuilxochitl. (1940).* Mexican Orchestra; Chavez, cond. Col. LL1015 Stereo LS-1016. *Toccata for Percussion. (1942).* Manhattan Percussion Ensemble; Price, cond. Urania 134 Stereo 5134. Concert Arts; Slatkin, cond. Cap. HBR21003. Los Angeles Percussion Ensemble; Temianka, cond. Col. ML5847 Stereo MS6447.

CHIHARA, PAUL. *Redwood for Viola and Percussion (1968).* Thomas and Watson. *Protone 145. Willow, Willow; Logs; Branches; Driftwood; Logs XVI.* Price, Watson, DesRoches, Fitz perc. CRI S-269.

CHOU WEN-CHUNG. *Soliloquy of a Bhiksuni. (1958).* Louisville Orchestra; Whitney, cond. Louisville Orchestra 641.

COLGRASS, MICHAEL. *Percussion Music. (1953)* Percussion Ensemble; Price, cond. Period 743 Stereo S743. *Three Brothers.* Phil Kraus, cond. Golden Crest 4004. American Percussion Society; Price, cond. Urania 106 Stereo 5106. *Variations for 4 Drums and Viola.* Firth, percussion Victor LSC 6184.

COLGRASS, MICHAEL. *Three Brothers.* Ohio State University Percussion Ensemble, Moore, cond. MES35747.

COWELL, HENRY. *Ostinato Pianissimo for Percussion Orchestra (1934).* Manhattan Percussion Ensemble; Price, cond. Mainstream 5011. *Set of Five.* Elden Bailey, Percussionist. MGM E 3454.

CRESTON, PAUL. *Concertino for Marimba and Orchestra. (1940)* Owen, Marimba. Philadelphia Orch; Ormandy, cond. Col. ML 6377 Stereo MS 6977.

CRUMB, GEORGE. *Night Music I.* Burge and McCluskey, Percussion CRI S-218.

CRUMB, GEORGE. *Ancient Voices of Children.* Contemporary Chamber Ens. Nonesuch 71255.

CRUMB, GEORGE. *Echoes of Time and the River (1968).* Mester, Louisville Orch. Lou. S-711.

DAHL, INGOLF. *Duettino Concertante.* Firth, Percussion. Victor LSC 6189. Ervin, Percussion. Crystal S641.

DALLAPICCOLA, L. *Canti di Prigionia.* Hamburg Monteverdi Chorus. Telefunken S-43095.

DIEMER, EMMA LU. *Toccata for Marimba.* Frazeur, Marimba. MRS 37070.

DUCKWORTH, WILLIAM. *Gambit.* Chamber Ens. and tape. Capra 1201.

EPSTEIN, ALVIN. *Dialogue for Double Bass & Percussion.* (1965). Medea m/s 1001.

ERB, DONALD. *Concerto for Solo Percussion.* Marvin Dahlgren, perc. Dallas Sym. Johanos, cond. Turnabout 34433.

ERB, DONALD. *Diversion for Two (other than sex) for Trumpet and Percussion. (1966).* Opus One I Stereo S1

ETLER, ALVIN. *Concerto for Brass Quintet, Strings & Percussion.* National Orch. Ass'n. Alumni. CHI S-229.

FARBERMAN, HAROLD. *Evolution. (1954). Impressions. (1954). Progressions (1959–60).* Boston Chamber Ensemble; Farberman, cond. Cambridge 805 Stereo 1805. *Trio for Violin, Piano and Percussion.* Farberman, Percussion. Serenus 1016 Stereo 12016.

FELDMAN, MORTON. *Durations.* (1960–61) Krause, Percussions Mainstream 5007. *King of Denmark.* Neuhaus, Percussion. Col. MS 7139.

FELDMAN, MORTON, *Chorus and Instruments (1967).* Bergamo, perc. Brandeis U. Chorus Odys 32160156.

FELDSTEIN, SAUL. *Variations on a Four Note Theme (1963). Insight (1967) Progression.* Potsdam Percussion Ensemble, Feldstein, cond. Golden Crest 1005.

FIRTH, VIC. *Encore in Jazz.* Ohio State University Percussion Ensemble, Moore, cond. MES35747.

FISSINGER, ALFRED. *Suite for Marimba.* Vida Chenoweth, Marimbist. Epic LC 3818.

FLAGELLO, NICHOLAS. *Concertino for Piano, Brass & Timpani (1963).* Serenus 1003 Stereo 12003.

FOSS, LUKAS. *Echoi for Four Soloists (1963).* Columbia University Contemporary Music Group. Epic LC-3886. Stereo BC-1286. *Time Cycle (1960).* Columbia Symphony; Bernstein, cond. Col. ML-5680. Stereo MS-6280. *Time Cycle (Chamber Version) (1963).* Improvisation Chamber Ensemble. Epic LC-3886. Stereo BC-1286.

FRAZEUR, THEODORE. *Uhuru.* Fredonia Percussion Ensemble, Frazeur, cond. MRS 37070. *The Quiet Place; Rondo for Marimba and Piano.* Frazeur, Marimba MRS 37070.

FUKUSHIMA, KAZUO. *Hy-Kyo for Flute, Strings and Percussion.* Rome Sym. Orch. Maderna, cond. Victor VICS-1313.

GABER, HARLEY. *Ludus Primus Kata.* DesRoches, perc. CRI 299.

GABURO, KENNETH. *Line Studies (1957).* Price, perc. Col. Special Products CMS-6421.

GINASTERA, ALBERTO. *Cantata para America Magica (1961).* Los Angeles Percussion Ensemble; Temianka, cond. Col. ML-5847. Stereo MS-6447.

GLANVILLE-HICKS, PEGGY. *Sonata for Piano and Percussion.* New York Percussion Group; Surinach, cond. Col. ML-4990.

GOODRICH, LORRAINE. *Octave Etude in D Minor.* Vida Chenoweth, Marimba. Epic LC-3818.

GOTTSCHALK, LOUIS. *Nuit des tropiques.* Vienna State Opera Orchestra, Buketoff, cond. Turnabout 34440/2.

GRAVES, MILFORD, *Nothing;* From You Never Heard Such Sounds ESP 1015.

GUTCHE, GENE. *Bongo Divertimento.* Dahlgreen, Percussionist. St. Paul Chamber Orchestra; Sipe, cond. St. Paul 96585/6. Stereo 96583/4.

HALFFTER, CRISTOBAL. *Espejos.* Madrid Conjunto Musica Contemporanea. RCA International LSC 16329.

HARRISON, LOU. *Canticle No. 1 for Percussion. (1940).* Manhattan Percussion Ensemble; Price, cond. Mainstream 5011. *Canticle No. 3 for Percussion. (1941).* American Percussion Society; Price, cond. Urania 106. Stereo 5106. *Song of the Queztecoatl. (1941)* Percussion Ensemble; Price, cond. Period Stereo S-743.

HARRISON, LOU. *Suite for Percussion.* Manhattan Percussion Ensemble, Price, cond. CRI S-252.

HARSANYI, TIBOR, *Histoire du Petit Tailleur for Seven Instruments and Percussion.* (1939). Paris Conservatory Orchestra; Pretre, cond. Angel 36357. Stereo S. 36357.

HASHHAGEN. *Pergiton IV.* Siegfried Find, perc. Behrend guitar. DG L 3034.

HAUFRECHT, HERBERT. *Symphony for Brass and Timpani.* (1956). New York Brass Ensemble Society; Karasick, cond. CRI 192.

HENRY, *Liberty Bell.* East Carolina Univ. Perc. Ens. Jones, cond. 12″ LP from East Carolina U. Greenville, N.C.

HENZE, HANS WERNER. *Der langwierige Weg in die Wohnung der Natasha Ungeheuer (1972).* Stomu Yamsh'ta perc. Deutsche Grammophone 2530 212.

HEUSSENSTAMM, GEORGE. *Tetralogue for 4 Clarinets and Percussion.* L.A. Clarinet Society. WIM 7.

HILLER, LEJAREN. *Avalanche for Pitchman, Primadona, Player Piano, Percussion and Tape.* Computer Music for Tape & Percussion. Heliodor 2549006.

HILLER, LEJAREN. *Machine Music for Piano, Percussion and Tape. (1964).* Siwe, percussion. Heliodor 25047. Stereo S25047.

HOVANESS, ALAN. *Fantasy on Japanese Woodprints. (1965).* Hiraoka, xylophonist; Kostelanetz, cond. Col. CL-2581. *"Khaldis" Concerto for Piano, Four Trumpets & Percussion.* Solomon Chamber Ensemble. Heliodor 25027. Stereo S25027. *Koke no niwa (Moss Garden).* Bailey, Rosenberger; percussion. CRI 186. *October Mountain.* Manhattan Percussion Ensemble; Price, cond. Urania 134. Stereo 5134. *Suite for Violin, Piano and Percussion. (1951).* Bailey, percussion. Col. ML-5179.

HUSA, KAREL. *Serenade for Woodwind Quintet with Strings, Harp and Xylophone.* Prague Sym., Husa cond. CRI S-261.

ISHII, MAKI. *Marimba Piece with 2 Percussionists.* Abe, marimba; Aruga and Sato, perc. Candide 31051.

IVES, CHARLES. *From the Steeples and the Mountains.* Am. Brass Quintet. Nonesuch 71222.

JOLIVET, ANDRE. *Concerto No. 2 for Trumpet, Brass, Piano and Percussion. (1948).* Lamoureaux Orchestra; Jolivet, cond. West. 19118. Stereo 17118.

JORGENSEN, ERIK. *Quintet for 2 Pianos, 2 Percussion Groups and Double Bass.* Jorgensen, cond. Chamber Ens. Odeon PASK 2004.

KABELAC, MILOSLAV. *8 Inventions Opus 45.* The Percussions of Strasbourg. Limelight LS 806051.

KAGEL, MAURICIO. *Transicion II for Piano, Percussion and Two Tapes.* Caskel, Percussion. Time 58001. Stereo 8001. *Match for 3 Players.* Caskel, Percussion. DGG 137006.

KARLIN, FRED. *Re: Percussion.* Saul Goodman and Ensemble. Col 1533. Stereo 8333.

KELLY, ROBERT. *Toccata for Marimba and Percussion Ensemble.* Ohio State University Percussion Ensemble, Moore, cond. MES 35747.

KNOX, CHARLES. *Symphony for Brass and Percussion.* Baldwin-Wallace Ensemble. Mark S-32565. *Symphony for Brass and Percussion.* Georgia St. Ensemble. Golden Crest S 4085.

KOTONSKI, W. *Musica per Fiati e Timpani (1963).* Warsaw National Philharmonic. Rowicki, cond. Muza 0336.

KOLB, BARBARA. *Solitare for Piano and Vibes.* Fitz, vibes. Turnabout 34487.

KRAFT, WILLIAM. *Contextures: Riots—Decade '60; Concerto for 4 Percussions and Orchestra.* L.A. Philharmonic; Mehta, cond. London 6613. *Triangles, Concerto for Percussion and 10 Instruments. Momentum for 8 Percussionists. Theme and Variations for Percussion Quartet.* Pacific Percussion Ensemble, Kraft, cond. Crystal S 104. *Morris Dance for percussion solo (1963).* Ervin, perc. Crystal S-821.

KRAFT, WILLIAM. *Nonet for Brass and Percussion.* L.A. Percussion Ens. Kraft, cond. Crystal S-821. *Encounters IV, a duel for trombone and percussion.* Ervin, perc. Crystal S641.

LESEMANN, FREDERICK. *Sonata for Clarinet and Percussion.* Ervin, Perc. Crystal 641.

LEWIS, ROBERT HALL. *Toccata for Solo Violin and Perc.* Goodman and Rosenberger, percussion. CRI S-263.

LOPRESTI, RONALD. *Sketch for Percussion.* Manhattan Percussion Ensemble; Price, cond. Urania 134. Stereo S 134.

LUTOSLAWSKI, WITOLD. *5 Dance Preludes for clarinet, strings, harp, piano and percussion (1955).* Berlin Sym., Gruber, cond. Candide 31035.

LYLLOFF, BENT. *Pieces.* Copenhagen Percussion Group. Cambridge 2824.

MACINNIS, DONALD. *Variations for Brass and Percussions.* Georgia St. Ensemble Crest S 4084.

MARTIN, FRANK. *Concerto for Seven Winds, Strings and Percussion. (1949).* Suisse Romande Orchestra; Ansermet, cond. Vic. LM 2914. Stereo LSC-2914.

MARTIRANO, SALATORE. *O O O O that Shakesperian Rag.* Newhaus, percussion. Princeton Chamber Singers and Instrumental Ensemble; Hilbish, cond. CRI 164.

MAYUZUMI, TOSHIRO, *Concerto for Percussion.* American Wind Symphony, Boudreau, cond. Point Park College 101.

MCKENZIE, JACK H. *Introduction and Allegro for Percussion.* American Percussion Society; Price, cond. Urania 106. Stereo 5106. *Nonet* and *Three Dances for Percussion.* Kraus, cond. Golden Crest 4004.

MCKENZIE, JACK. *Nonet for Percussion.* East Carolina University Percussion Ens. Jones, cond. 12″ LP from East Carolina U. Greenville, N.C.

MESSIAEN, OLIVER. *Couleurs de la Cite Celeste.* Domaine Musicale Orchestra and Strasbourg Percussions, Boulez, cond. Col. MS 7356.

MESSIAEN, OLIVER. *Et Expecto Resurrectionem Mortuorum.* Orchestra Paris Percussion, Soloists, Baudo, cond. Angel S-36559; Col. MS 7356. *Seven Haiku.* Domaine Musicale Orchestra and Strasbourg Percussions; Boulez, cond. Everest 3192.

MIKI, MINORU. *Concerto for Marimba and Orchestra I.* Abe, Marimba. New Music Orch. Wakasugi, cond. Candide 30151.

MILHAUD, DARIUS. *"Lent" from Concerto for Marimba and Vibraphone.* East Carolina University Percussion Ens. Jones, cond. 12″ LP from East Carolina U.

MILHAUD, DARIUS. *Concerto for Percussion and Small Orchestra.* Concert Arts Orchestra; Slatkin, cond. Cap. HBR 21003. Concerto for Percussion and Small Orchestra. Daniel, Percussions Candide 31013.

MILLER, MALLOY. *Prelude for Percussion.* Price, cond. Percussion ens. Orion 7276.

MISSAL, JOSHUA. *Hoe-Down.* Ohio State University Percussion Ensemble, Moore, cond. MES 35747.

MIYOSHI, AKIRA. *Concerto for Marimba and String Ensemble. Torse III. Conversation.* Abe, marimba. New Music Orch. Wakasugi, cond. Candide 31051.

MOZART, W. A. *Divertimenti Nos. 5 and 6 in C, K. 187 & 188.* For Flutes, Trumpets and Timpani. Salzburg Wind Ensemble; von Zallinger, cond. Dover 5223.

MUSSER, CLAIR. *Prelude in G Major Opus 11, No. 3. Prelude in B Major Opus 6, No. 9. Prelude in C Major Opus 6, No. 10. Prelude in Ab Major Opus 6, No. 2* Vida Chenoweth, Marimba: Epic LC 3818.

NELHYBEL, VACLAV. *Chorale for Brass and Percussion.* Orchestra of Sinfonia Roma; Flagello, cond. Serenus 1008. Stereo 12008.

NIELSON, CARL. *Concerto for Clarinet and Orchestra.* Gould, cond. Chicago Symphony Orch. RCA Vic. LSC 2920. Maga, cond. Hungarica Phil. Turnabout 34261. Bernstein, cond. New York Phil. Col. MS-7028.

NODA, TERUKI. *Quintet for Marimba, 3 flutes and Contrabass. "Mattinata"* Abe, Marimba and ensemble Candide 31051.

NONO, LUIGI. *Epitaffio per Garcia Lorca: Part 2, Y su sangre ya viene cantando for Flute, Strings and Perc.* Rome Symphony Orch. Maderna, cond. Victor VICS-1313.

NORGAARD, PER. *Waves; Rondo.* Copenhagen Perc., Group Cambridge 2824.

NOWAK, LIONEL. *Concert Piece for Kettledrums.* Calabro, timpani. Bennington String Ens. Nowak, cond. CRI S-260.

OHANA, MAURICE. *4 Choreographic Etudes.* The Percussions of Strasbourg. Limelight LSS 86051.

OLIVEROS, PAULINE. *Outline for Flute, Percussion and String Bass.* N. & B. Turetzky, and George. Nonesuch 71237.

PARTCH, HARRY. *Windsong. (1958). Plectra and Percussion Dances: Castor & Pollux. (1953).* Gate 5 Ensemble CRI 193. *And on the Seventh Day Petals Fell on Petaluma.* Partch and the Gate 5 Ensemble. CRI S 213. *Plectra and Percussion Dances: Castor and Pollux.* Mitchell's Ensemble. Col. MS 7207. *Delusion of the Fury.* Mitchell, cond. Unique Instrumental Ens. Col. M2-30576.

PENDERECKI, K. *Anaclasis (1960).* Warsaw National Philharmonic; Markowski, cond. Muza 0260.

PERKINS, BILL. *Textures for Musical Saw and Percussion.* Jim Turner, Saw. Electronic Percussion Ens. Galm and Kiteley, Perc. Owl Records ORLP 22.

PERRY, JULIA. *Homunculus C. F. for 10 Percussionists.* Manhattan Percussion Ensemble; Price, cond. CRI S-252.

PETERS, GORDON. *Swords of Moda-Ling.* Eastman Percussion Ensemble, John Beck, cond. University of Rochester ES 72001. Ohio State University Percussion Ensemble, Moore, cond. MES35747.

PILLIN, BORIS. *Duo for percussion and piano (1971).* Ervin, perc. WIM 5.

POULENC, FRANCIS. *Concerto for Organ, Strings & Timpani. (1941).* Hinger, Timpanist, Philadelphia Orchestra; Ormandy, cond. Col. ML-5798. Stereo MS 6398. National Radio Orchestra; Pretre, cond. Angel 35953. Firth, Timpanist, Boston Symphony Orchestra; Munch, cond. Vic. LM 2567. Stereo LSC 2567.

RILEY, TERRY. *In c.* Buffalo, New York. State University Ensemble. Col. MS7187.

ROGERS, BERNARD. *Three Japanese Dances. (1933).* Eastman Wind Ensemble; Fennell, cond. Mer. 50173. Stereo 90173.

ROLDAN, AMADEO, *Ritmicas for Percussion: Nos. 5 & 6 (1930).* Manhattan Percussion Ensemble; Price, cond. Time 58000. Stereo 8000.

ROREM, NED. *Lovers, for Harpsichord, Oboe, Cello and Percussion. (1964).* Farberman, Percussion. Dec. 10108. Stereo 710108.

RUSSELL, WILLIAM. *3 Dance Movements. 3 Cuban Pieces.* Manhattan Percussion Ensemble; Price, cond. Mainstream 5011.

SALZEDO, CARLOS. *Concerto Pour Percussion.* London Percussion Ensemble. Phillips 839280.

SCHAT, PETER. *Signalement.* The Percussions of Strasbourg. Limelight LS 86064.

SCHIFFMAN. *Musica Battuta.* East Carolina University Percussion Ensemble. Jones, cond. 12″ LP at East Carolina U. Greenville, N.C.

SCHMIDT, WILLIAM. *Septigams, for flute, piano and percussion.* Remsen, perc. WIM 2.

SCHMIDT, WILLIAM. *Ludus Americanus for Percussion and Narrator (1971).* Ervin, perc. WIM 5.

SCHWARTZ, ELLIOT. *Arias: Nos. 1, 2, 4.* Thraikill, percussion. Advance 7.

SHAPEY, RALPH. *Evocation for Violin, Piano and Percussion. (1959).* Price, percussion. CRI 141.

SHINOHARA. MAKOTO. *Alternances.* The Percussions of Strasbourg. Limelight LS 86064.

SIEGMEISTER, ELIE. *Sextet for Brass & Percussion.* Am. Brass Quintet. Desto 6467.

SIFLER, PAUL. *Marimba Suite for solo Marimba (1970).* Ervin, Marimba WIM 5.

SKAVANINSKI. *Scherzo for Xylophone and Piano.* East Carolina University Percussion Ens. Jones, cond. 12″ LP available from East Carolina, Univ. Greenville, N.C.

STIBILJ, MILAN. *Epherview de ta Faiblesse, Domine.* The Percussions of Strasbourg. LS 8664.

STOCKHAUSEN, KARLHEINZ: *Kontakte. (1960).* For Electronic Tape, Piano and Percussion, Wcrgo WER60-009. Stereo 60-009. *Momente. (1962 rev. 1965).* For Four Sopranos, Four Choruses, and Thirteen Instrumentalists. Members of the Cologne Radio Orchestra; Stockhausen, cond. Nonesuch 1157. Stereo 71157. *Refrain for Piano, Celesta, and Vibraphone. (1950). Zyklus for Solo Percussion. (1959).* Caskel, Percussion. Mainstream 5003. Neuhaus, Percussion. Col. MS-7139.

STOLZER, GOTTFRIED. *Concerto in D for Six Trumpets, Four Kettledrums, Two Harpsichords and Double String Orchestra. (C. 1730).* Vienna State Opera Orchestra; Scherchen, cond. Westminster 19047. Stereo 17047. Wuttemberg Chamber Orchestra; Faerber, cond. Mer. 50385. Stereo 90385.

STRANG, GERALD. *Percussion Music for Three Players.* *(1935).* Percussion Ensemble; Price, cond. Period 743, Stereo S 743.

STRAVINSKI, IGOR. *L'histoire du Soldat. (1918)* (complete) Chamber Group; Markevitch, cond. Philips 500046 Stereo 900046. *L'histoire du Soldat.* Stokowski, cond. Vangard 71165. *L'histoire du Soldat.* *(Suite).* London Symphony; Carewe, cond. Everest 6017. Stereo 3017. Chamber Ensemble; Rozhdestvensky, cond. Angel 40005. Stereo S40005. Columbia Symphony; Stravinski, cond. Col. ML 5672. Stereo MS 6272. *Les Noces.* (1917-23). Columbia Percussion Ensemble. Col. MS 6991. Suisse Roman Orchestra; Ansermet, cond. Lon. 9288, Stereo 6219. Chamber Ensemble; Stravinski, cond. Col. ML 5772. Stereo MS 6372. French National Opera Orchestra; Boulez, cond. Nonesuch 1133. Stereo 71133.

SYDEMAN, WILLIAM. *Music for Flute, Guitar, Viola, and Percussion. (1960).* Contemporary Chamber Ensemble; Weisberg, cond. CRI 181.

TAKEMITSU, TORU. *Miniature: Stanza No. 1—Sacrific—Ring—Valeria.* Abe, percussion and chamber ens. DG 2530088.

TANNER, PETER. *Sonata for Marimba and Piano.* East Carolina University Percussion Ens. Jones, cond. 12″ LP from East Carolina U. Greenville, N.C.

TELEMANN, GEORG. *Canonic Sonata in A Major.* Vida Chenoweth, Marimba. Epic LC 3818.

THOMPSON, VIRGIL. *Concerto for Flute, Strings, and Percussion. (1954).* Louisville Orchestra; Whitney, cond. Lou 663 Stereo S663. *Mass for Two-part Chorus and Percussion. (1934).* Chorus; Thompson, cond. Cambridge 412.

THORNE, FRANCIS. *Songs and Dances.* Rosenberger, perc. Op. One 9.

VARÈSE, EDGARD. *Ameriques. (1926).* Utah Symphony Orchestra; Abravanel, cond. Vangard 1156. Stereo 71156. *Arcana. (1927).* Chicago Symphony Orchestra; Martinon, cond. Vic LM-2914. Stereo LSC-2914. *Ionisation. (1931).* American Percussion Society; Price, cond. Urania 106. Stereo 5106. Julliard Percussion, Orchestra; Walsman, cond. EMS 401. Aarhus Conservatory Percussion Ensemble Cambridge 2824. Die Reihe Ens. Cerha, cond. Candide 31028. *Integrales. (1925).* Julliard Percussion Orchestra; Waldman, cond. EMS 401. Complete Works of Varese. *Arcana, (1927). Deserts, (1954). Offrandes, (1922). Ionisation, (1931). Integrales, (1925),* and *Hyperprism, (1923).* Chamber Ensemble; Craft, cond. Col. ML 5762. Stereo 6362. Col. ML 5478. Stereo MS 6146.

WALTON, WILLIAM. *Facade (1926–48).* Dec. 10097. Stereo 710097. Lon. 4104. Col. ML 5241. Philadelphia Orchestra; Ormandy, cond. Col. ML 5849. Stereo MS 6449.

WILLIAMS, CLIFTON. *Concertino for Percussion and Band. (1959).* North Texas Band Austin 6164.

WIMBERBER, GERHARD. *Stories fur Blaser und Schlazeug (1962).* Vienna Symphony; Wimberger, cond. Amadeo 5017.

WOLPE, STEFAN. *Sonata for Violin; Passacaglia;* Percussion or Chamber Orchestra. Counterpoint 530 Stereo 5530.

WUORINEN, CHARLES. *Janissary Music.* DesRoches, Percussion. CRI S 231. *Prelude and Fugue for Percussion.* Kraus Ensemble Golden Crest 4004.

YTTREHUS, ROLV. *Music for Winds, Percussion and Viola (1961).* Capra 1202.

ZACHER, GERD. *Re.* Deutsche Gram. 139442.

Folk Music

Africa Drums of the Yoruba of Nigeria Folkways 4441.

African & Afro-American Drums Folkways 4502.

African, Latino Voodoo Drums. Audio Fidelity 2102 Stereo 6102.

Bali Gamelan Music Lyrachord 179. Stereo 7179.

Brazil Batucada Fantastica RCA 1079001.

Caribbean Islands Federators Steel Band Miniter 355. Stereo S355. Wong Steel Band. Folkways 8367.

China Chinese Drums & Gongs Lyrachord 102.

Guatemala Marimba Gallito RCAP8S 1369 (tape). Guatemalan Marimbas. Maderas De Mi Tierra Orchestra. Cap. T10170.

Haiti Drums of Haiti. Folkways 4403.

India Drums of North & South India. World 1437. Stereo 21437. Lal, Chatur—Drums of India. World 1403.

Japan Temple Music Lyrachord 117.

Japan Buddhist Drums, Bells and Chants Lyrachord 7200.

Java Court Gamelan Nonesuch 72044.

Mexico Marimbas South of the Border, Cap. ST 10358. Marimbas Mexicanas, Cap. T 10043. Mexican Marimba Music, Cap. T 10183.

Mexico Marimba from Oaxaca. Folkways 8865.

Scotland Shotts and Dykehead Caledonia Pipe Band-World Championship Pipes and Drums London 99012.

Tahiti Drums of Bora Bora. Criterion 1600 Stereo S 1600.

Instructional

Snare Drum:

Haskell W. Harr Drum Method No. 2. Slingerland Drum Co. Chicago, Illinois.

Mervin Britton. Sounds for Success. Rogers Drum Co., Fullerton, CA.

The Thirteen Essential Rudiments.

Learning Unlimited Audio-Visual Band Series: Let's play Percussion. Level I and Level II.
James Moore.
Charles Merrill Publishing Co.
1300 Alum Creek
Columbus, Ohio 43216.

The Twenty-six Standard American Drum Rudiments. Ludwig Drum Company, Chicago, Illinois.

Jazz Drums:

Jim Chapin. Modern Jazz Drumming. Music Minus One Records 4001.

For Drummers Only. Music Minus One Records 4002.

Klock, Bob, Latin Time. Klock's House of Music, 200 2nd Street, Highspire, Pa. 17034.

Shelly Mann Drum Folio No. 1. Music for Percussion, New York.

Blue Drums MMO 4005.

Drummer Delights MMO 4004.

8 Men In Search of A Drummer MMO 4003.

Fun With Drum Sticks MMO 125.

The Sound of Brushes—The Sound of Jazz MMO 175.

You're On Drums URS Productions BDE 1002.

Funk and Soulful Sound Cassette Dictionary for Drums.
J. C. Combs
Universal Dynamics Corp. 8361 Woodward.
Overland Park, Kansas 66212.

Shelly Elias, For Vibists Only MMO 4076.

Shelly Elias, Good Vibrations MMO 4077.

Tom Brown, Vibist, Clinician Series Golden Crest Records CR 1012.

Miscellaneous:

Spotlight on Percussion. Vox DL 180 Saul Goodman, Kenny Clark and Others.

Mervin Britton. Percussion Performance No. 1 (Tambourine, Castagnets and Triangle)
Lyons Band Instrument Co., Chicago, Ill.

Bongo Drum Instruction Folkways 8320.

Dick Schory and Percussive Art Ensemble. Re-Percusssion. Everest 5232 Stereo 1232.

Latin Rhythms MMO 10240.

Jazz Collection Featuring Drummers

Gretsch Drum Night (Blakey, E. Jones, etc.) Roulette 52049 Stereo S 52049.

Original Drum Battle. (Krupa, Rich) Verve 8484. Stereo 68484.

Percussive Jazz Vol. 1. Audio Fidelity 3002. Stereo 7002.

Percussive Jazz Vol. 2. Audio Fidelity 3007. Stereo 7007.

Taste of Drums (Roach, Stoller, Bunker, etc.) Time 52140. Stereo 2140.

Louis Bellson. Explorations. Roulette Record SR 52120.

Giants of Jazz Vol. VIII: The Jazz Greats, Drum Role Mer. M G 36071.

Popular and Miscellaneous

Marimba Masters, Gordon Peters, director. Kendall LP 341.

Spirit of 1776. Eastman Wind Ensemble. Mer. MG 50111.

Ruffles and Flourishes. Eastman Wind Ensemble Mer. GM 50112.

Percussion in Hi Fi (David Carroll) Mer. MG 21006.

Bell-Drum-Cymbal (Saul Goodman) Angel 35269.

The Percussive Phil Krause. Golden Crest. 3004.

Holidays for Percussion. New York Percussion Trio Vox VX25-740.

Music for Bang, Baaroom and Harp (Dick Schory) RCA Vic. LPM 1866.

Steel Drums. Pete Seeger Folkways CRB-7.

Fife and Drum March Music Major 1007.

Schory, Dick, Holiday RCA LSA 2485.

Runnin' Wild RCA LSA 2306.

Stereo Action Goes Broadway RCA LSA 2382.

Dick Schory Carnegie Hall Ovation OV/14-10-2.

N.B. This discography lists recordings currently available and is not a complete, historical listing. With the exception of the Concert Music section, the listings are representative of the categories and not complete. [It would be a major work just to list all the jazz and rock recordings that use a percussionist (s)].

GLOSSARY OF PERCUSSION TERMS

Including Some of the More Common French, German and Italian equivalents.

(For names of percussion instruments, with their foreign equivalents, see table of percussion instruments Chapter 2.)

English	French	German	Italian
(with) brush, brushes, wirebrushes	brosse (avec) brosses balai métallique	Besen or Stahlbesen	spazzola
buzz roll (a snare drum roll so closed that individual sounds blend into a continuous tone)			
cadence (marching beat for drums, usually 8 measures long)			
change tuning (timpani)	changez	nach-umstimmen	muta
choke (damp cymbal quickly)	étouffé	dämpfen	secco
clashed (pair of cymbals)	a l'ordinaire	becken gewöhnlich	a 2
closed (closely spaced individual strokes, taps and bounces—snare drum rudiments)			
collar (that portion of a drum or timpani head which extends from the flesh hoop to the edge of the shell)			
damp, dampen (stop vibration suddenly by contact with fingers or hands)	étouffé	dämpfen	secco
double, double stroke (successive *pairs* of stick alternations RRLL etc.)			
double drums (snare and bass drums played by the same player, through use of the bass drum foot pedal)			
double stops (two-note chords on the mallet-played instruments)			
double tension (drums with separate tension casings attached to the shell for each tuning rod. Heads tune independently)			
drum (generic term)	caisse, tambour	trommel	cassa, tamburo

English	French	German	Italian
hammering (patterns of alternated or successive R or L strokes—mallet-played instruments, timpani)			
handhold (manner of grasping the stick, beater or mallet)			
hand-to-hand (alternating the snare drum sticking patterns in playing the rudiments)			
hard sticks	baguettes dures	schwerer schlagel	bachette duro
idiophone (percussion instrument whose tone is produced by the body of the instrument vibrating, through striking, shaking, scraping, or friction)			
mallet (heavy)	marteau	Holzhammer	maglio
membranophone (percussion instrument whose tone is produced by one or two stretched membranes [heads, skins] vibrating through being struck)			
motor off (vibraphone)	non vibrez		
muffle with cloth (timpani)	voilé couvert(e) voilēe couvertes	Gedampft	coperto, coperti (plural)
near rim	au bord	am Rand	sul bordo
on the knee (tambourine)	avec le genou	auf dem Knie	col ginocchio
on the shell (of the drum)	sur la cadre du tambour	auf dem Holzrand der Trommel	sulla cassa del tamburo
on the skin (head)	sur la peau	auf das Fell	sulla membrana
on the snares	sur les timbres	auf den Saiten	sulla corde
open (widely spaced individual strokes, taps and bounces—snare drum rudiments)			
pedal off (vibraphone)	sans pedal	ohne pedal	senza pedale
percussion (section)	batterie	schlagewerk	batteria
piatti (the pair of clashed cymbals)	cymbales á 2	becken	piatti
playing spot (point on the head, bar, tube or surface where the beater should strike for maximum resonance)			

English	French	German	Italian
press roll (a short snare drum roll made by pressing both sticks onto drumhead simultaneously)			
rim (play on rim of drum)			
rim shot (drumstick contacts head and rim simultaneously)	sur le bordure or sur L'ourlet		
roll (technique of sustaining the tone of a percussion instrument by rapid alternations (single strokes) or successions (double strokes) of the sticks, beaters or mallets.	roulée	wirbel	rullo

rubbed together
(clashed cymbal roll)
	agitees I'une
	   contres l'autre
		triller
		   (zu 2)
			trillo (à 2)

rudiments (prescribed sticking of traditional snare drum rhythm figures and techniques)	rudiments	anfangsgründe	
shake (tambourine)	agite	schütteln	agitare, trillo
single, single stroke (alternated sticking RLRL etc.)			
single tension (drums whose heads tension by means of single tuning rods connected to both counterhoops [rims])			
snare, snares (set of four to twenty wire, gut, or combination wire-gut cords which pass under the bottom head of the snare drum and rattle against it when the drum is struck)	cordes, timbres	saiten	corde
(with) sponge-headed sticks (timpani)	(avec) baguettes d'eponges	mit dem schwamnschlagel	bachelle di spunga
stick beat (note, or notes, played by striking the shoulders of the snare drumsticks together in mid-air)			
stick, beater, mallet	mailloche baguette	schlag, Klopper	mazza, bachetta
sticking, stickwork (patterns of alternated or successive R or L strokes or taps—snare drum, timpani)			
strike	frappée	schlag	colpo
street beat (marching cadence for drums, usually 8 measures long)			

English	French	German	Italian
stroke (action of fingers, hand and arm, and stick, beater or mallet used to produce sound of percussion instruments)			
take drumstick	prenez la mailloche	mit der Schlagel	colla mazza
tap (a light stroke initiated by wrist action only)			
tap step (marching cadence for drums, usually 8 measures long)			
(with) timpani sticks	(avec) baguettes de timbales	(mit) paukenschlagel	(con) bachette di timpani
Tog. (abbr. of *together*) (bass drum and cymbals to play from the same notes)			
traps (the numerous small percussion instruments, as triangle, woodblock, etc.)			
with the fingers (light tambourine stroke)	avec les doigts	mit den fingern	col il dita
with the thumb (tambourine thumb trill)	avec le pouce	mit dem daumen	col pollice
without snares (muffled drum)	sans timbres	ohne Schnarrsaite	senza le cordes
(with) wood sticks	(avec) baguettes en bois	(mit) Holzschlagel	Col legno, bachetto